I0824814

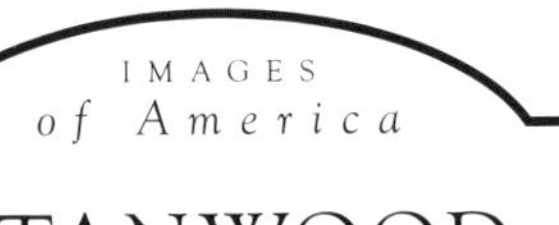
IMAGES
of America
STANWOOD

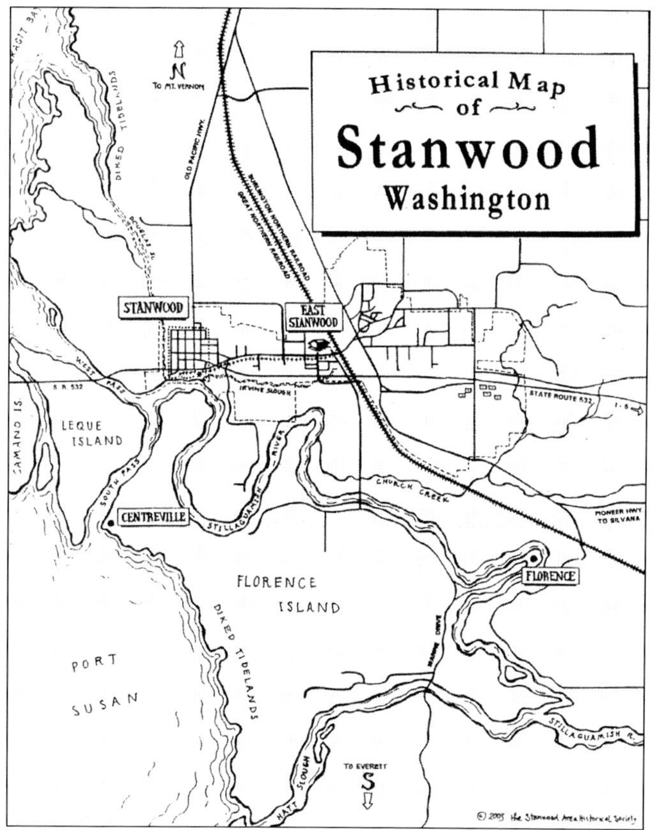

HISTORICAL MAP OF STANWOOD. This map features the delta of the Stillaguamish River, where Stanwood was established. One mile east, the winding river flows out of the Cascade Mountains and diverges into several sloughs and two main channels. In the 1860s, there was a Coast Salish village opposite where settlers established what was to become Stanwood. The main channel diverges again north toward Skagit Bay and south toward Port Susan in the Puget Sound of Washington State. This formed Florence Island, part of which is now known as the Zis A Bas Estuary. The South Pass was a fork of the Stillaguamish River that flowed south into Port Susan where Centreville, the first name of Stanwood, was originally established. The West Pass forked into Skagit Bay to the north. (Map by Renee Marquette.)

ON THE COVER: PARASOLS ON PARADE. A Fourth of July parade proceeds south toward Broadway past the Stanwood Hotel and the Stanwood Meat Market. The elaborately decorated automobiles were proudly displayed and part of a long parade tradition. The largest number of photographs in this book are by local photographer John T. Wagness. He created many of the best-quality views of Stanwood streets and businesses and hundreds of portraits. They have become part of the collective memory of the community. (Courtesy of the Stanwood Area Historical Society.)

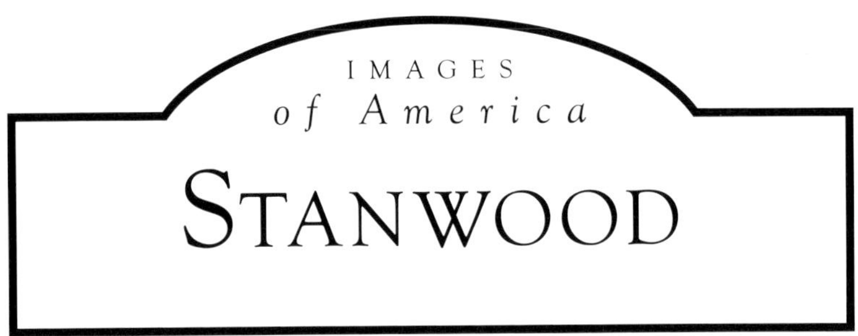

Karen Prasse and the
Stanwood Area Historical Society

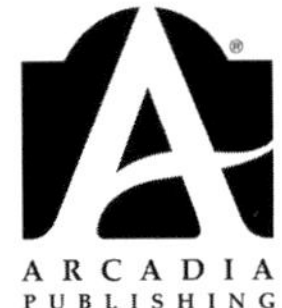

Copyright © 2025 by Karen Prasse and the Stanwood Area Historical Society
ISBN 978-1-4671-6230-2

Published by Arcadia Publishing
Charleston, South Carolina

Printed in the United States of America

Library of Congress Control Number: 2024948418

For all general information, please contact Arcadia Publishing:
Telephone 843-853-2070
Fax 843-853-0044
E-mail sales@arcadiapublishing.com

Visit us on the Internet at www.arcadiapublishing.com

This photographic history is dedicated to Margaret Riddle, whose career at the Everett Public Library Northwest Room provided an amazing resource for all of us who write the history of Snohomish County. She endlessly encouraged and supported all the researchers who had wandered into the Northwest Room since the 1970s until she officially retired. She has carried on as a writer, researcher, and historian for many publications and projects since.

Contents

ACKNOWLEDGMENTS

This book is a photographic history of Stanwood, Washington, from 1879 until 1960. Unless otherwise noted, all images are from the Stanwood Area Historical Society collections. Because it is a historical photographic interpretation, some major historical events are left out because we do not have photographs depicting the places. The most popular topics were those that inspired professional and amateur photographers to bring out their cameras during floods, snowstorms, and parades. The photographs illustrate the town's development primarily through businesses and street views as this community grew and replaced itself.

The Stanwood Area Historical Society (SAHS) is indebted to the donors of original photographs and other printed materials along with other types of museum artifacts that help us interpret the local history of the Stanwood and Camano Island area. Some of those donors were Kenneth Wagness, Clarence Wagness, Gordon and Bonnie Pedersen, Jesse Hall, Cliff and Shirley Danielson, Dave Pinkham, Evan Caldwell, Ivy Hansen, Carol Schmidt, June Iverson Orth, Grace Cornwell, Ole Eide, Neil and Diane Hampson, John Taubeneck, Nolen Sill, the Von Moos family, Dan Logen, Jim Palmquist, Barbara Stave, Ruth Anne Rose, Dolores Fure Marx, the Amundson family, Naomi Payton, Penny Buse, and several unknown donors. I am also very grateful to Michele Heiderer of the Stillaguamish Valley Museum and Bill Blandin, SAHS member volunteer and genealogist, for their research assistance and to Dave Eldridge for proofreading.

This book features photographs primarily by our local and regional photographers: John T. Wagness, John A. Juleen, J. Boyd Ellis, Robert Young, O.S. Van Olinda, Gilbert D. Horton, Edward A. Johnson, Hellick Aas, Charles Wightman, and Herman Siewert. More contemporary photographers include Howard Hansen and Cliff Danielson.

Special recognition goes to Alice Essex (1900–1986), author of *The Stanwood Story*, whose three volumes were published in 1971, 1975, and 1998 by the *Stanwood News*. Alice Essex was the daughter of D.G. Bennie, owner and manager of the Stanwood Lumber Company. She attended Stanwood schools and graduated from the University of Washington School of Journalism.

Many thanks also to publishers Cliff and Shirley Danielson, who donated many photographs, and to Dave Pinkham, who owned the *Stanwood Camano News*. The *Stanwood Story* encompasses the Stanwood area, including the Milltown, Cedarhome, Camano Island, Silvana, Warm Beach, and Florence communities. Unlike the *Stanwood Story*, this volume focuses only on Stanwood and East Stanwood. Much of the information was found in issues of the *Stanwood Tidings*, *Stanwood News*, and *Twin City News*, early names of the current *Stanwood Camano News*. The clippings are on file at the Stanwood Area Historical Society. The *Daily Herald* (Everett) was also a source of confirming events and dates.

Introduction

The town now known as Stanwood, Washington, was established at the mouth of the Stillaguamish River on the eastern shoreline of Puget Sound. The word *Stillaguamish* means "people of the river," and the river was named for the local Coast Salish people of the Stillaguamish tribe. In the 1800s, one of their encampments was located near the mouth of the river. A trading post was established near this site along the shoreline of Port Susan.

Like many communities after the Civil War and the following westward expansion, a trading post with a saloon and a post office was started. It was first called Centerville and was located on the South Pass of the river. The nearby Utsalady Lumber mill on Camano Island was operated by Lawrence Grennan and Thomas Cranney of Coupeville almost continuously from 1858 until 1891. Their mill workers and loggers were among those who were immigrants looking for a new start, and many found their way to Centerville.

Diking began in 1864, and an 1873 survey map shows properties of W.B. Moore, James Caldon, Henry Oliver, Robert Freeman, George Kyle, Thomas Ovenell, Peter Wilkinson, J. Hatt, and several others. Others including Henry Marshall, Willard Sly, G.D. Neville, and Daniel Marvin were settling upriver at what became known as Florence as early as October 1864. Robert Fulton had started the saloon and trading post in 1866. It served farmers and loggers who were staking claims upriver. Mail was brought from Utsalady because there was no regular steamboat service yet. George Kyle officially registered the post office on his claim on the South Pass in 1870. Steamers navigating the river delta and Port Susan depended on tides, as Capt. George Vancouver discovered was necessary in 1792 when he grounded briefly in Port Susan during his exploration of the Puget Sound.

In 1873, the post office was moved to a lodging house on the northern shoreline of the Stillaguamish River on the claim of Robert Freeman. Four years later, in 1877, D.O. Pearson arrived on the steamer *Fanny Lake* with capital and goods for a store worth $4,000. He also built a wharf to make it possible for a steamboat to dock along the Stillaguamish River. In 1877, he became the sixth postmaster in seven years. At the request of the postal service, Pearson also gave the town a less common name, Stanwood, honoring his wife, Clara Stanwood Pearson, who came through the Isthmus of Panama by herself in 1868 to join him.

As early as 1871, diking, logging, and land clearing had begun along the river and sloughs. They were usually commissioned by farmers collectively. Leque Island, Steamboat Slough, and Florence Island were all eventually diked. In 1876, Bengt Johnson from Sweden was hired by Francis Hancock north of Stanwood to build dikes. Later, he also diked along the slough that ran eastward later named Irvine Slough. After diking, farmers grew hay and oats for cash. Some had large ranches with many cattle, but they all had a few cows, chickens, fruit trees, and berries and survived as they could doing this back-breaking work. In the 1880s, logging camps and shingle mills surrounded the Stillaguamish River valley area.

In a 1908 article in *The Coast* magazine, Andrew Klaeboe, mayor of Stanwood in 1907–1909, proclaimed Stanwood to be among the richest oat and grain lands in the world. He went on to say it was the metropolis and center for a "miniature Holland" located in the northwestern part of the county where thousands of acres of land had been reclaimed from the sea by a system of dikes reaching for miles.

Stanwood employed a "town diker," "Big" Peter Arentzen from Denmark, who lived in Cedarhome. In 1892, the dike on the Skagit River to the north broke, and Stanwood was deluged with four feet of water. At the end of a workday, Peter trudged through town with his high hip boots turned down, a spade held on his right shoulder, and always a black felt hat. Dikers used slip scrapers and horses. A few years later, they were run by gas engines with several men to attend them.

In 1900, the Stanwood Precinct had 767 people. The surrounding communities of Cedarhome, Florence, Port Susan (Warm Beach), and the Stillaguamish Precinct (Silvana) accounted for about 1,765 more in the area. In 1910, the Stanwood population was 544; in 1920, it was 704, and East Stanwood had a population of 476. In 1930, Stanwood had 715, and East Stanwood's population was at 330. In 1940, Stanwood had 600, and East Stanwood had 359. In 1950, Stanwood had 710 and East Stanwood had 359. When the towns merged again, the population was 646 in 1960; 1,347 in 1970; 1,646 in 1980; 1,961 in 1990; 3,923 in 2000; 6,231 in 2010; and 7,705 in 2020.

In the period between 1922 and 1960, Stanwood was two separate towns, Stanwood and East Stanwood. Several reasons contributed to the separation of the communities. At that time, the area had several school districts, and the location of a new high school was being decided. The area became known informally as the Twin Cities. Businesses and the newspaper took on the name: *Twin City News*, Twin City Foods, Twin City Dairy, Twin City Lanes, Twin City Grain, Twin City Bakery, and Twin City Auto Parts. Even the high school was named Twin City High School from 1945 until 1962.

New development was occurring in East Stanwood, between the towns, and eastward on the highlands. In the following decade, Highway I-Y, now State Route 532, bypassed the old highway through the town to Camano Island. The new road through Stanwood was built with an overpass over the railroad tracks. It was also built high enough to act as a levee to divert water and help keep it from threatening the town. South of town, the residents still suffered, and many houses were raised above the 100-year flood level. Though Stanwood has not been flooded since 1959, the threat continues. There have been many high-water events and one in 1990 that inundated homes on the "river road" south of the city limits.

In 1945, Twin City Foods was incorporated as a new food processing company and, soon after, installed new machinery and space for freezing and storage. In 1959, it demolished the old cannery building operated by the Lien Bros. Packing Co. and added a cold storage unit. Its home office building was constructed in 1975, and the structure dominates the waterfront operated by a new food-processing company, the No Meat Factory.

Because of the industrial nature of the Stillaguamish River waterfront, there was little public access to the river over the years. There is now a new (in 2024) small boat launch and park below "the Hamilton Stack," the Port Susan Trail, and the Leque Island Trail where residents and visitors can appreciate the expansive and spectacular waterfront views between two mountain ranges, the Cascades and the Olympics Mountains.

One

Territorial Times

In 1877, Daniel Orlando "D.O." Pearson moved to Centerville and established a mercantile on the Stillaguamish River waterfront. He commissioned a wharf to accommodate the steamboats and store and took over the post office as the sixth postmaster in seven years. To make farming hay and oats possible, land was cleared and the settlers built dikes to keep out the saltwater. In the 1880s, logging camps and shingle mills surrounded the Stillaguamish River valley area.

D.O. Pearson followed his father, also named Daniel Pearson, who with his two daughters (D.O.'s sisters) arrived two years earlier on Asa Mercer's first expedition. Daniel Orlando arrived in Coupeville, Washington, on Whidbey Island in 1866 from Lowell, Massachusetts, on the second Mercer Expedition. Two years later, Clara Stanwood came through the Isthmus of Panama in 1868. Daniel and Clara were married in June 1868. Though a lonely place, their location offered spectacular views of two mountain ranges and an open sky.

In 1888, the plat of Stanwood was recorded by W.R. Stockbridge. He also brought the first mill to Stanwood near the mouth of the Irvine Slough, a tributary of the Stillaguamish River. He also brought in Otto Rabel, who managed it until 1899. The slough was named for Jack Irvine, who operated a ranch to feed mill workers and loggers. His ranch was at the mouth of the slough, where it flowed into the Stillaguamish River.

Waterfront photographs of the wharf and shoreline show Stanwood built of the plentiful timber. There was a small but growing cluster of storefronts facing the south toward the shoreline at that date. Most of these buildings burned to the ground in 1892, a devastating setback that fortunately took no lives. Fires were frequent events despite Western Washington's reputation for rain, as this was three years after the Great Seattle Fire of 1889, which was the year Washington became a state.

A personal account by O.B. Iverson, a surveyor and territorial legislator, described the town when he first saw it as a surveyor in 1876: "[Henry] Oliver had a barn about where the post office was and a pig house on the site where the first church was built and later the Ketchum's store. The town did not interest me much but the river did. When we crossed it there was a strong current downstream like any sane river would run. The next time I looked at it the insane thing ran just as furiously upstream. I began to think that either I or the country was crazy."

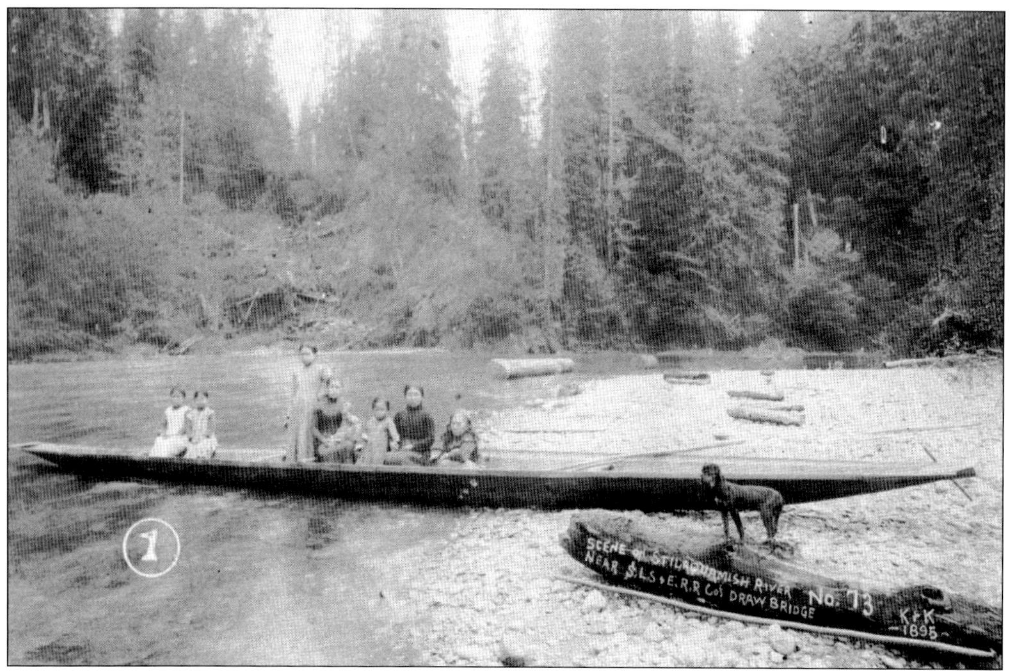

SCENE ON THE STILLAGUAMISH RIVER. Native Americans navigated their canoes expertly. This shovel-nose canoe was the type used on a river. This unidentified family is posing for K+K (Clark and Darius Kinsey) in 1895, as indicated in the handwriting. It was taken near the Seattle, Lake Shore & Eastern Railroad Company drawbridge about 12 miles upriver east of Stanwood. (Courtesy of the Stillaguamish Valley Museum.)

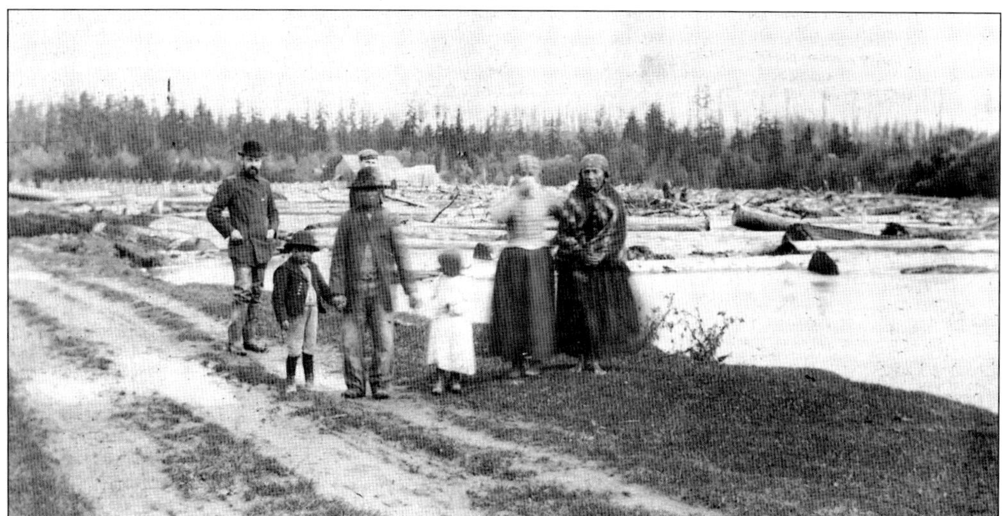

ALONG THE STILLAGUAMISH RIVER, ABOUT 1898. The view looks upriver across toward the Joergenson Farm. The river bank in the foreground shows Einar Juel and unidentified Native Americans. The logjam could be part of a flood or just an early logjam. Juel was the business manager and secretary of the Stanwood Cooperative Creamery, established in 1895. The Matterand Farm, across the river, is now owned by the Stillaguamish tribe. In 2017, the tribe converted much of the farmlands into a flood plain to restore original salmon and other wildlife habitat. The photographer, Oliver S. Van Olinda, worked at the *Stanwood News* for D. Carl Pearson from 1897 to 1900.

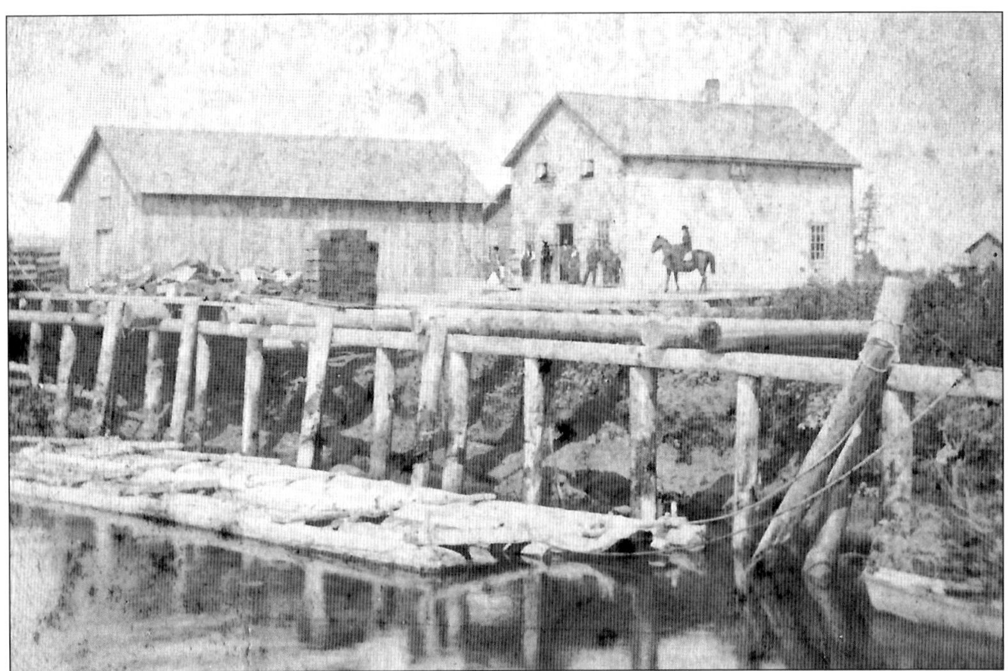

Pearson Store, Built in 1877. The buildings in this photograph are the Pearson Store and its warehouse at the mouth of the Stillaguamish River. Note the timber pilings on the shore with a log raft in the foreground. The plank-sided building on the left was the warehouse, and the two-story building on the right was the store. This photograph was from a Pearson family scrapbook labeled "Building built in 1877; store and home burned here."

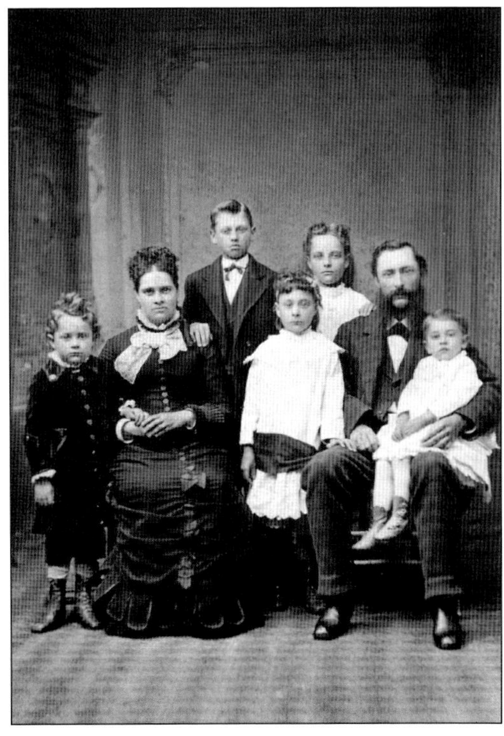

D.O. Pearson Family, 1879. D.O. Pearson began his mercantile to supply local farmers during the height of activities at the Utsalady Mill on Camano Island. This family portrait includes, from left to right, Fred Wallace Pearson (1875–1954), Clara Stanwood Pearson (1949–1910), Guy Stanwood Pearson (1869–1906), Bertha May Pearson (1870–1895), Eva Marian Pearson (1873–1972), and Daniel Orlando (1846–1929) holding Daniel Carlton Pearson (1877–1971). Rachel Pearson (1883–1963) was not yet born when this was taken. (Photograph by D.R. Judkins.)

Stanwood, April 1886. The photograph looks across the tidal marsh on the Zis A Bas Estuary, once the Matterand family farm, from the South Pass of the Stillaguamish River. It shows the waterfront of Stanwood with its wharf, early hotels, mercantile stores, hardware stores, blacksmiths, and the Irvine Ranch. At this time, John H. "Jack" Irvine bought property and raised cattle for beef for the local mills. In 1879, he opened the second store in Stanwood after

Pearson. In the foreground are the tidal flats that were diked, now known as Florence Island. From left to right are the Robert Freeman barn, the Pioneer Hotel, known as "Caldon's," the Scandinavian Lutheran church, Peter McLaughlin's shop and house, the O.K. Saloon, the D.O. Pearson Store, the Dimick Hardware Store, a blacksmith shop, the Irvine Store and warehouse, and a schoolhouse. (Photograph by Gilbert D. Horton.)

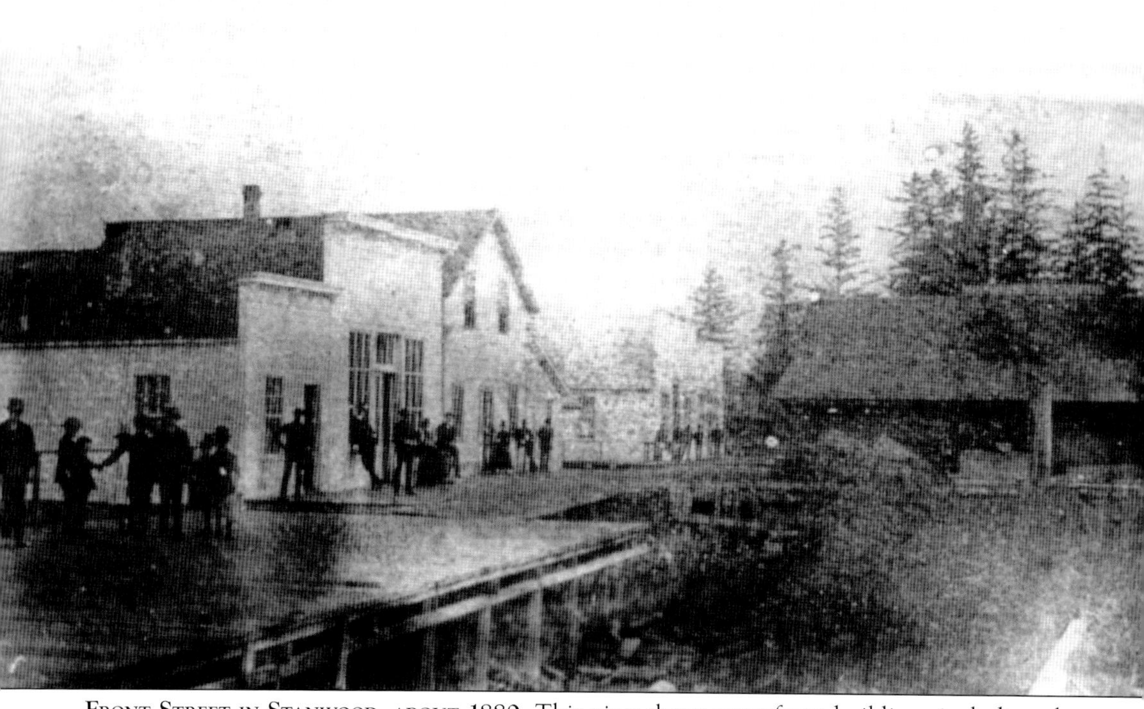

Front Street in Stanwood, about 1880. This view shows waterfront buildings including the Irvine Store (second from the left). On the left is the Pearson warehouse. Early surveyor O.B. Iverson while visiting Centerville noted the "city" in 1876 consisted of Jim Caldon's hotel and saloon, which stood on the bank of the river with the dike for the front porch.

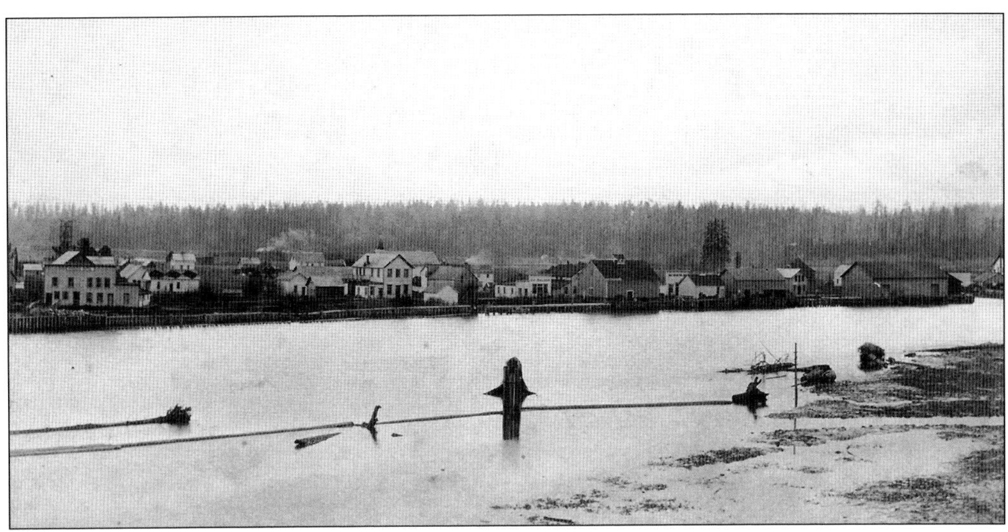

STANWOOD WATERFRONT, 1889. The large pilings and logs in foreground of the Stillaguamish River were to divert logs out to Skagit Bay rather than Port Susan. The area had many diked channels or sloughs including the Irvine Slough, a tributary of the river. The river at the time was wide enough for floating logs to the boom where they were sorted. On the far left is the Pioneer Hotel, and the scaffolding of the Methodist church is behind it. D.O. Pearson's store is in the center. Other businesses include saloons, hotels, a hardware, and a blacksmith.

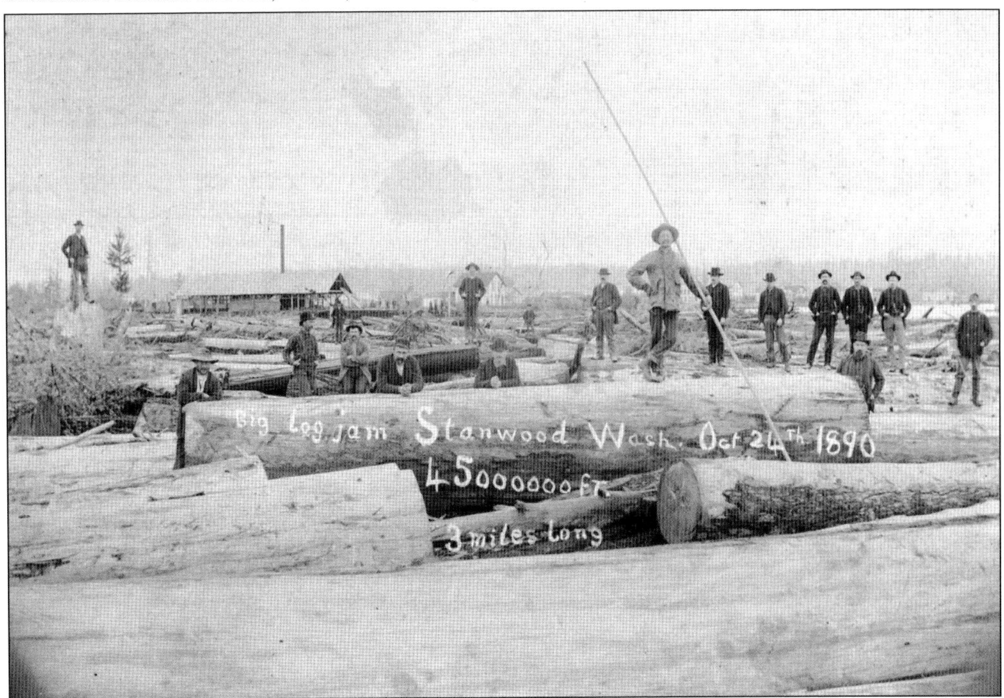

BIG LOGJAM, 4.5 MILLION FEET, 1890. Few details are known of this view, but the date is October 24, 1890. The *Anacortes American* reported in November 1890 that four million feet of logs came down in three days and were boomed at the mouth of the river by the Chinook Boom Company. In 1887, a logging crew of 15 men run by Jasper Sill of Florence pulled 144,000 feet of logs, some 60 inches in diameter, with a single team of 10 oxen.

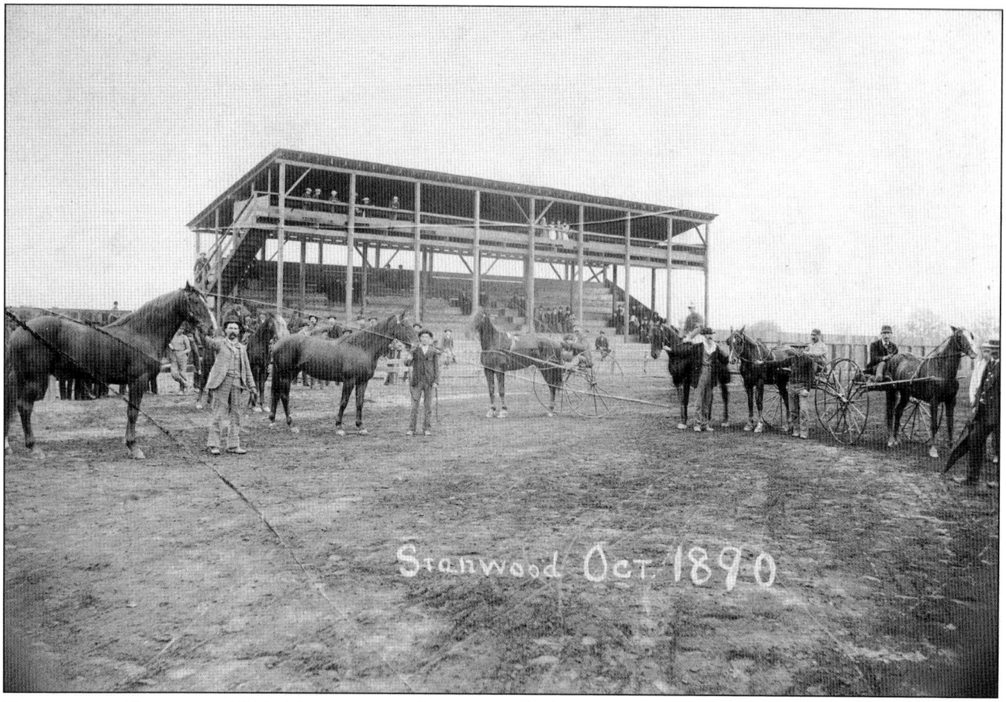

Stanwood, October 1890. Harness racehorses with their carts or carriages, known as sulkies, are lining up in front of the bleachers. Not much is known about the track except it lasted only one or two seasons. The photographs of the racetrack came from Willow Sill Johnson. She was the granddaughter of Jasper and Susie Sill, who operated a store in Florence.

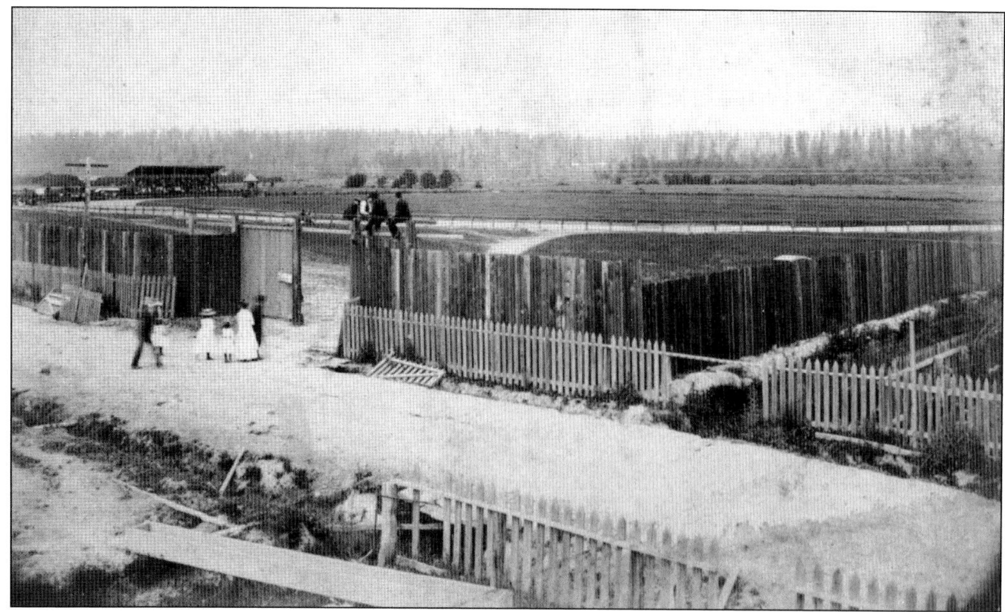

The Stanwood Racetrack. The racetrack was located on the "flats," as the river delta was known, north of the waterfront just east of Market Street toward what became the Josephine Sunset Home. In the distance are the hillsides above the newly diked fields between the Skagit and Stillaguamish Rivers. (Photograph by Charles Wightman.)

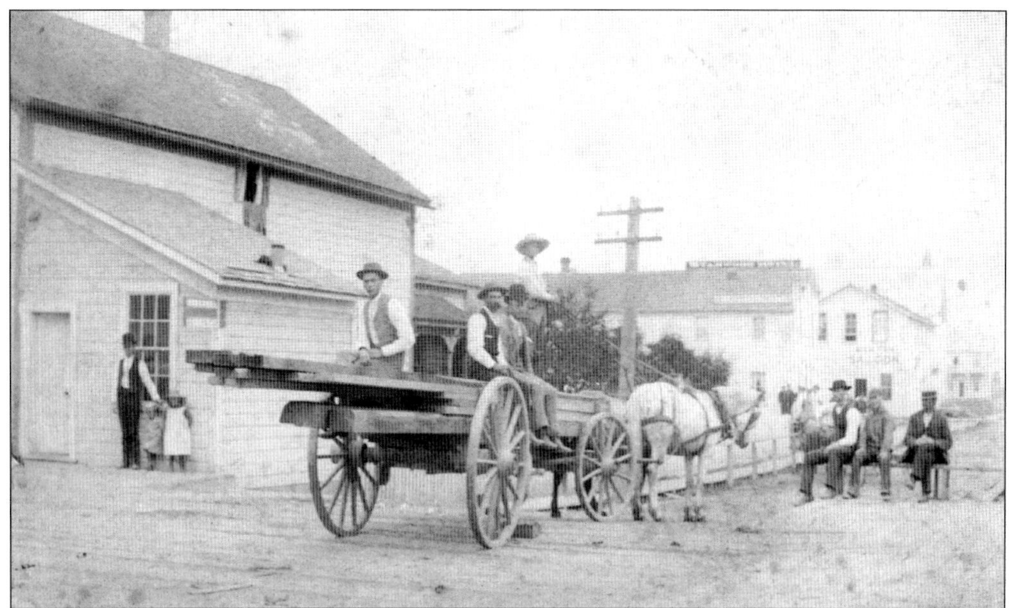

STANWOOD, JUNE 21, 1889. Pictured is a horse-drawn wagon with lumber planks for road building and sidewalks. Sidewalks had to be staked to keep from floating off during floods. The buildings were the first Stanwood Hotel and the Bonton Saloon, seen in the distance prior to the 1892 fire.

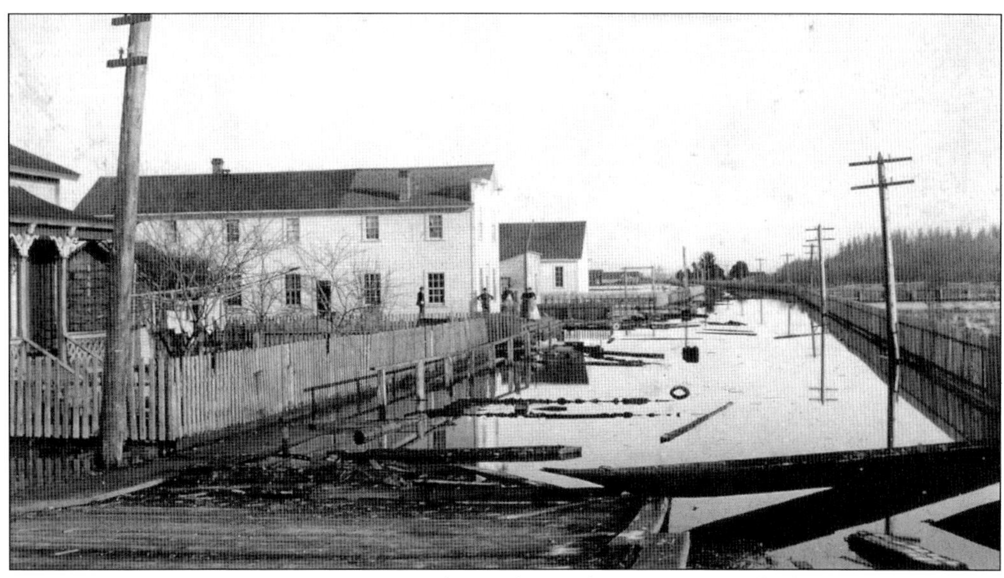

EARLY FLOODING IN STANWOOD, 1886. This early Market Street view looks north before the Pearson family built their third home in 1891. These buildings would have burned in the 1892 fire. Note the shovel-nose Indian canoe, picket fences, and the wooden sidewalks in the foreground. (Photograph by Gilbert D. Horton.)

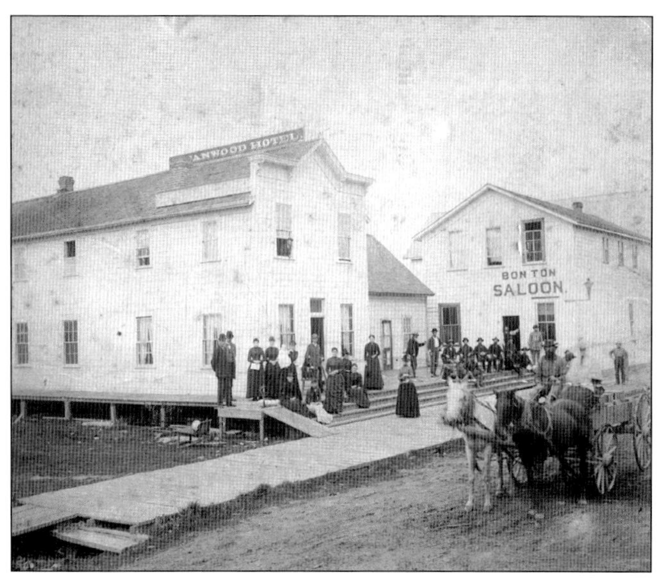

Stanwood's Market Street, 1889. Washington became the 42nd state of the United States of America on November 11, 1889. The sign on the top of the building indicates it is the first Stanwood Hotel, which burned down in an 1892 fire. The Bon Ton Saloon is beyond it, one of at least six saloons in town. The hotel was informally called Armstrong's for John H. Armstrong, who apparently left town soon after. He had been a logger from Maine. The group meeting in the hall at the time, the local Good Templars, was compelled to rescue Armstrong's stock of whiskey.

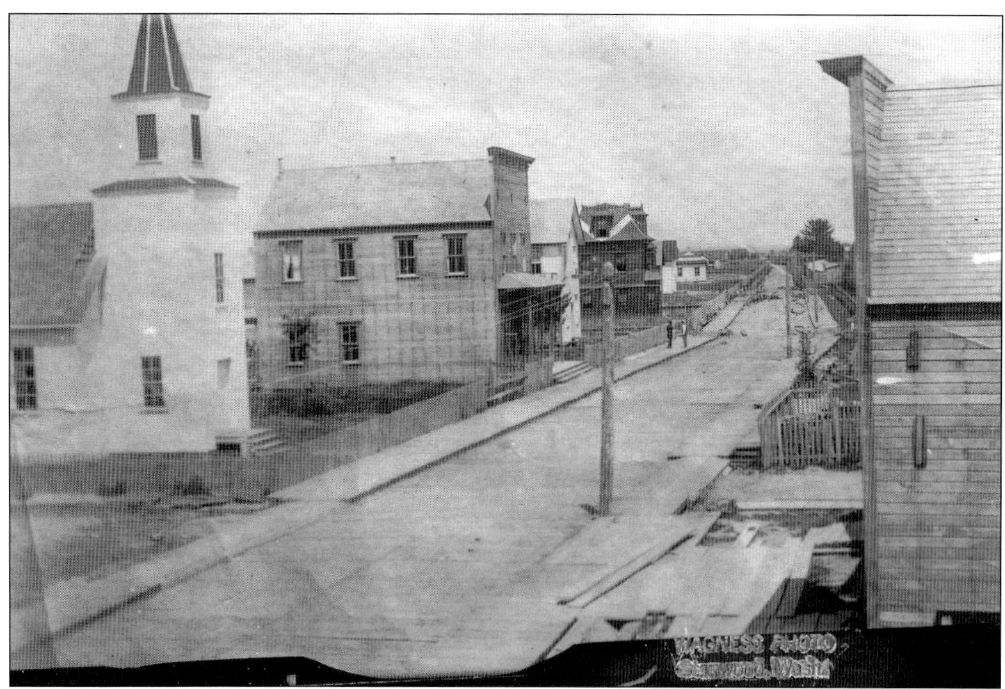

Stanwood's Market Street, about 1891. This view of early Market Street looks north on what was to become the first highway north. It became Market Street and took travelers toward Skagit County; it was the first land route before the railroad. The Our Saviour's Trinity Lutheran Church is in the foreground on the left and is said to be the first church built by Lutherans on the Pacific Coast. Its first services were held in October 1879. Beyond is the Melby Hotel and the newly built 1891 D.O. Pearson Home, which is now a house museum. The church did not survive the 1892 fire, nor did the building next to the Melby Hotel.

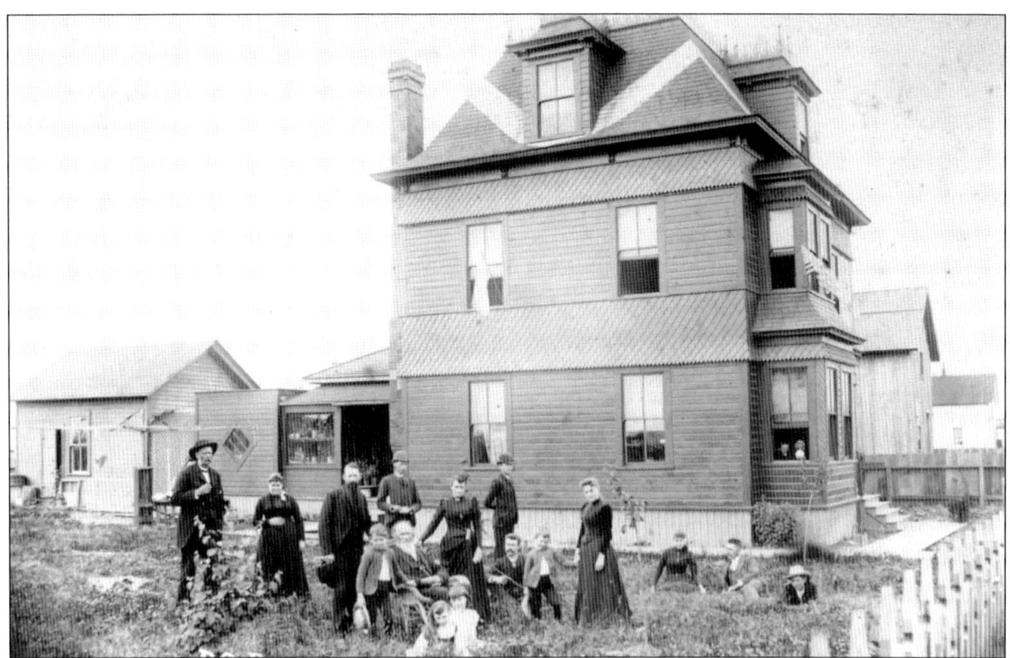

Family Members of D.O. Pearson, 1891. The family is gathered at their third residence in Stanwood, Washington. Daniel Pearson the elder is seated with other Pearson family members from Coupeville on Whidbey Island. This photograph shows a side view of the Second Empire Victorian house with three stories and a mansard roof with cresting along roofline. The siding has shingles in a diamond pattern painted by their son Guy. From left to right are Charles Terry, husband of D.O. Pearson's deceased sister Georgia, Clara Stanwood Pearson, Daniel Orlando Pearson, and his father, Daniel Pearson, who is seated in the center. Next to him are Flora Pearson Engle; Pearson's son Guy; George Ketchum, a clerk in the Pearson Store; and Pearson's daughters Rachel and Eva.

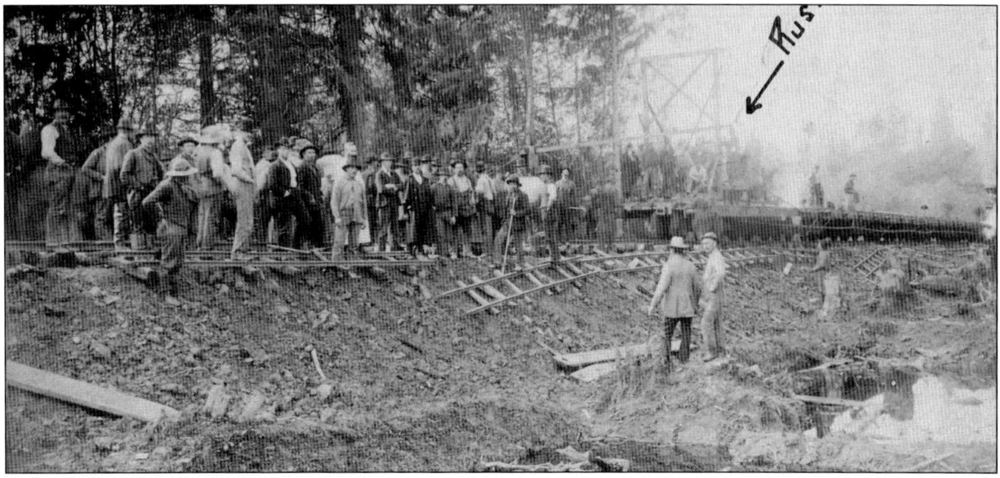

Last Rail Laid, October 23, 1891. On November 28, an excursion train of the Great Northern Railroad with passengers finally connected Seattle and South Westminster in Canada. Handwriting on the photograph indicates the last rail was laid on October 23, 1891, near Stanwood. On December 1, 1891, passenger service into Everett began, and the transition to rail for carrying food, passengers, and freight was made possible, though it bypassed the Stanwood townsite one mile east.

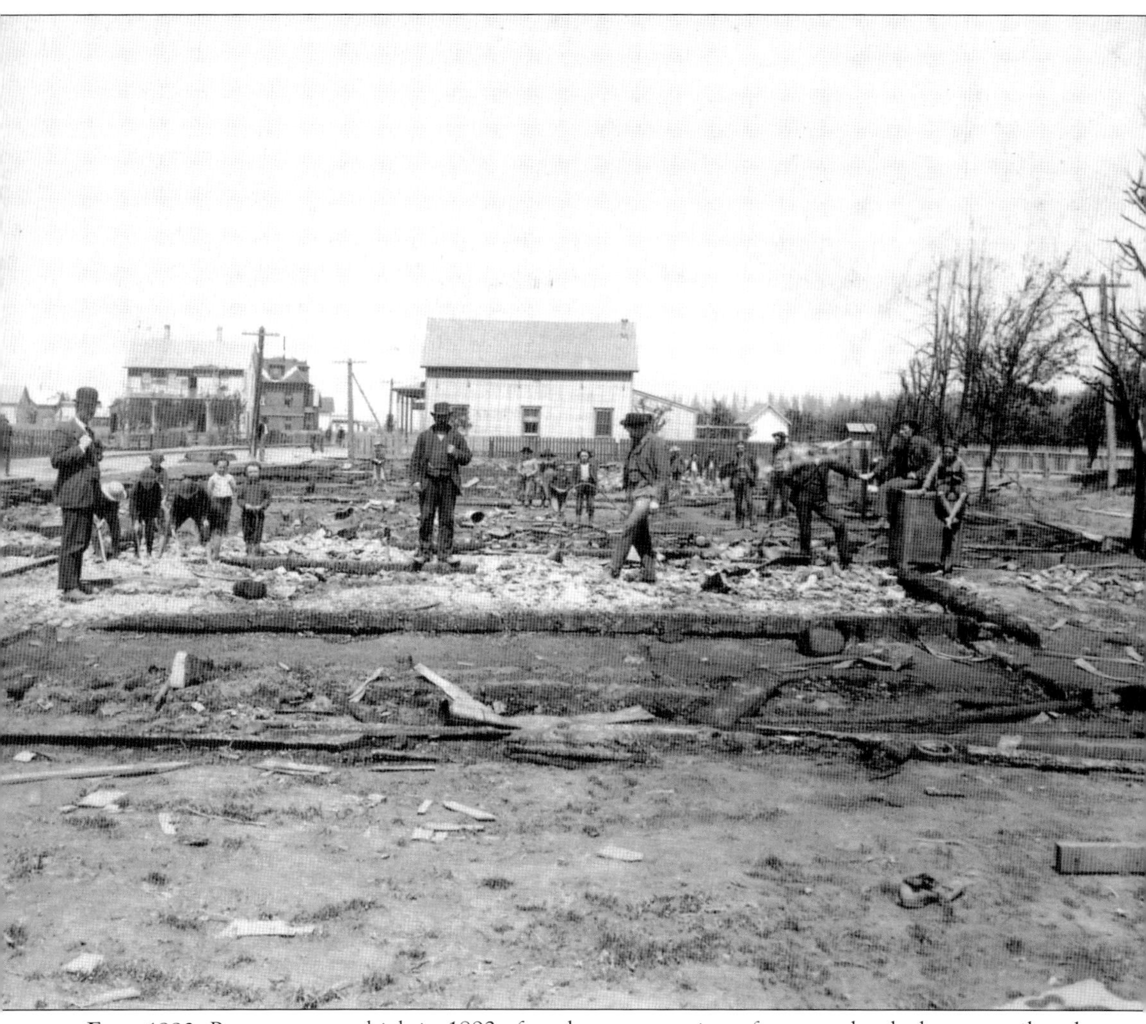

Fire, 1892. Prospects were high in 1892 after the construction of a new school, the new railroad connection, and the first cannery. It was platted in 1899 by W.R. Stockbridge, who was selling many new lots for homes. Farmers were bringing in bumper crops on the newly diked tidelands converted to farm fields. In May 1892, a fire destroyed at least eight buildings on the waterfront, including the first Stanwood Hotel. Another major loss was the L.H. Smith market, the second mercantile in Stanwood on the corner of Market Street (102nd Avenue NW) and Irvine Street (270th Street NW). On the left, the Melby Hotel and the D.O. Pearson house survived.

Two

Klondikers and the Hall & Hall Railroad

The town rebounded quickly after the fire despite the Panic of 1893. After the Seattle & Montana Railroad, a subsidiary of the Great Northern Railroad, the major rail connection north to Bellingham and south to Seattle began to change the nature of transportation and commerce for the Puget Sound. At the end of the decade, many of its local men found their fortunes in the Klondike Gold Rush.

In the late 1880s, Henry C. Anderson and John P. Anderson (not related) went north to work for the North American Transport and Trading Company in Alaska. Henry moved on to the Klondike, where he delivered mail with a dog team. He filed a claim on the Eldorado River, where he struck gold, and then sold the mine. When the steamer *Portland* docked in Seattle in July 1898, Henry C. Anderson was one of those carrying over $200,000 in gold nuggets. Meanwhile, other Stanwood residents followed. Several others came back successfully, most notably Francis Giard, whose son Francis Giard Jr. wrote an account of the adventures.

Francis Giard Sr. climbed Chilkoot Pass, and later, he and a partner built a raft with a tent on it and floated it down the Yukon River to the ocean. On one of his trips, he carried $25,000 of gold dust in each of two suitcases to the mint in San Francisco. He exchanged it for money and returned to Stanwood with the money in them on the train. He returned for the last time in 1904 and bought and platted the area around the depot as East Stanwood in 1906.

After braving the cold, snow, and nightlife, many of the miners came back to Stanwood more successful than they left. H.C. Anderson became president of the newly established Bank of Stanwood and a primary investor in the Stanwood Lumber Company. To make use of the railroad, John W. Hall and his son Jesse N. Hall operated the Stanwood Feed and Livery, which provided carriage service to and from the depot. In 1903, John W. established the Hall & Hall (H&H) Railroad to connect Stanwood mills and passengers with the depot one mile east. Sometimes, schoolchildren used it to get to school. It became known for a time as the "Shortest Railroad in the World."

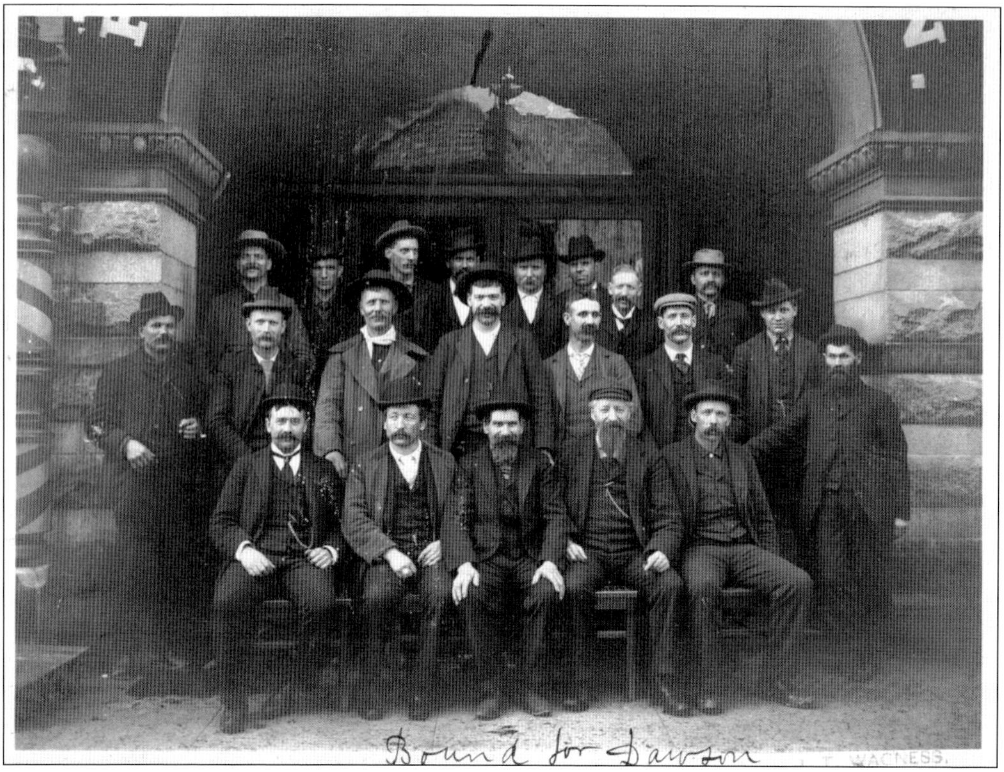

Bound for Dawson, 1895–1899. Handwritten on the photograph is "Bound for Dawson—Lee and Anderson Party, C.J. and John Lee Party." Most came back successful. H.C. Anderson, who became known as "Klondike" Anderson, had preceded the party of gold-seekers. The 21 men in this photograph include C.J. Anderson; John Lee; Ole Larsen; Ed Hamilton; A.E. Klaeboe (Stanwood druggist); E.O. Anderson; John Ness; Anders, Severt, and Hans Engseth; and John Ware. Others not included in the photograph were Peter Henning, Francis Giard, James Esary, George Ovenell, William Gunderson, Dan McDonald, and Andrew Olson. (Photograph by John T. Wagness.)

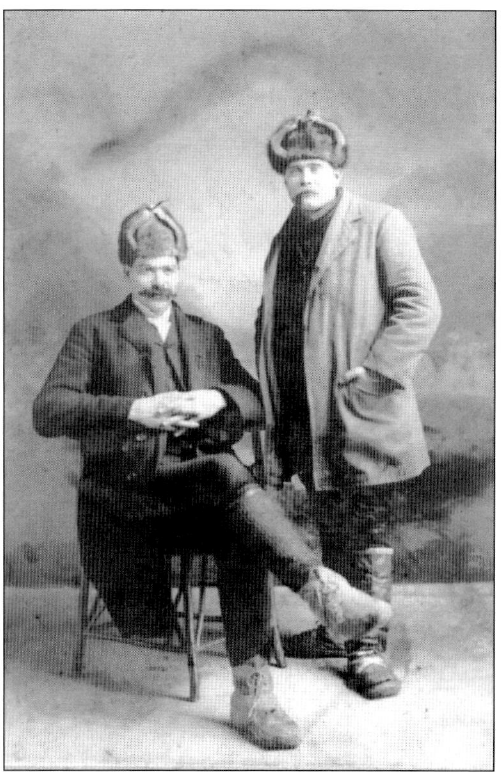

John T. Wagness and John B. Lee. Brothers-in-laws Wagness (standing) and Lee (sitting) are wearing fur hats and heavy coats for this portrait as part of the required Alaskan attire. Lee was the miner, and Wagness went along at his request to document the adventure. Lee came back with his wife, Lillian, whom he married in Dawson, and established a farm upriver from Stanwood in 1903.

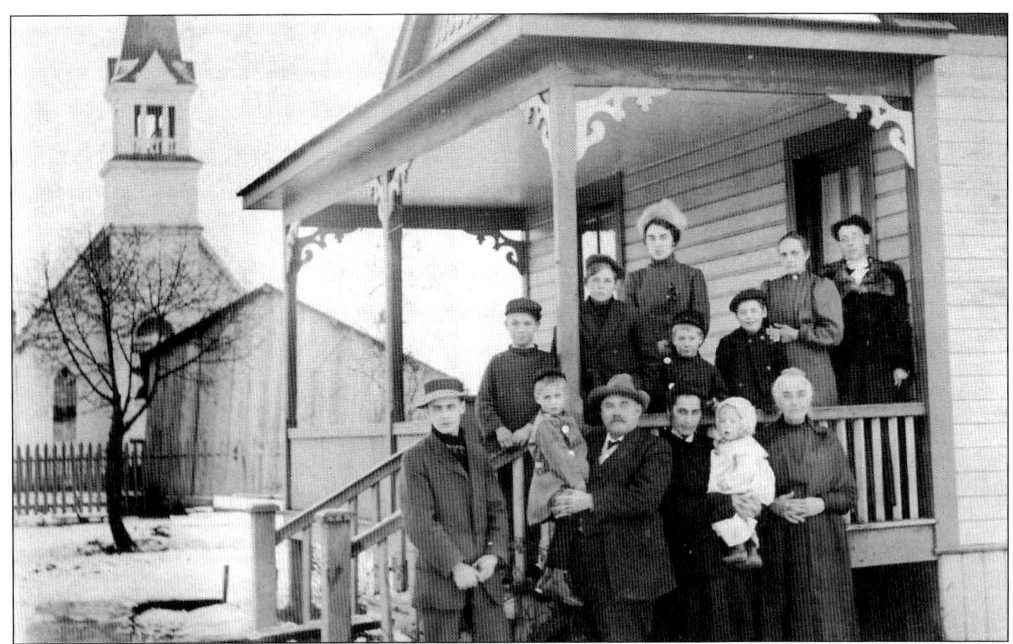

John and Mary B. (Lee) Wagness Family. John T. Wagness is standing below holding one of his nine children surrounded by his family. The small house is just east of the second Our Saviour's Lutheran Church. His son Kenneth made prints from glass negatives. He donated many of these photographic prints to the Stanwood Area Historical Society.

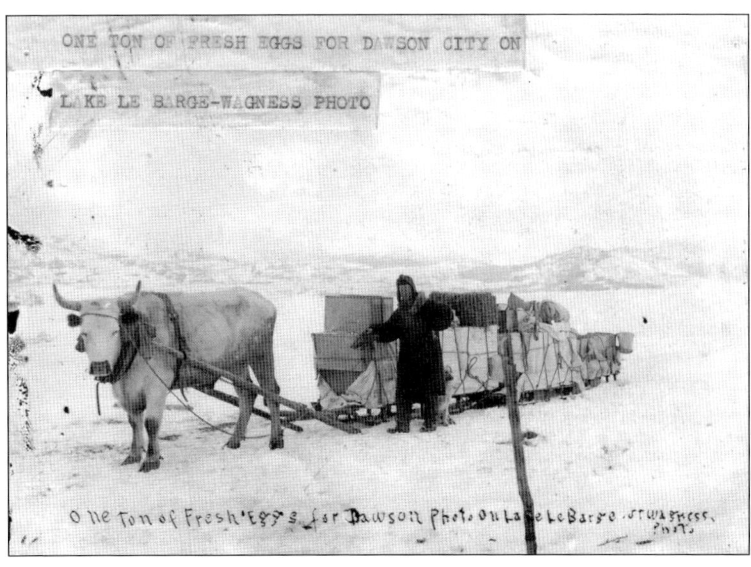

Eggs, a Delicate Cargo. The caption reads, "One ton of fresh eggs for Dawson City on Lake Le Barge." Dogs were most often used to carry supplies, but John T. Wagness captured this photograph among his 50 photographs of the commercial activity around the Klondike Gold Rush and often wrote on the negatives of the photographs.

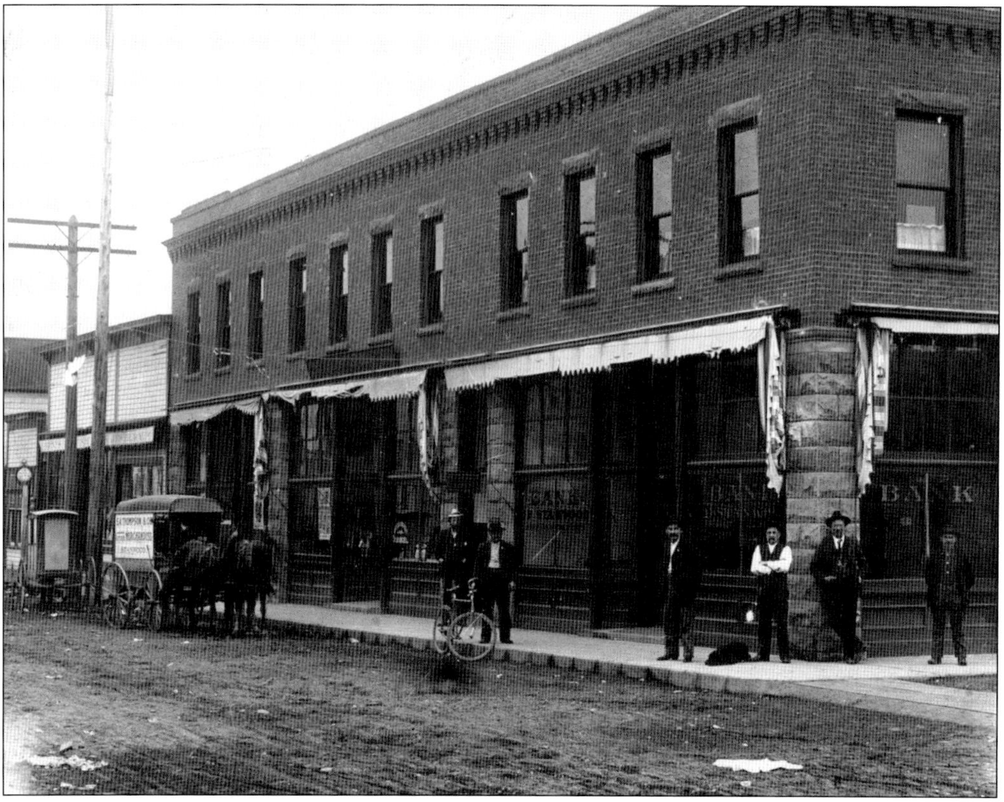

Bank of Stanwood, 1904. In 1904, twelve years after the 1892 fire, the Bank of Stanwood built a two-story brick building on the southwest corner of Market Street (102 Avenue NW) and Broadway Street (State Route 532). It was organized by H.C. Anderson with Peter Leque, Sven A. Thompson, Alfred Densmore, Whitfield C. Brokaw, and Francis Giard. S.A. Thompson's delivery wagon is on the left with the mail wagon on the far left. Local men in the photograph include, from left to right, Andrew Klaeboe (pharmacist), Francis Giard, unidentified, Ben Willard, Louis Hanson, and Edward Husby (mail carrier). Knud Knudson's jewelry and watch store is on the far left. The barely visible sign leads to an upstairs dentist's office for Dr. Edward L. Hogan.

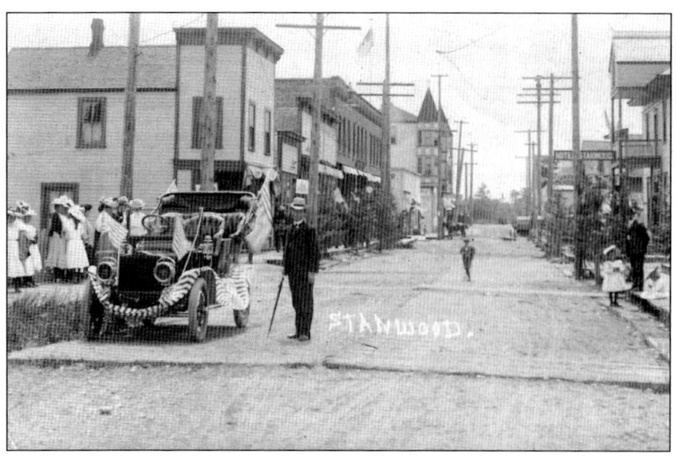

Parade on Plank Roads. Fourth of July parades were and are a strong tradition in Stanwood. The plank roads were built before the town could afford to brick them in 1912. In 1904, the two-story building on the left was a meat market with a stationery shop and jewelry store beyond it. On the right is the Hotel Stanwood. The Palace Hotel in the distance with towers.

Parasols on Parade. Parades were a break from the farmwork and time off from the mill for ice cream and cake. In this photograph, the automobiles proceed south on Market Street toward Broadway past the Stanwood Hotel and the Stanwood Meat Market. The elaborately decorated automobiles were proudly displayed with cedar boughs, flags, and flowers. (Photograph by John T. Wagness.)

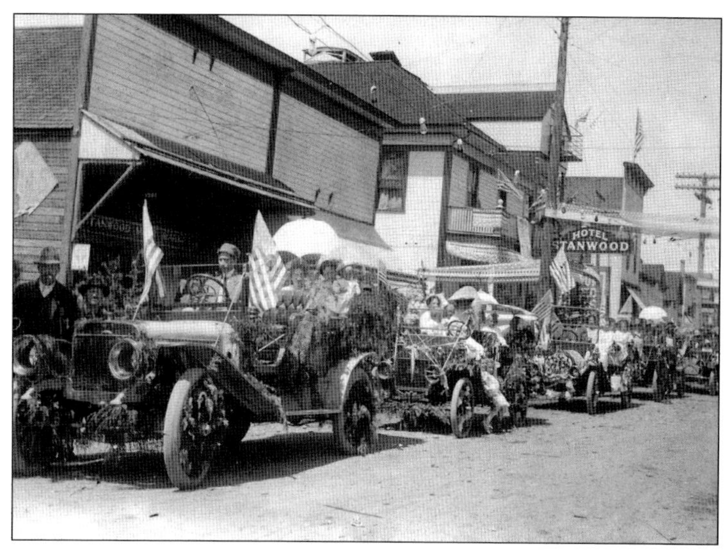

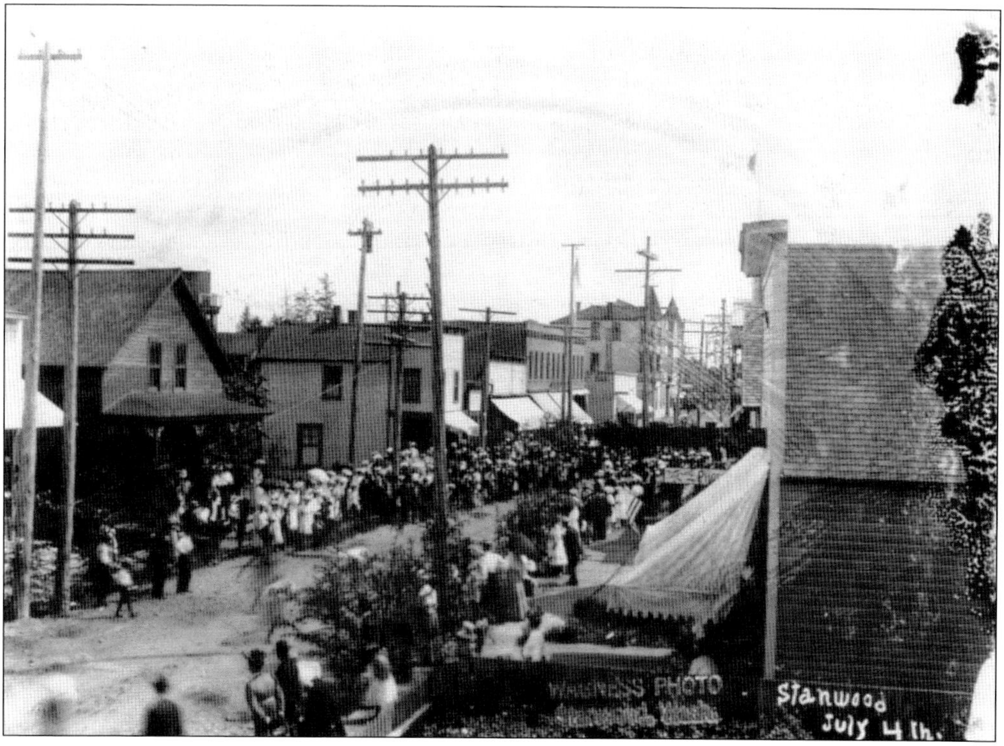

Crowds along Market Street. Wagness captured this Fourth of July celebration that clearly attracted a large crowd. This view looks south toward the east side of Market Street. On the left is the edge of the Pearson Store, built in 1906, a residence and restaurant, Knudson's jewelry storefront, the Bank of Stanwood, and the Palace Hotel in the distance. Hafstad Hardware is on the right with the awning, and beyond is the Wagness studio sign. (Photograph by John T. Wagness.)

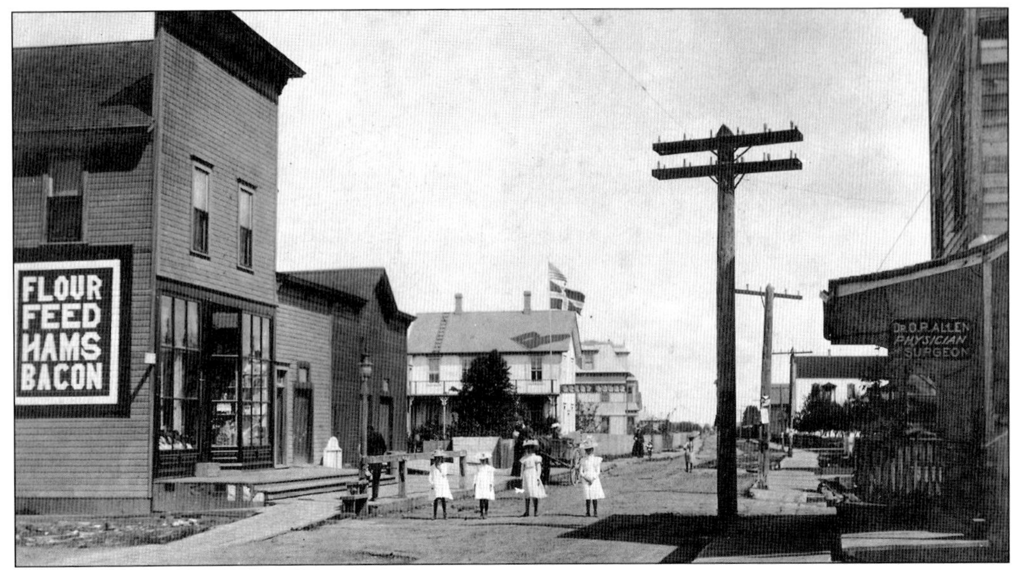

STANWOOD, MAY 17, 1900. Another occasion for celebrating in 1900 was Norwegian Independence Day. Though many Scandinavian immigrants were among the early settlers, the Norwegians seemed to celebrate more. Sytennde Mai is still celebrated to commemorate Norway's independence after long complicated alliances and dissolutions of Norway, Sweden, and Denmark. In Stanwood, the Sons and Daughters of Norway still celebrate it. Note the Ketchum Store, the Melby Hotel, and the Masonic Hall in the distance. Dr. Orville Reid Allen had an office before building his new one on Broadway. (Photograph by John T. Wagness.)

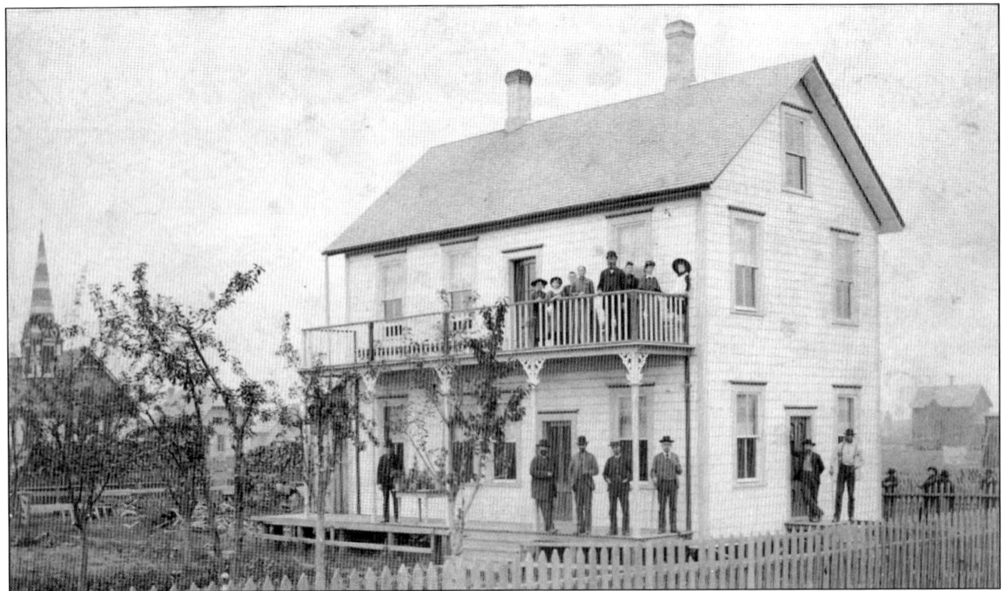

THE MELBY HOTEL, AN EARLY VIEW. The two-story Melby Hotel in Stanwood, Washington, was an early hotel for travelers built in 1889. The Methodist church is in the distance with a striped steeple. The hotel survived the fire of 1892 and added a large walkaround second-story porch. The Melbys came to Stanwood from Norway through Wisconsin, Chicago, and British Columbia and farmed in the valley first. They moved upriver in 1882 and soon moved to Stanwood. Ole K. Melby died in 1911. (Photograph by C.E. Wightman.)

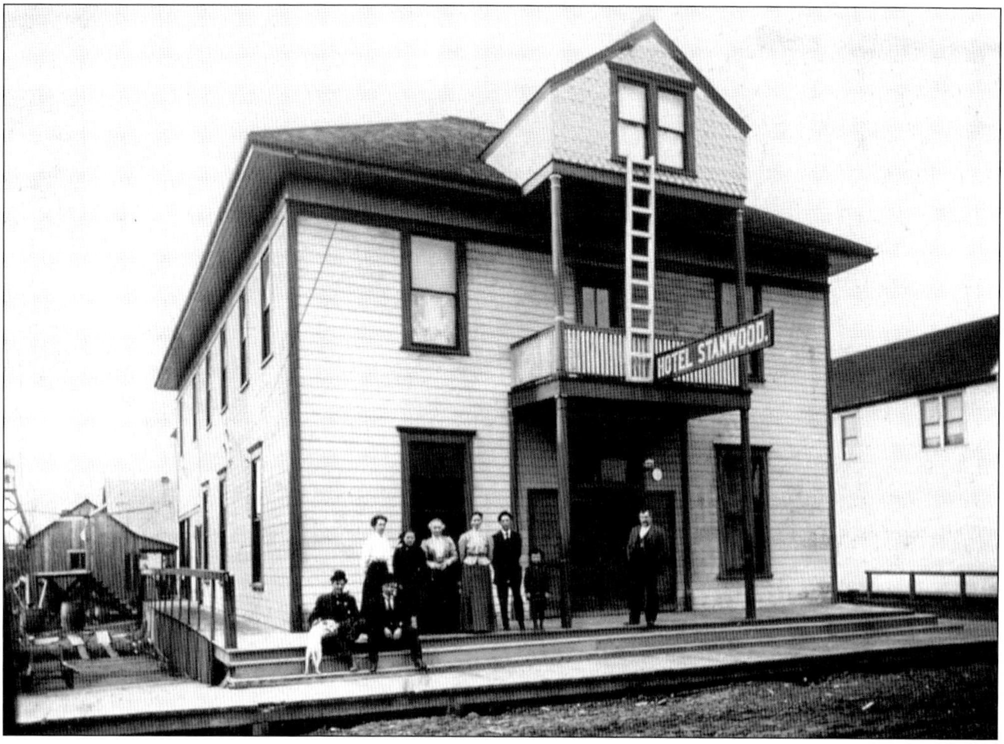

Hotel Stanwood. The second Stanwood Hotel building still remains at the corner of Market and Main Streets. It no longer has the third-floor room in the front. It remains a busy institution that has had many owners and proprietors over the last 120 years. In the earliest years, mill workers purchased meal cards to eat there. It became a tavern with a card room after Prohibition. Its first owners are said to have been Ira and Clara Galloupe. (Photograph by John T. Wagness.)

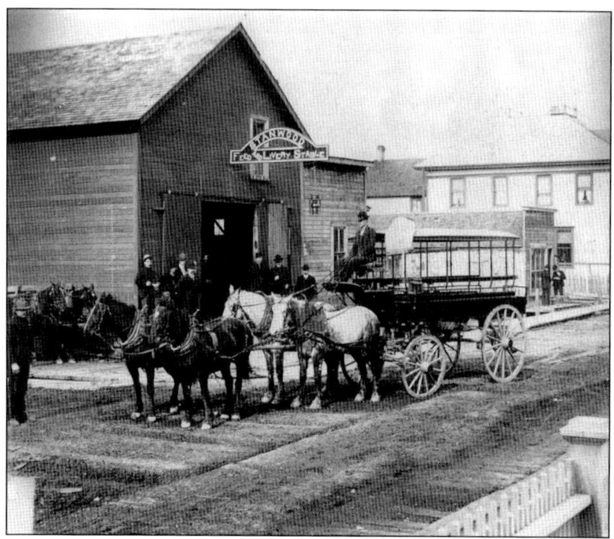

Stanwood Feed & Livery Stable. The Hall's Transfer Co. & Stanwood Feed & Livery Stable was operated by John W. Hall, who came to Stanwood in 1890 on his wedding trip from Kansas. He first worked for Robert Bates and later took on the livery. The Stanwood Feed & Livery building was located south of the Stanwood Hotel. The livery delivered mail and passengers between the waterfront and the Great Northern Railroad station. Later, John W. Hall was called on to establish the H&H Railroad between Stanwood and the depot one mile east. (Photograph by John T. Wagness.)

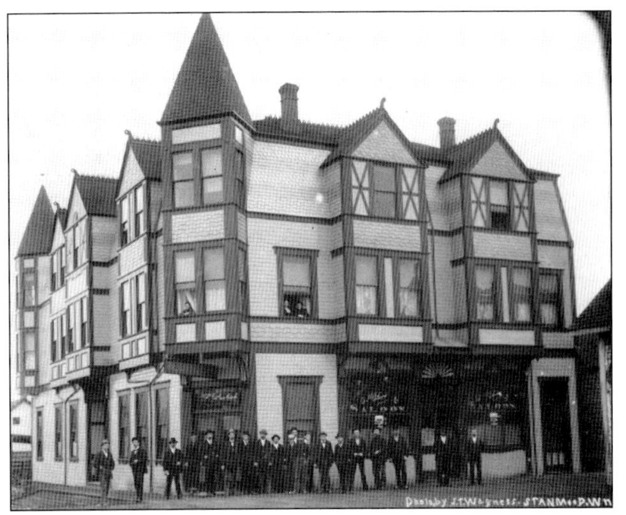

The Palace Hotel. The Palace Hotel dominated the waterfront of Stanwood for many years. Its first owner is thought to have been Sam Gilpatrick. Bill Conners took over with H.C. Whalen as proprietor in 1916 with a billiard hall and confectionery. In 1920, it was moved to the corner of Broadway and Market Streets with Bill Conners still as manager. In 1926, it became the Hotel Graham, and it was again remodeled and renovated. (Photograph by John T. Wagness.)

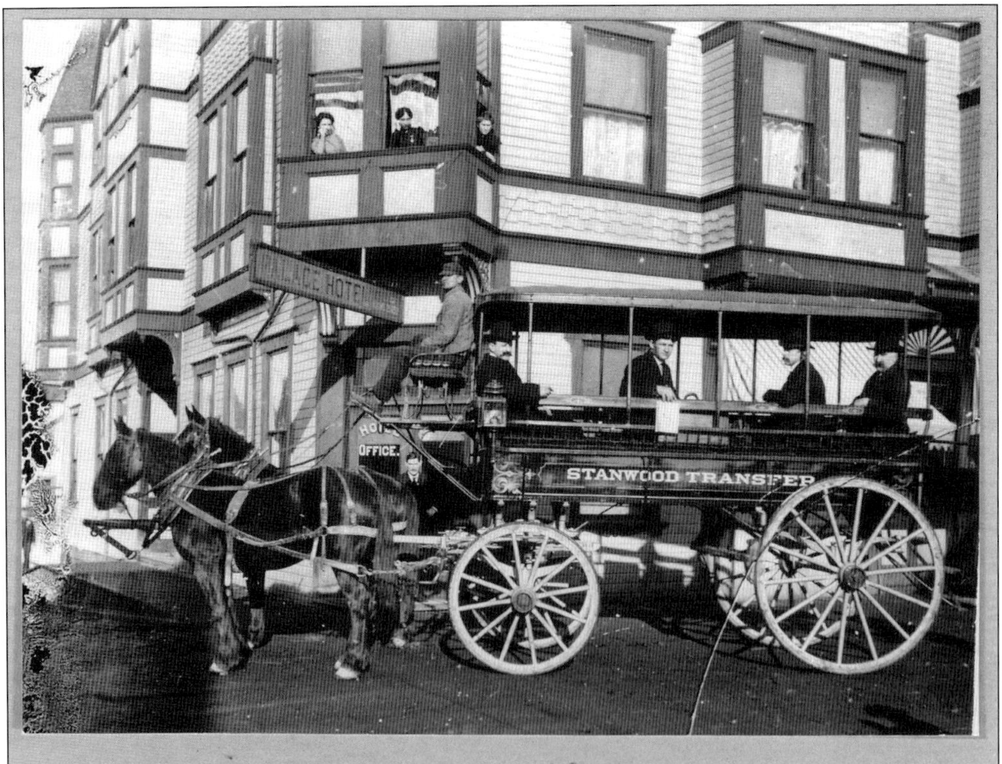

Stanwood Transfer. This beautiful carriage was operated by John W. Hall, who owned the livery stable. The livery is posed in front of the Palace Hotel with the ladies looking out the windows. The photograph inspired many assumptions about the reputation of the hotel. In a 1903 advertisement, the Palace Hotel was promoted as a "Headquarters for Commercial Men, The best fish and hunting in close vicinity. Boats and Attendants furnished. First class bar in connection." The carriage driver was Faye Miller. It was sometimes referred to as "Hall's Hack." (Photograph by John T. Wagness.)

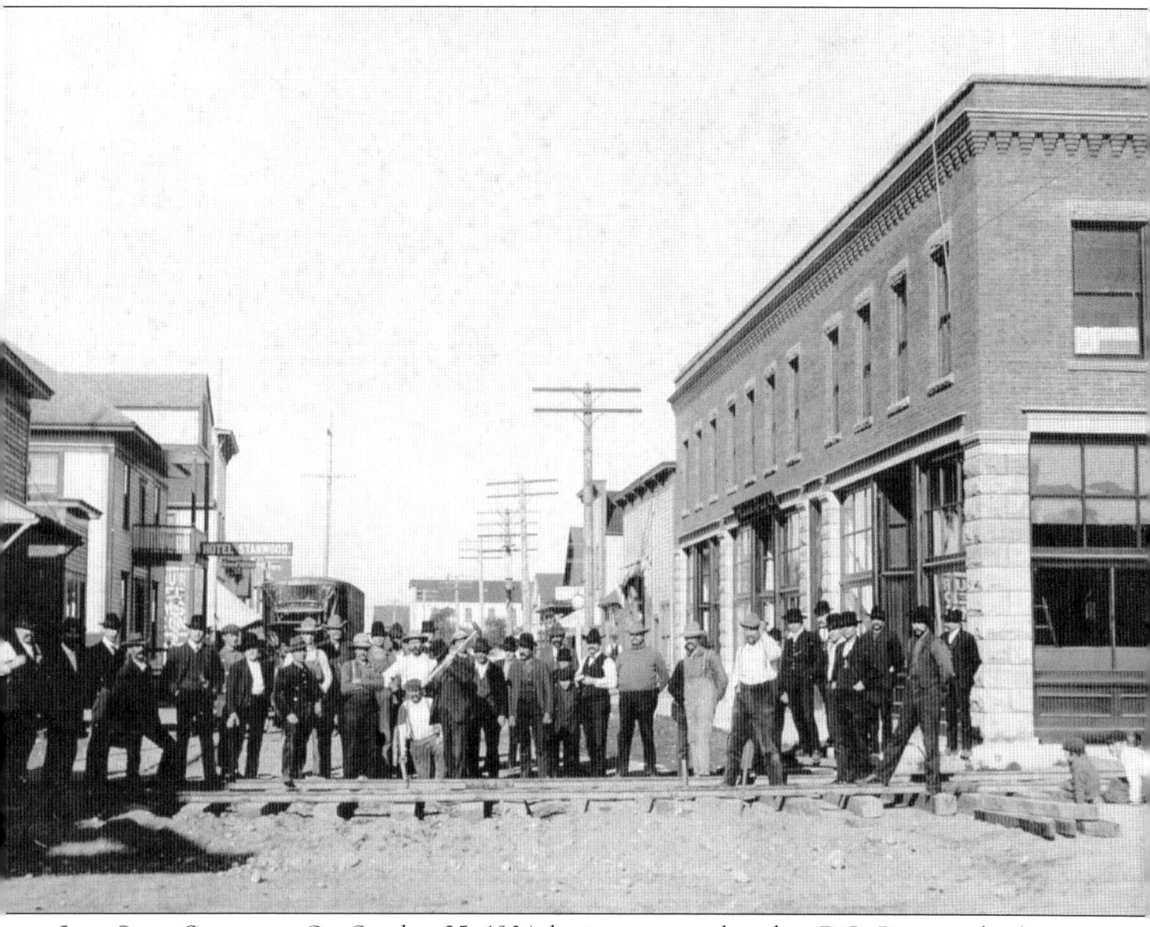

Last Spike Ceremony. On October 25, 1904, businessmen gathered as D.O. Pearson, the first mayor of Stanwood, drove the last spike into the railroad crossing at Market Street and Broadway. Not exactly the transcontinental connection but important to Stanwood, it was built ultimately to transport goods from the sawmills to the Great Northern Railroad at the depot in what was to become East Stanwood. This view looks north with the Hotel Stanwood on the left, and in the distance is the two-story Masonic Hall. On the right is the Bank of Stanwood. (Photograph by John T. Wagness.)

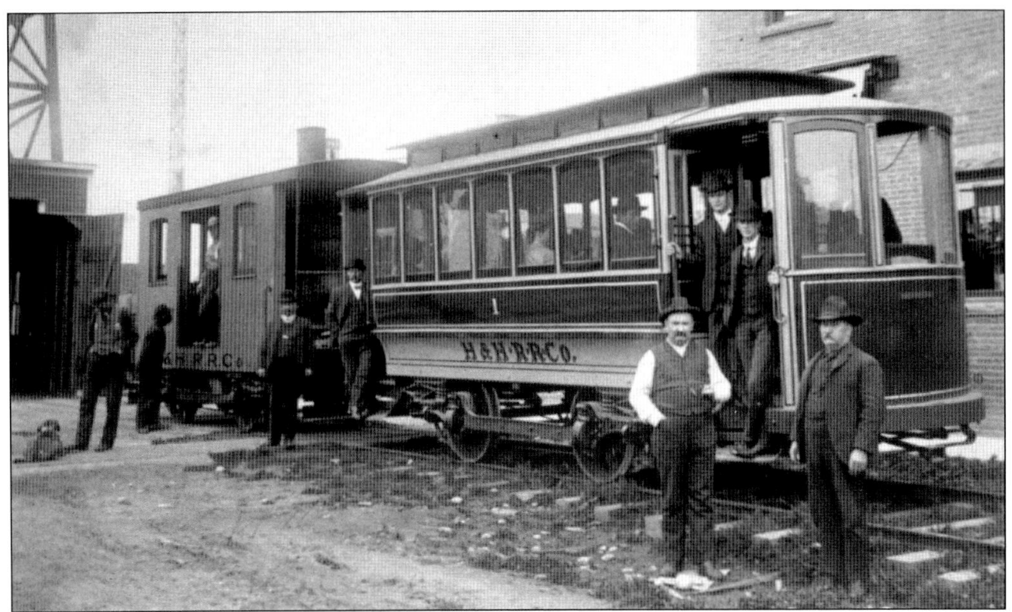

H&H Railroad Co. The trolley and first engine of the H&H Railroad streetcar are seen here with local store owner Charlie Hancock on the left and John W. Hall, the owner, on the right. For its first year or so, it ran from the bank building and the Palace Hotel, which was the livery route, and carried US mail. The gasoline engine was not a success, so it was replaced a year later. (Photograph by John T. Wagness.)

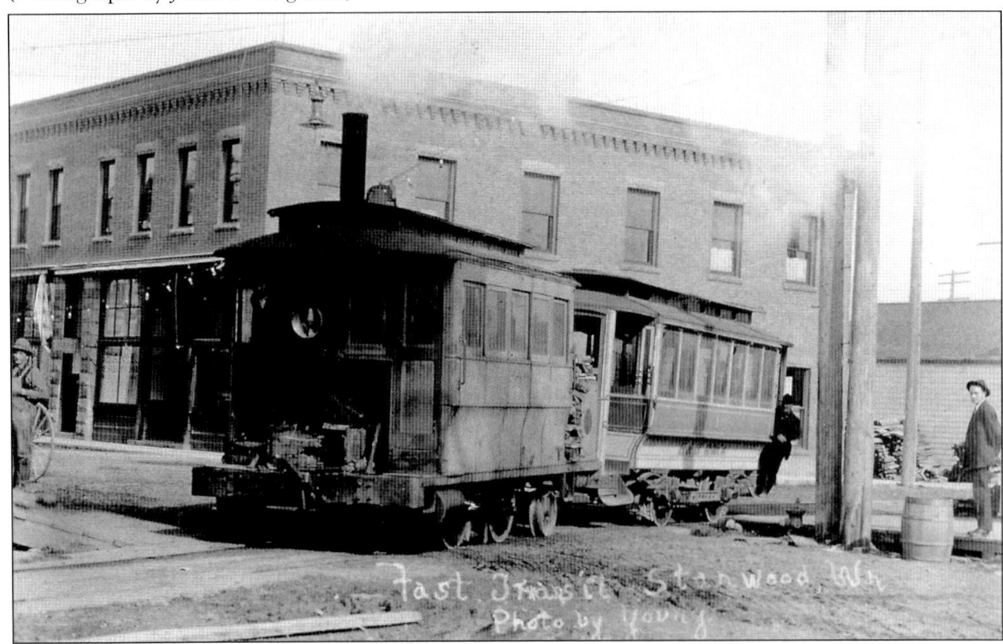

Fast Transit, Stanwood. In 1905, Hall acquired a new 18-ton Shay engine. It is shown here at the intersection of Market Street and Broadway. In 1907, because of the narrowness of Saratoga Street, part of the corner of Hall's livery barn on Market Street had to be cut to extend the railway down to the Stanwood Lumber Company's mill. He had so far invested over $10,000. (Photograph by Robert A. Young.)

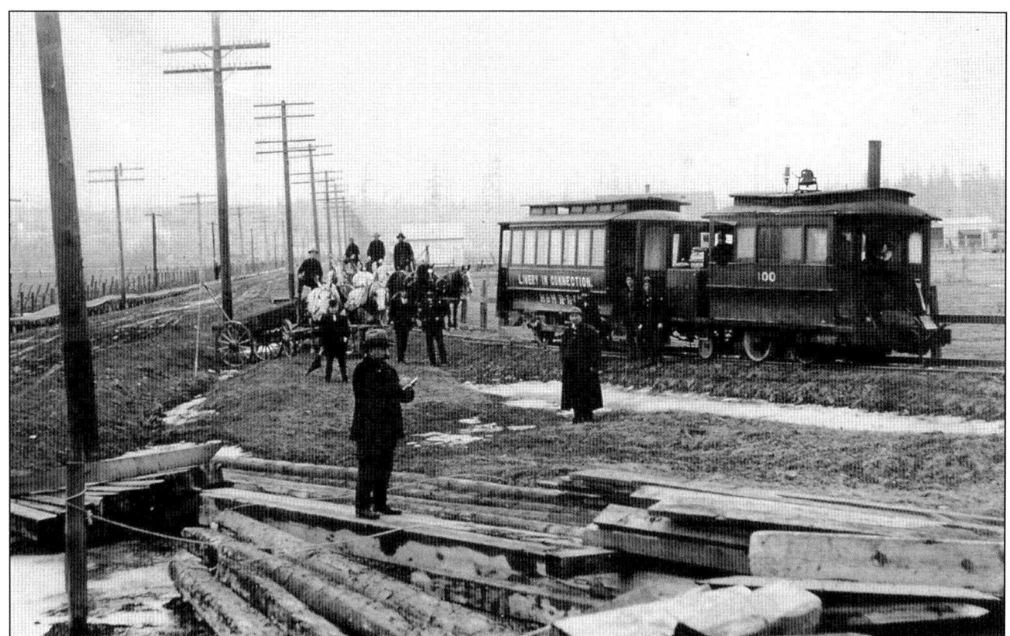

The H&H Railroad Rounding Another Curve. The route of the H&H tracks curved again just east of the original Stanwood city limits, where it met the road between Stanwood and East Stanwood, sometimes called Burnway. In the faint distance is the hillside east of the Great Northern Railroad tracks and the telephone lines. From here, it passes between the two large farms of the Lien family and Francis Giard.

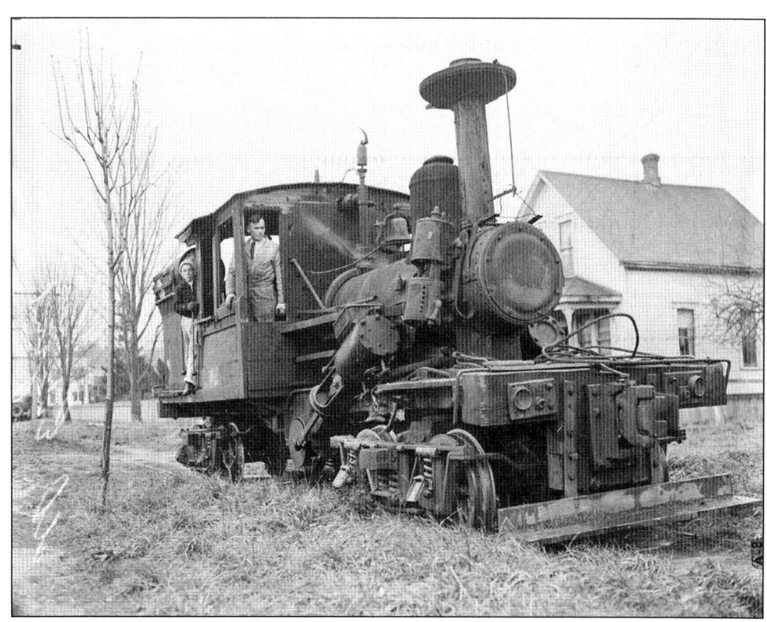

Climax Engine and Jesse Hall. This is one of the last runs of the old Climax engine of the H&H Railroad. Jesse N. Hall is standing running the engine through the grassy tracks. Behind is Jesse Hall, grandson of John W. Hall, the original builder of the railroad.

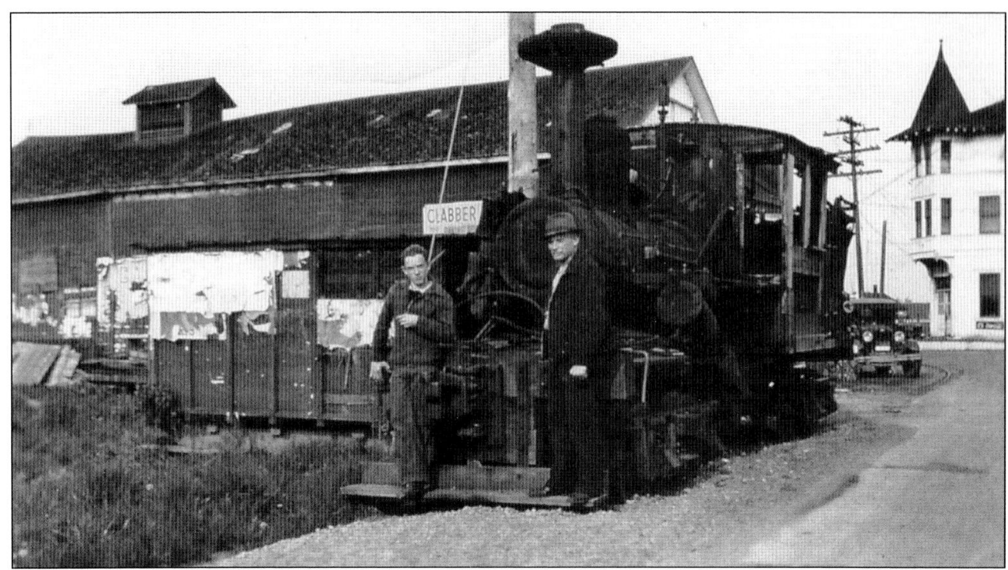

The Climax Engine. After its last run, the Climax engine sat along the waterfront for many years until it was scrapped for metal for World War II. Jesse Hall is on the right. Beyond the engine are one of the packing plant buildings soon to be torn down and the Palace Hotel with its distinctive towers when it was known as the Hotel Graham.

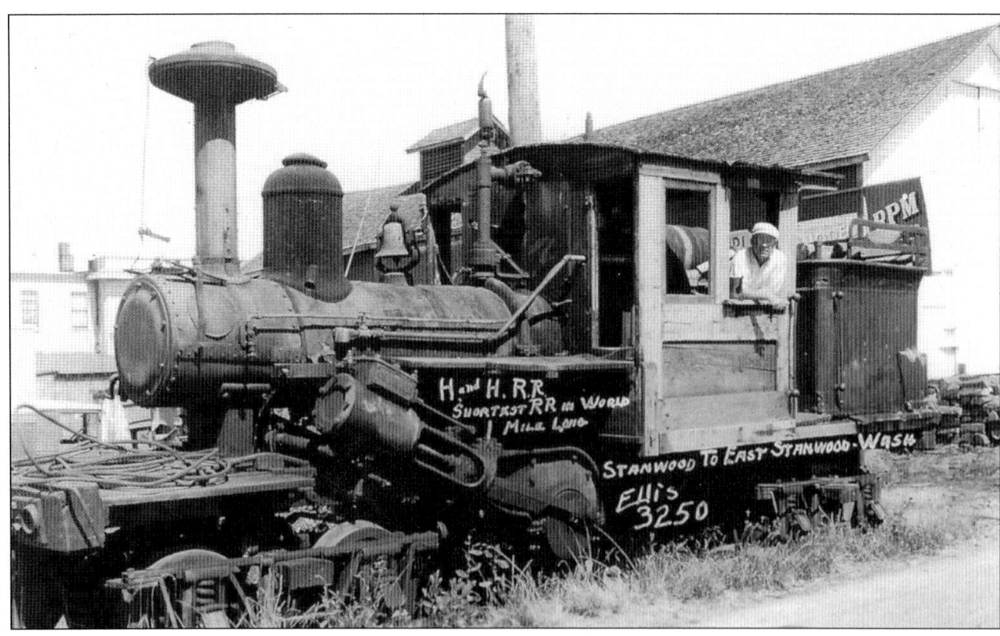

Shortest Railroad in the World. This small railroad started with a used steam engine and trolley in 1905 and ran until the 1930s. It changed engines and did not carry passengers in its later years. In the late 1920s and 1930s, its operation depended on the needs of the mills. The last run of the H&H Railroad was in January 1938. The Climax engine sat in disuse along Broadway until it was scrapped. This image was published as a postcard. (Photograph by J. Boyd Ellis.)

Three

WORKING WATERFRONT

In spite of the shallowness of the Stillaguamish River, Stanwood had and continues to have an active but mostly industrial waterfront. The river is tidal, and steamboats not only had to navigate the river but also consider the tides at all times. This chapter focuses on the age of steamboats, the small Matterand Boatyard, and the local lumber industry. Later, the industrial use continued as food processing grew and Twin City Foods dominated the waterfront. Only recently is the City of Stanwood trying to create public access points beginning with a small park and small boat access at the Hamilton Stack.

In 1868, there was a logging camp on the hillside near the depot to the east. The logs were driven down the Irvine Slough to the Stillaguamish River where the Hamilton Lumber stack now towers over Stanwood. The slough was a tributary of the Stillaguamish that ran east toward the hillside.

In March 1888, the steamer *Bob Irving* took a load of lumber as far as Norman, about four miles up the river. On its way down, it picked up a load of hay, grain, and groceries at Stanwood and Utsalady and traveled to the Skagit River, where the boiler exploded. The captain and fireman were instantly killed. According to historian Gus Joergenson, the *Harvester* was the last big steamboat to go up the river as far as Florence in 1916.

The course of the river began to change by this time. As early as 1923, when the Clough mill bought the Wisconsin Timber Co., it almost immediately began to experience difficulty shipping out lumber. Shipping out of Stanwood was decreasing rapidly because of the channel in front of Stanwood becoming more and more shallow. An *Everett Herald* article reported in 1923 that local businessmen from the Stanwood Commercial Club wrote that silt and debris accumulated in the river mouth to such a depth that boats could make this stop only at high tide. This caused the river to seek other outlets, and in one case, the current has been directed into Hatt Slough, which has become the main river channel. As a result of the lobbying, a dredger, the *Swinomish*, scooped out a change from Clough to the mouth of the river.

Robert Davis, lifetime resident and son of the Davis Hardware owners, wrote that in 1932 or 1933, a heavy spring freshet changed the channel of the river three or four miles up so that it emptied through Hatt Slough into Port Susan. The original channel gradually filled with sediment.

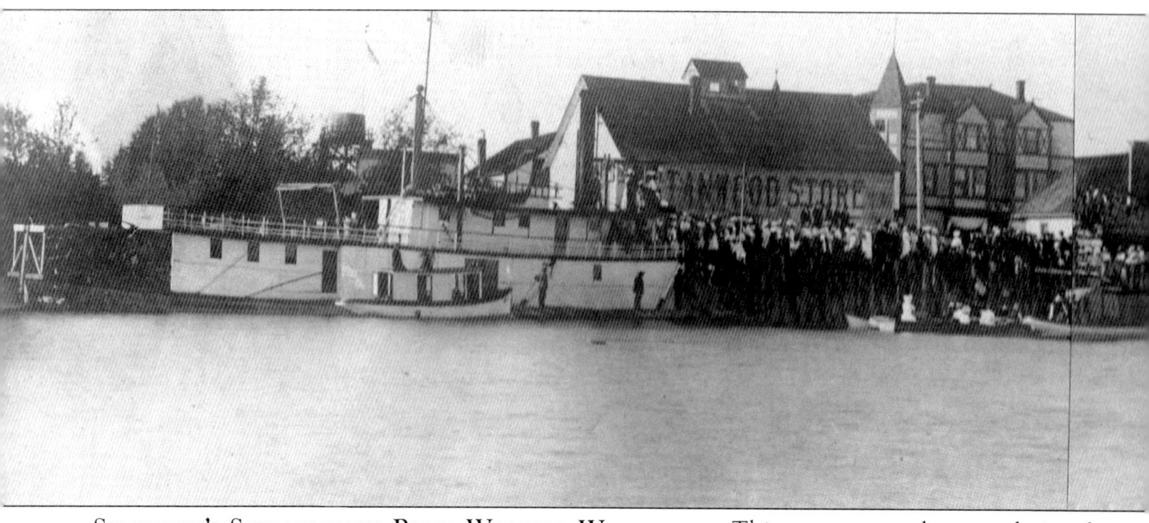

STANWOOD'S STILLAGUAMISH RIVER WORKING WATERFRONT. This panorama photograph is of Stanwood's waterfront on a celebration day, possibly the Fourth of July, about 1905. The views are perhaps of the same event as the swimming photograph below. From the left, note the water tower, the second D.O. Pearson's Stanwood Store, the Palace Hotel, and various forgotten commercial

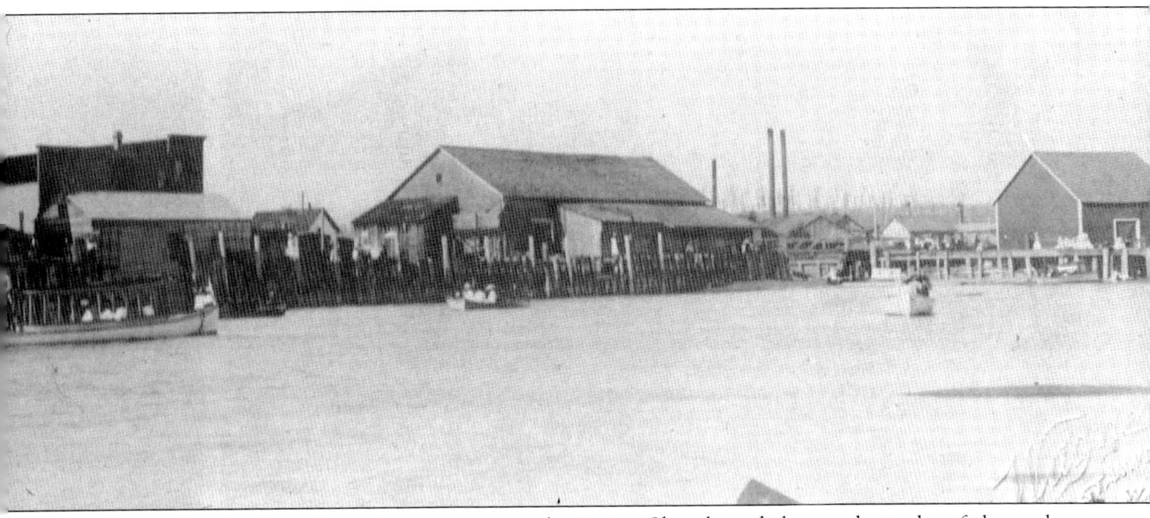

buildings. On the far right is the entrance to the Irvine Slough and the smokestacks of the early shingle mill. Note the variety of watercraft and the expanse of the river's width. (Photograph by John T. Wagness.)

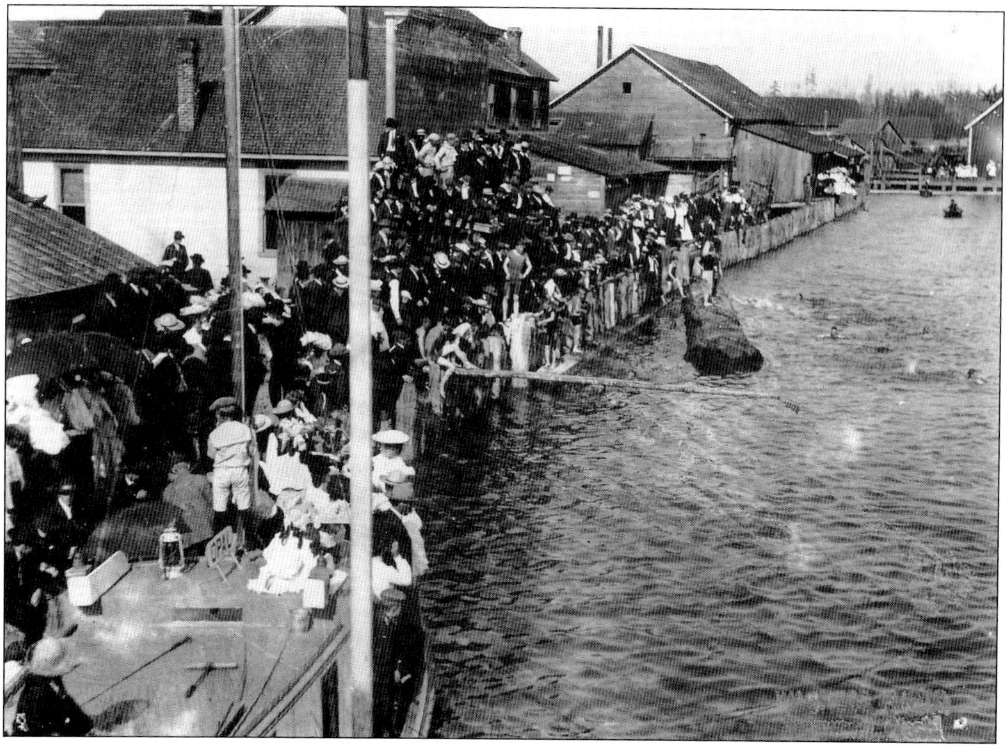

Logrolling Contest? Swimming in the Stillaguamish River is no longer encouraged, nor is the water as deep. Future loggers are perhaps learning to walk on logs. The *Opal* was a large launch often seen on the waterfront. It was owned by Charlie Johnson to carry fish to buyers. (Photograph by John T. Wagness.)

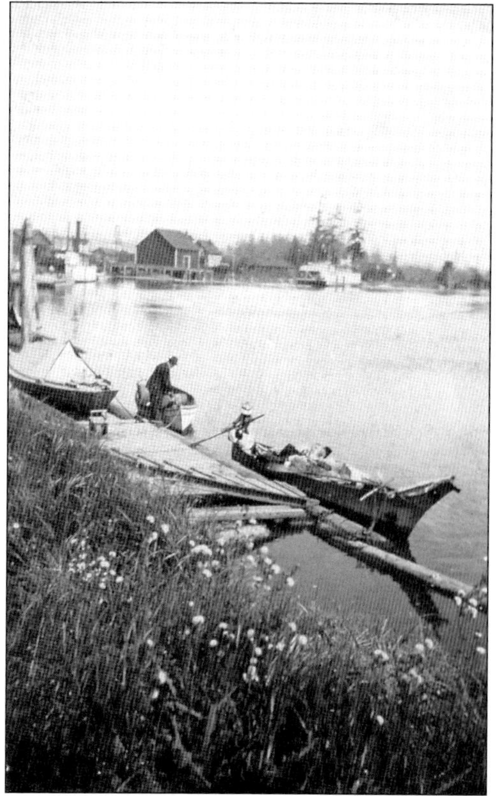

West Coast Indian Canoe. The waterfront was active with rowboats, riverboats, launches, and occasionally with canoes, like this Coast Salish Indian canoe. The Coast Salish canoe was common and used on more open waters than the river canoes. Made of western red cedar, they were carefully selected, carved, and spread from 22 inches to 29 inches. Canoes were used by Indians to transport passengers and carry the belongings of homesteaders upriver.

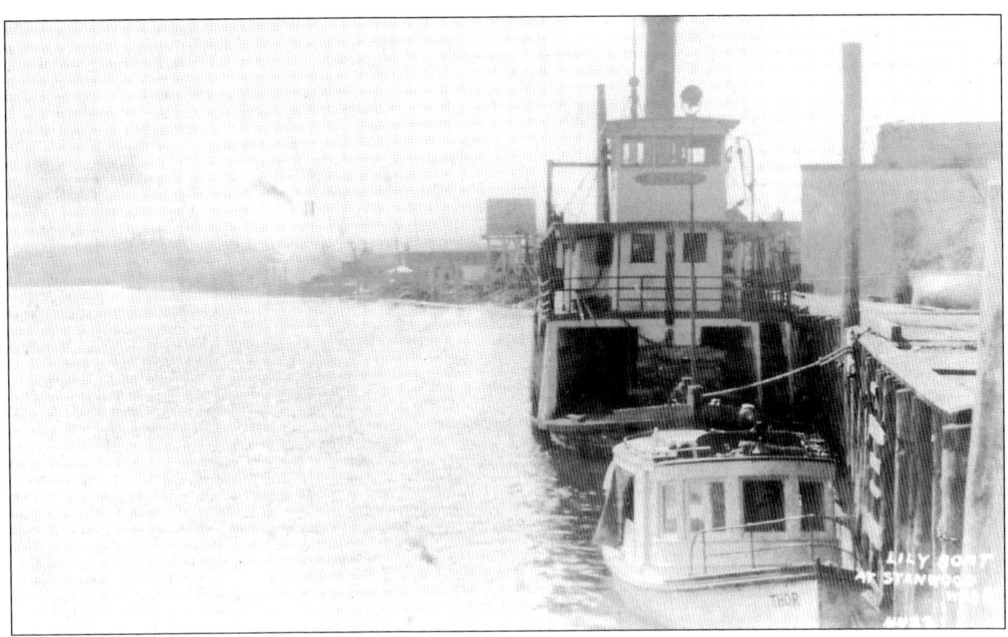

LILY BOAT, STANWOOD, WASHINGTON. The *Lily* was used as a tugboat that brought logs to Stanwood, where it was stationed. Other steamboats usually would not layover. The *Thor* is the smaller boat in the foreground. The *Lily* was built in 1881 and was 73 feet long and had a 16-foot beam with a 3-foot hold. Capt. Charles R. Durgan of Stanwood was captain until 1913. Captain Durgan came from Ireland in about 1859 and arrived in Stanwood in about 1888. He did log towing for the Florence and English Lumber Companies and the Stillaguamish Boom Co. The *Lily* was abandoned in 1930.

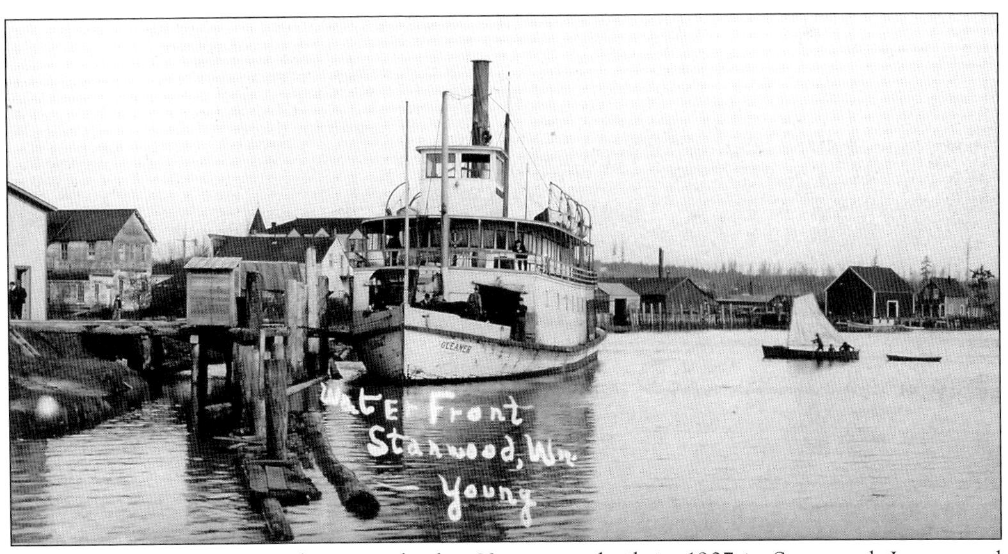

WATERFRONT, STANWOOD. The sternwheeler *Gleaner* was built in 1907 in Stanwood. It operated between Tulalip, Stanwood, Fir, Skagit City, Mount Vernon, and Avon. In 1908, it was christened, and in 1924, it was enlarged. This view looks east along the Stanwood City Dock. The shingle mill is just beyond on the right of the stern. This mill was the first mill along the waterfront at the mouth of the Irvine Slough. (Photograph by Robert J. Young.)

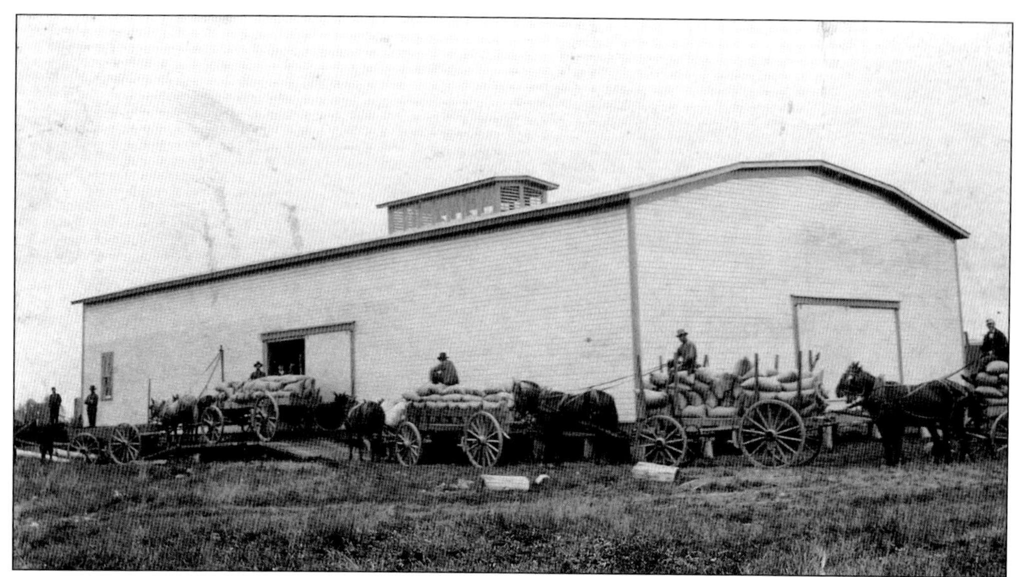

GRANARY ALONG WATERFRONT. Wagons lined up at the granary to weigh, store, and sell their sacks of grain. The granary, owned by W.R. Stockbridge and H.C. Anderson, was where farmers stored grains, primarily oats, for the steamers to pick up. The grain company brokered the grain. The company moved to East Stanwood along the railroad tracks in 1914 and became the Stanwood Grain Company and, later, the Twin City Grain Company. (Photograph by John T. Wagness.)

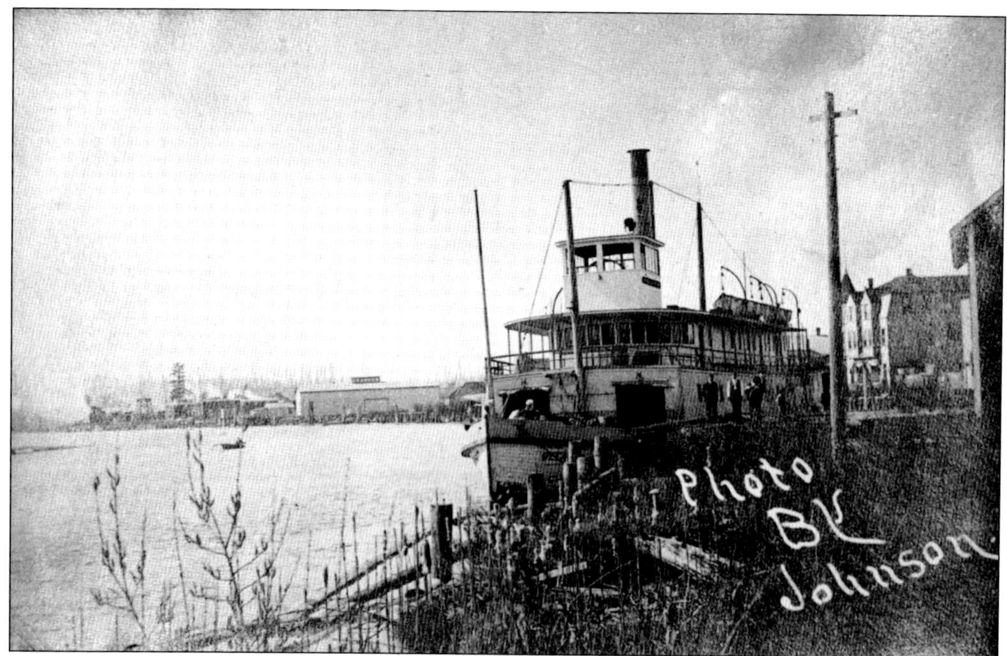

STEAMBOAT *GLEANER* ALONG THE WATERFRONT. The 422-ton, 145-foot *Gleaner* replaced the *Skagit Queen* and *Lily*. The Palace Hotel is at right, and the granary is in the distance. In the distance is the smoke from the mill buildings and the faint silhouettes of trees on Camano Island. (Photograph by Edward A. Johnson.)

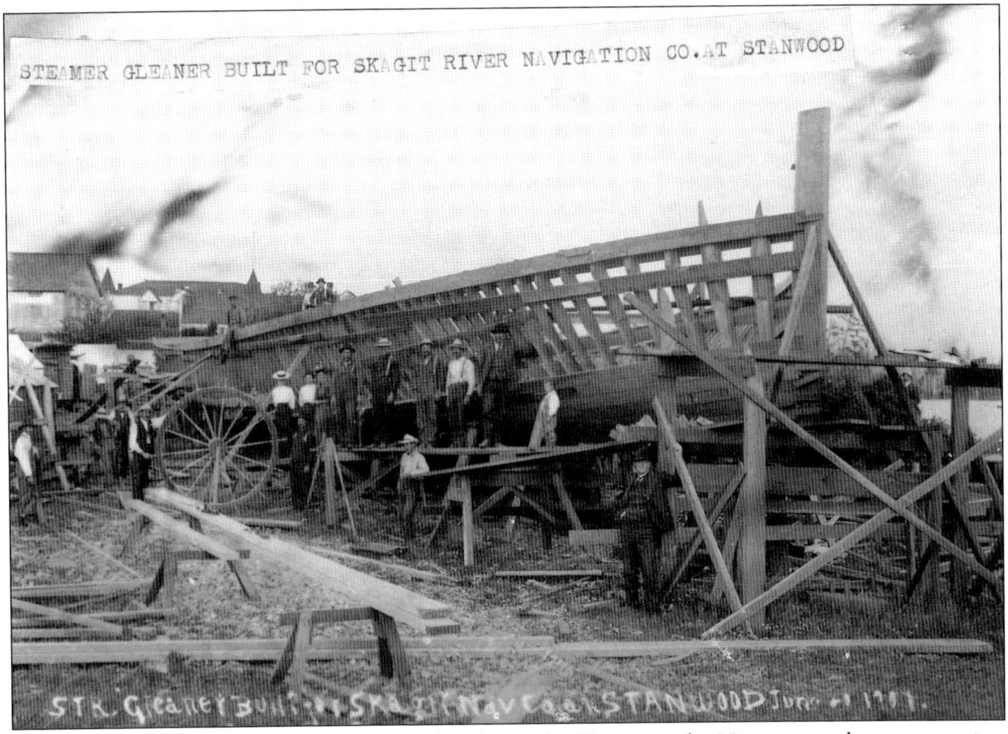

Steamer *Gleaner*, Built in Stanwood. This shows the *Gleaner* or the *Harvester* under construction by the Skagit Navigation Company. The well-known paddle wheeler had a 30-foot beam but drew only 22 inches of water. She carried freight and a few passengers to many ports in the area, including Seattle.

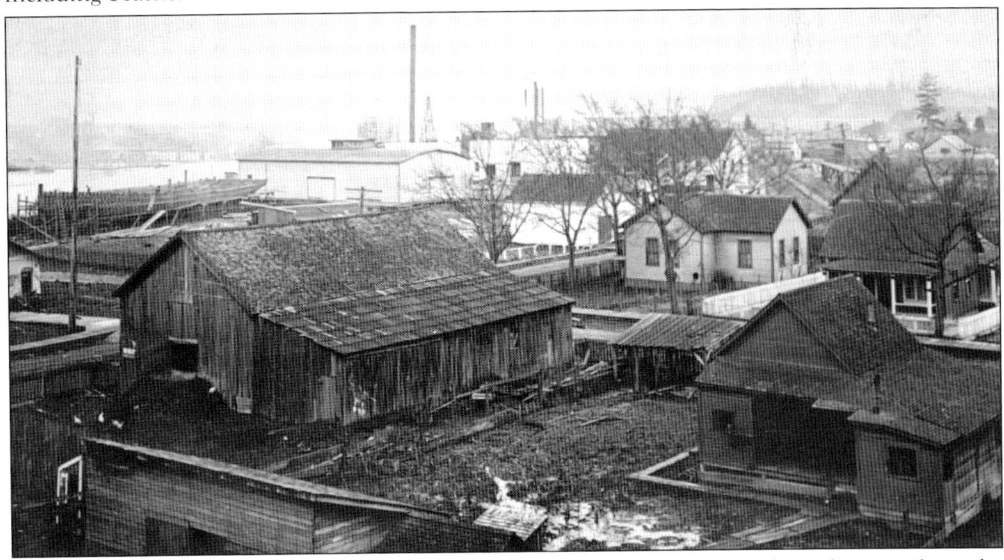

Steamboat under Construction. This is another view that shows where along the waterfront the *Gleaner* was built. The *Harvester* was christened in June 1912 and was larger than the *Gleaner*. The road is Saratoga Street, which curves following the waterfront around to the Stanwood Lumber Company and in 1909 to the bridge to Camano Island. The road went past the Ovenell Farm buildings owned now by the City of Stanwood.

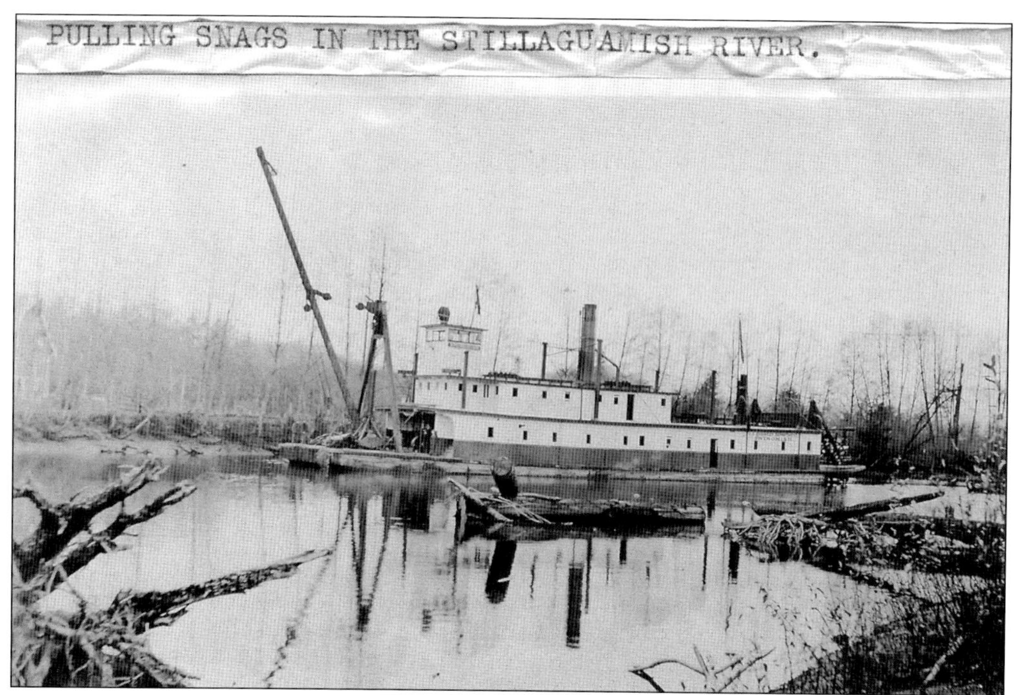

Pulling Snags in the Stillaguamish River. The steamboat *Swinomish*, above, was a sternwheeler built at LaConner in 1903. In 1884, the first snagboat, the *Skagit*, was put into service to remove snags by the US government. She served until 1914, when she was replaced by the *Swinomish*. The *Swinomish* was later replaced by the *W.T. Preston* in 1929. When the *W.T. Preston* needed replacement because of her wooden hull, the Corps of Engineers built a new steel-hulled snagboat. The second 1939 *W.T. Preston* is preserved in Anacortes as a national landmark.

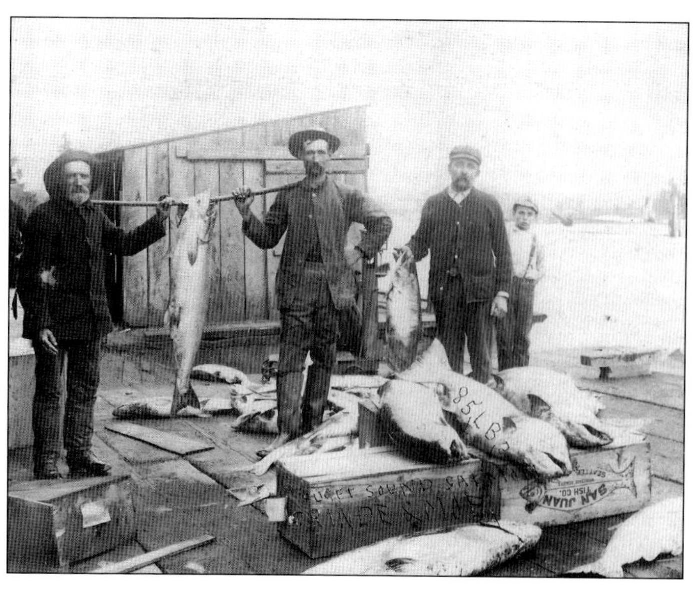

Puget Sound Salmon. The fishermen on the wharf pose for Wagness with their 85-pound salmon. The fishermen were "Grinde & Moe" for the San Juan Fish Co. Fishing was not a large industry for Stanwood, but in 1898, F.P. Friday established a salmon cannery. From left to right are Eric Grinde, Peter Moe, Albert Moe, and an unidentified boy. Everett Canning Company owned the cannery, but it was locally known as the Friday's Fish Cannery in the news.

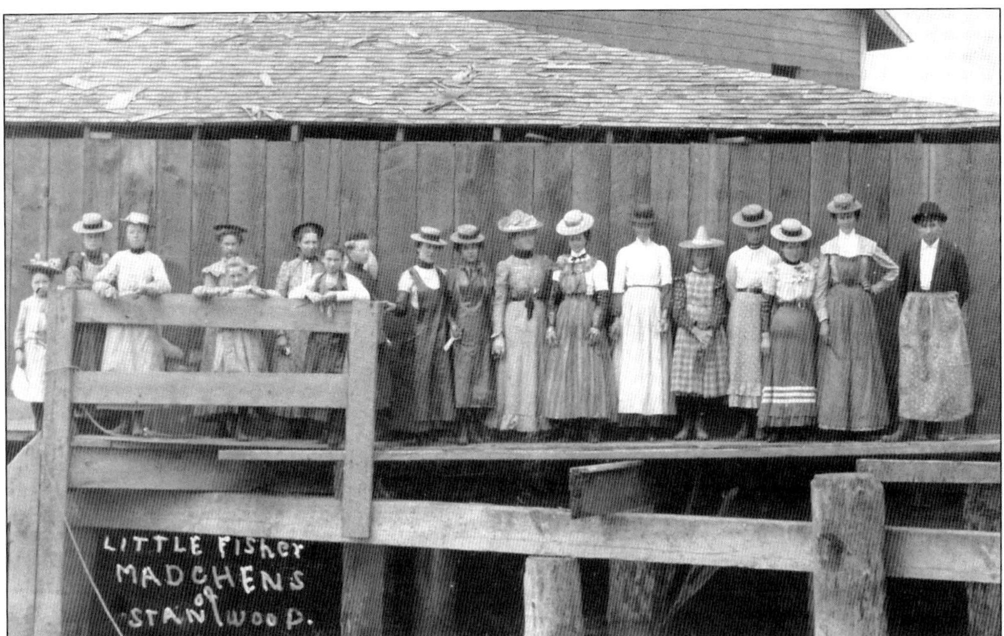

LITTLE FISHER MADCHENS, STANWOOD. This group of women were fish cannery workers on the Stanwood wharf. Their names included Margaret Parker, Isabel Bensen, Gilma Tjerne, Gertrude Miller, Rita Moran, Olive Gilchrist, Minna Shervin, Elsie Lien, Lena (Inions) Gilchrist, Ella (Martine) Olson, Malfa Tjerne, Hattie Chapman, and Emma Foss.

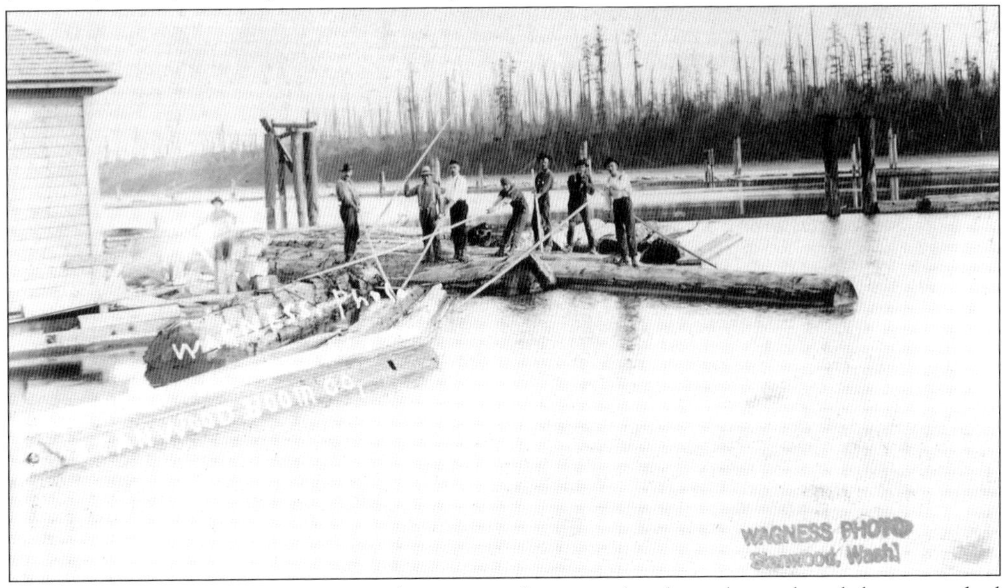

STANWOOD BOOM COMPANY, 1895. This group of men with pike poles and cork boots worked for the Stanwood Boom Company. It was active in 1895 according to a map showing permission granted by the State of Washington for clearing out, driving, sorting, organizing, holding, and delivering logs and other timber products. The boom logs kept the logs from hanging up on the bank as the tide fell. The men wore cork or calk shoes so they could have secure footing while poling the logs. The boom company was said to be operated by George Kunze of the Wisconsin Lumber Company. (Photograph by John T. Wagness.)

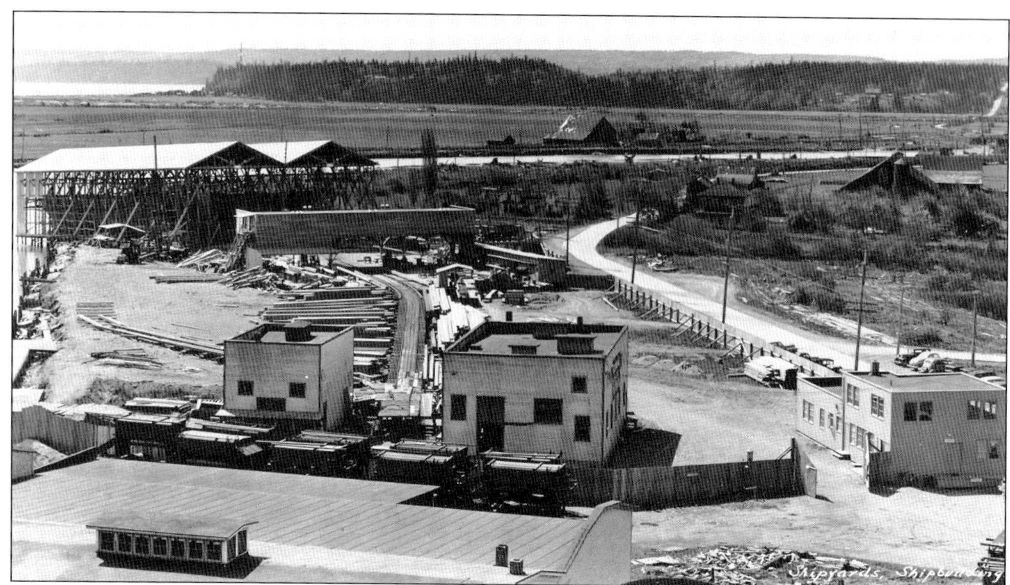

Shipyards during World War II. This view of the mouth of the Stillaguamish River shows the West Pass of the river as it flowed out to Skagit Bay. In the distance are Leque Island and Camano Island. In December 1942, the Carl E. Edlund Shipyard was established on the Stanwood Lumber Company property. From 1942 to 1944, seven ocean-going wooden barges were built for the Army at the shipyards with different contracts. They launched the first barge shortly before they changed names to the Stanwood Shipyards. (Photograph by Soren Sorensen.)

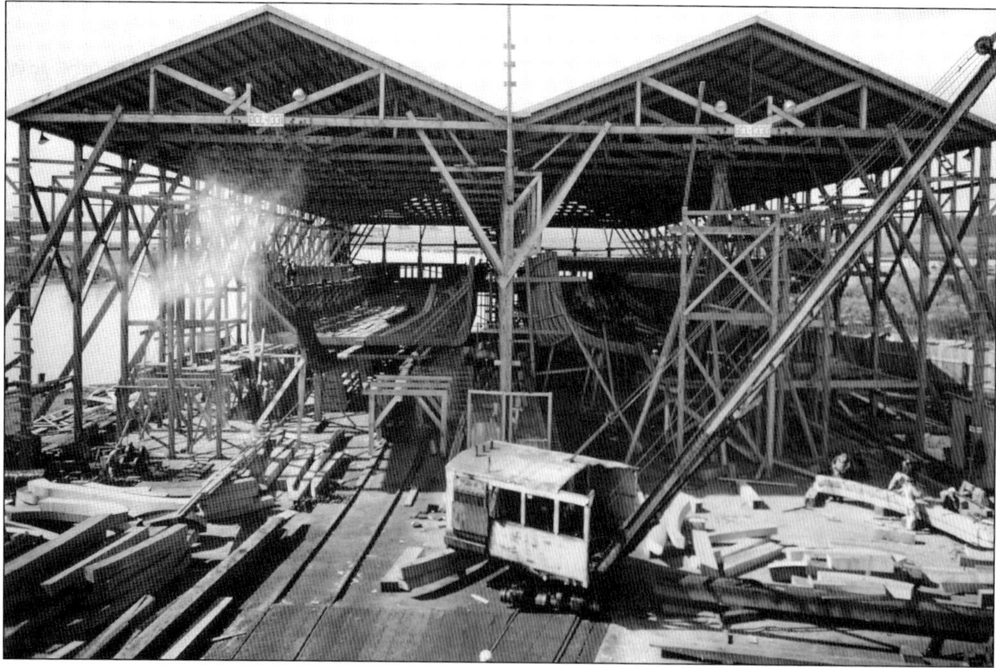

Stanwood Shipyards. In July 1943, the US Army Transport Corps barge *BCL-1330* was launched; it was reported the second barge, *BCL-1331*, was christened in September. The third barge was launched in December 1943. Ultimately seven barges were launched. The barges proved to be difficult to control, and many ended up on breakwaters along the sound. (Photograph by Soren Sorensen.)

BCL-1601 Launch, June 30, 1944. "BCL" stands for Barge Cargo Large (dry) for barges built during World War II. More than 6,000 barges were built during this war. They were nonpropelled 203-foot barges. The fourth barge was launched in January 1944. (Photograph by Ray Krantz.)

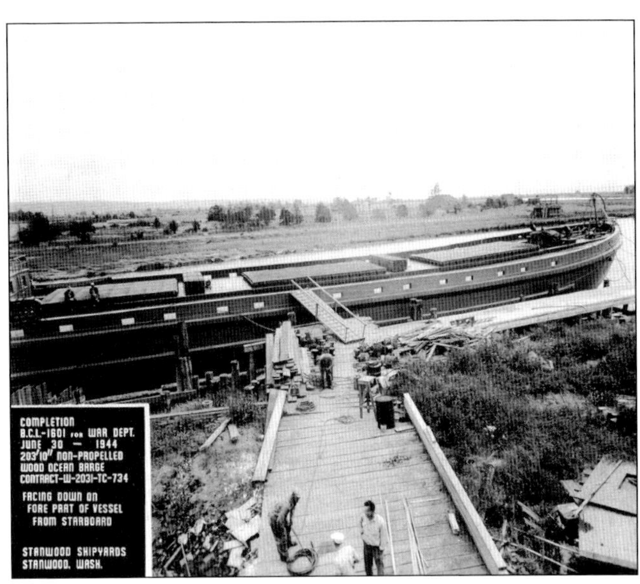

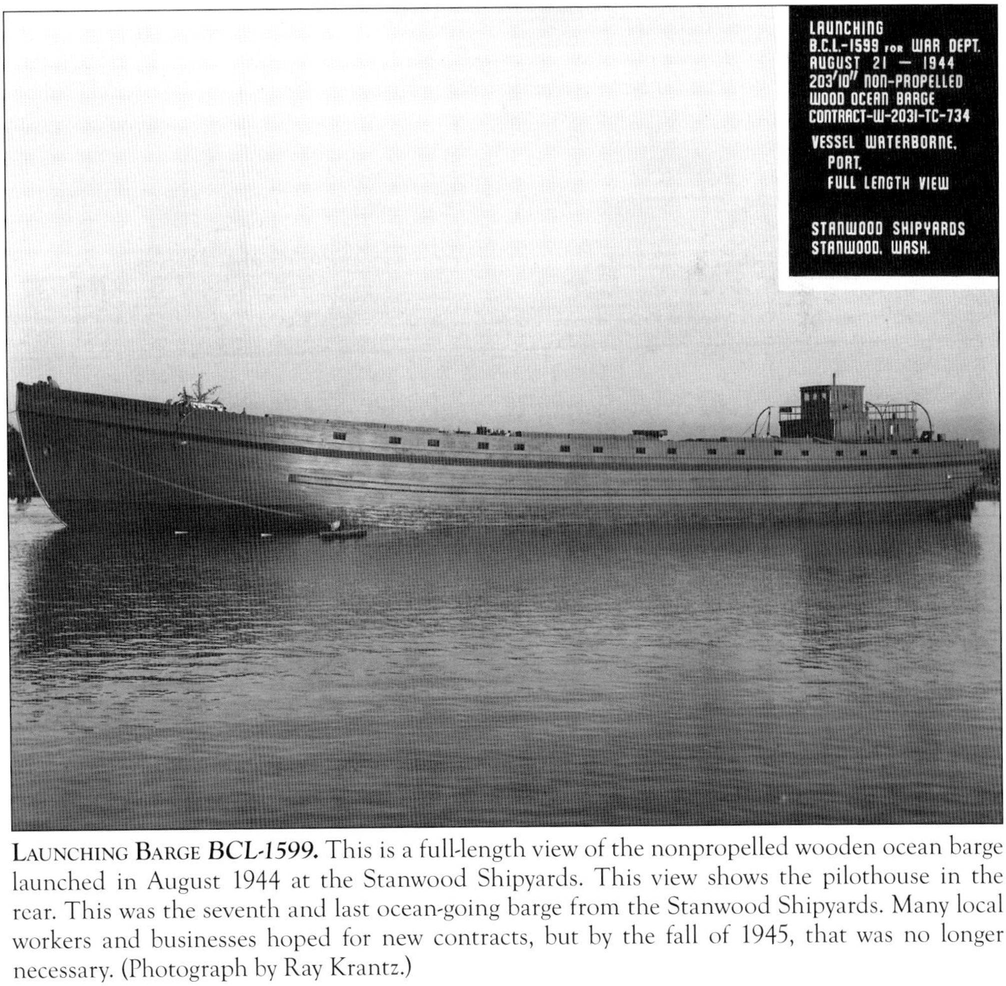

Launching Barge *BCL-1599*. This is a full-length view of the nonpropelled wooden ocean barge launched in August 1944 at the Stanwood Shipyards. This view shows the pilothouse in the rear. This was the seventh and last ocean-going barge from the Stanwood Shipyards. Many local workers and businesses hoped for new contracts, but by the fall of 1945, that was no longer necessary. (Photograph by Ray Krantz.)

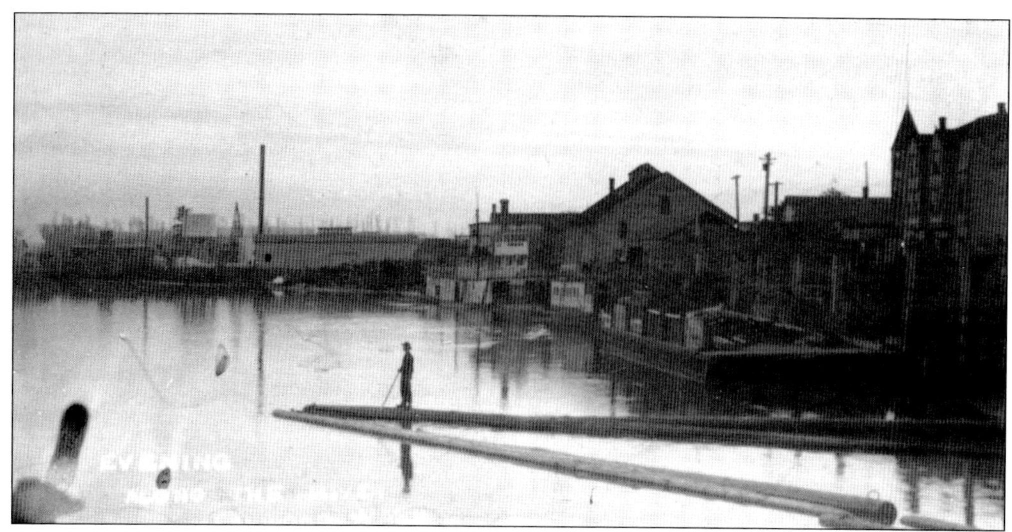

Evening along the River, Looking West. To capture this quiet calm moment on the river, the photographer was probably standing on the deck of a steamboat. The boom logs mark the Irvine Slough entrance into the Stillaguamish River. On the far right are the third-story turrets of the Palace Hotel. All of the buildings in this photograph are now gone. In their places are the buildings of the Twin City Foods Company. A boom company worker stands with a pike pole to divert wayward logs coming down the river. (Photograph by Evans.)

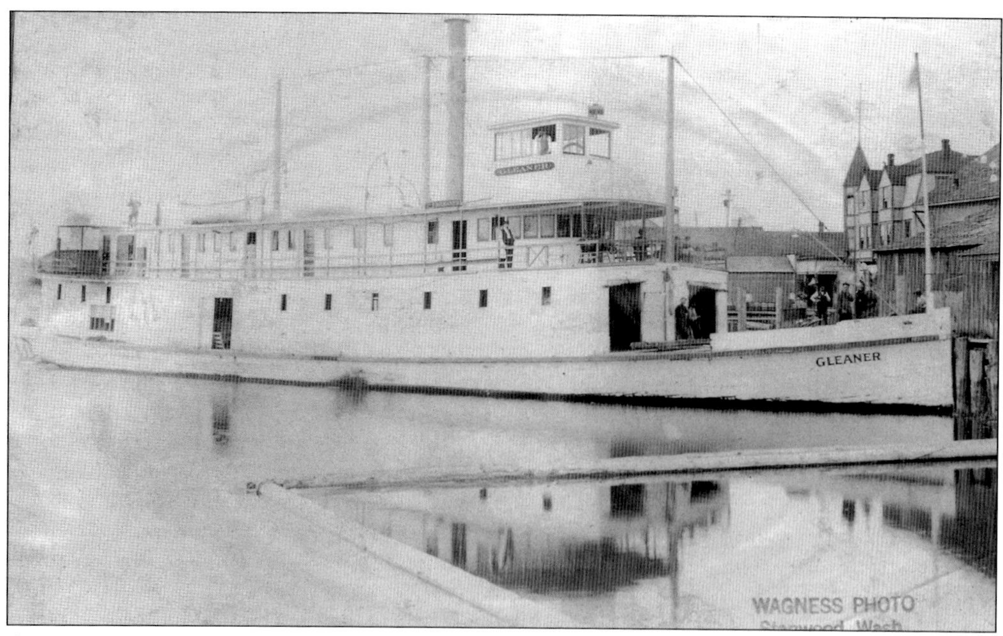

Gleaner at the Log Boom. The *Gleaner* is docked at the Irvine Slough log boom. Her captain, H.H. MacDonald of the Skagit River Navigation Company, would stop at family farm docks to load sacks of oats, the primary crop in the early days. The *Gleaner* hit a snag in December 1940 upstream from the North Fork Bridge on the Skagit River and sank. Her machinery and fittings were removed, and she was dismantled.

Four

Lumber Companies

Stanwood was a mill town. The mouth of the Stillaguamish River was active with a large shingle mill that began in about 1885 and operated until 1899, when Albert S. Howard took over the site and established the Stanwood Lumber Company. Unlike many of the local newcomers, Howard was from North Carolina. In 1884, at the age of about 23, he came to the Puget Sound. He first started a mill and farmed near Edison and Milltown until about 1896. He arrived in Stanwood in 1899 and took over a mill that was at the mouth of the river. He came with much logging experience in Skagit County. The location of water access was important. He recognized the need to ship to the railroad when that became inevitable. He died young at the age of 52 leaving the business in the hands of David Bennie, already a manager and part owner of the mill.

Shingle mills surrounded Stanwood. In Stanwood, there was a shingle mill that also became a lumber mill at the mouth of the Irvine Slough across from the Irvine Store. Christian Rabel ran it from 1888 until 1899, when he moved to Seattle. The mill was later taken over by Robert J. McLaughlin, followed by other owners. Around the beginning of World War I, George Kunze bought the land that had a giant burner used to generate power for an electric company at the mouth of the Irvine Slough. He established the Wisconsin Timber Company with the machinery of the Lincoln mill in Arlington to start operations. Though successful for a few years, Kunze's untimely death in 1921 brought the sale of the mill. The mill was taken over by the Clough Lumber Company in 1923 in Everett in a receiver's sale, and Clough built the Hamilton Stack that exists now. It was said to be 154 feet of reinforced concrete sections. The Clough mill did not succeed for long, though for a time it employed 75 to 100 men. Meanwhile, James E. Hamilton, born in New Brunswick, Canada, came to Seattle in 1888. Around 1930, he established the J.E. Hamilton & Sons Lumber Company on 271st Street in Stanwood and took over the old Clough mill and began improvements. Then in 1945, he added the finishing mill. The company opened an all-electric sawmill in 1954. It was plagued by fires and was finally taken down so the State Road 532 highway could bypass the town.

In East Stanwood, a branch of Seattle's Columbia Lumber Company was established in 1927. About 1947, this property was turned over to Andrew Floe Transfer Company, which had a large fleet of trucks.

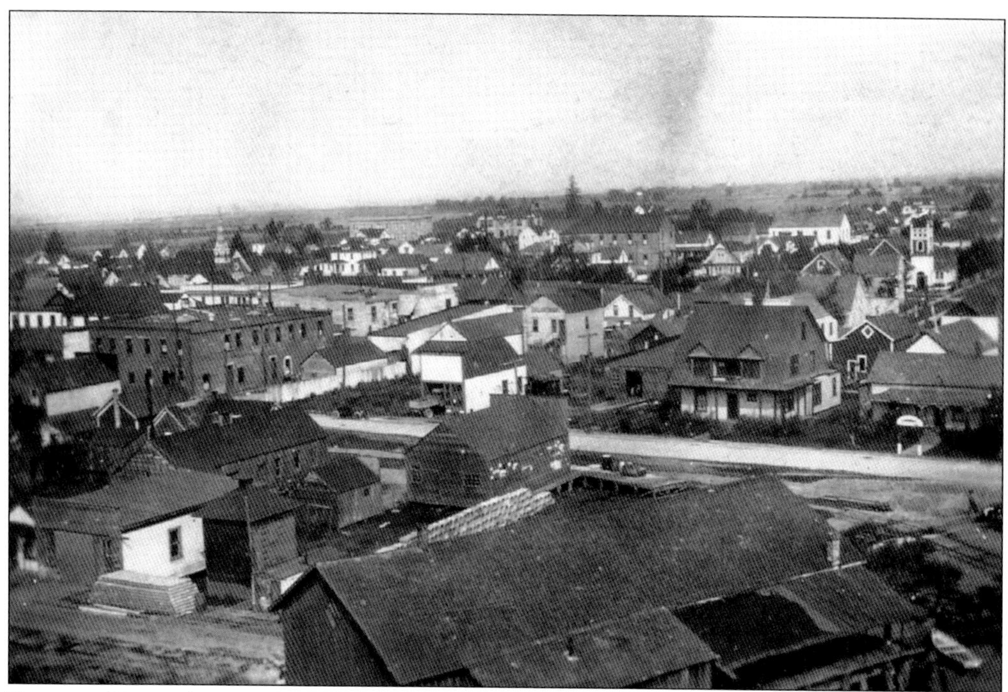

Rooftop View. The rooftop at the bottom of the photograph is the shingle mill operated in the 1880s by Otto Rabel. It was established at the mouth of the Irvine Slough, where logs were floated from logging camps. On the right side of the photograph are the home of Dr. Orville Reid Allen and his hospital. On the left is the brick bank building. In the distance are the steeples of the Methodist church and Presbyterian church. In the center is the three-story Oddfellows Hall and the Masonic Hall.

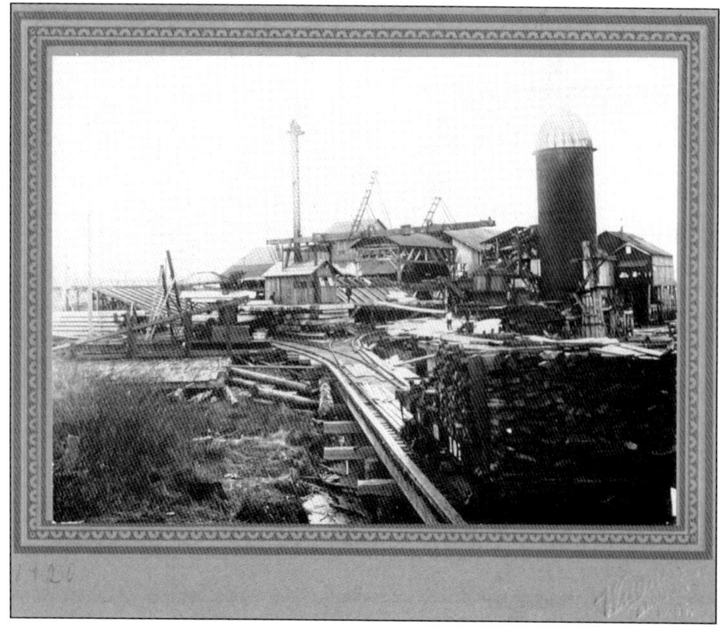

The Wisconsin Timber Co. This view of the mill is between 1917 and 1923, when Wisconsin Timber Co. owned it. The mill buildings are shown here with their new large wood burner. The tracks in the foreground are part of a short spur from the H&H Railroad line connecting the mill to the Great Northern Railroad in East Stanwood. The tracks were also used to move around a huge crane for loading lumber and sawdust onto the steamers on the river.

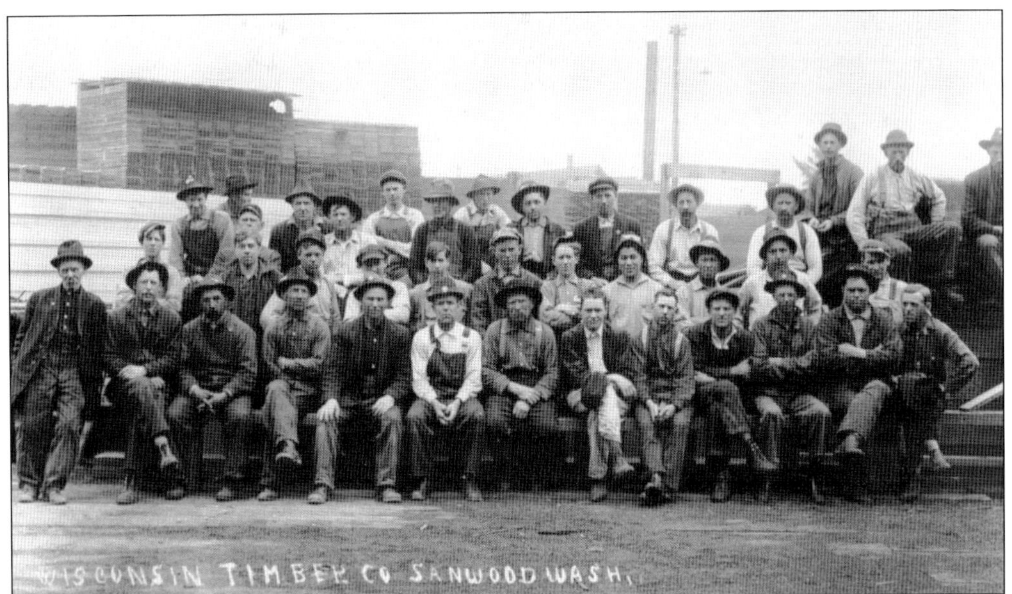

MILL WORKERS, THE WISCONSIN TIMBER CO. The Wisconsin Mill was purchased by Everett's Clough mill in 1923. Herbert Clough and Herbert W. White of the Clough Lumber Company began operating the Wisconsin Timber Co. plant at Stanwood in 1923. The Clough mill built what is now known as the Hamilton Stack, still a city landmark. (Photograph by John T. Wagness.)

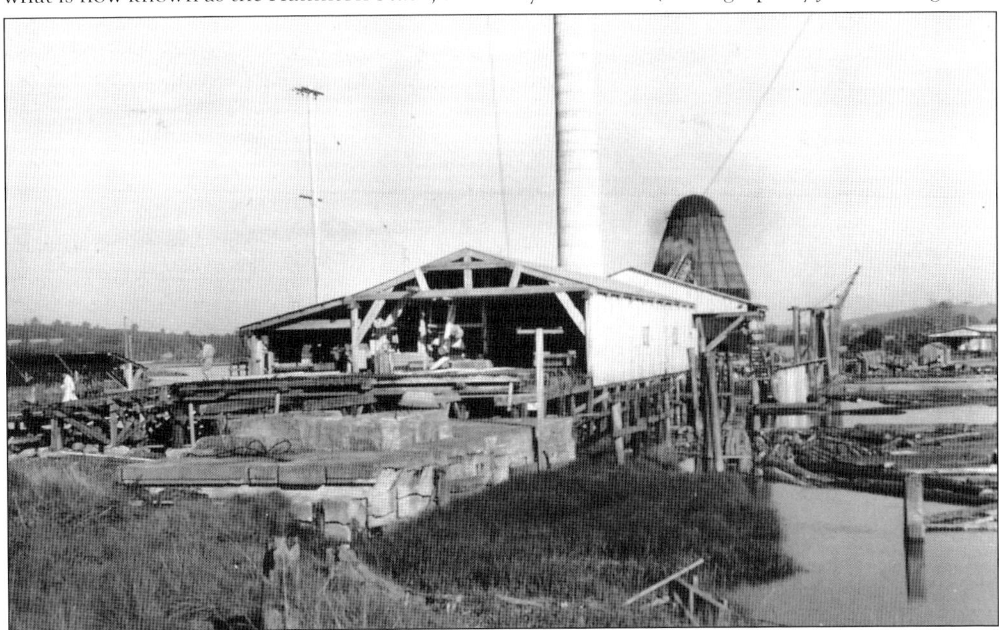

WISCONSIN, CLOUGH, HAMILTON. This is a later photograph taken soon before it was demolished for the new highway to Camano Island. Lifetime resident Ole Eide described working as a teenager with Dan MacDonald, who owned a cement contracting company in Stanwood. MacDonald was hired by a company that specialized in building smokestacks. Ole helped mix the cement to the exact specifications inside the foundation forms. The bottom of the stack was placed on the base, and the stack went up in sections. The stack, now known as the Hamilton Stack, still dominates Stanwood's skyline and river.

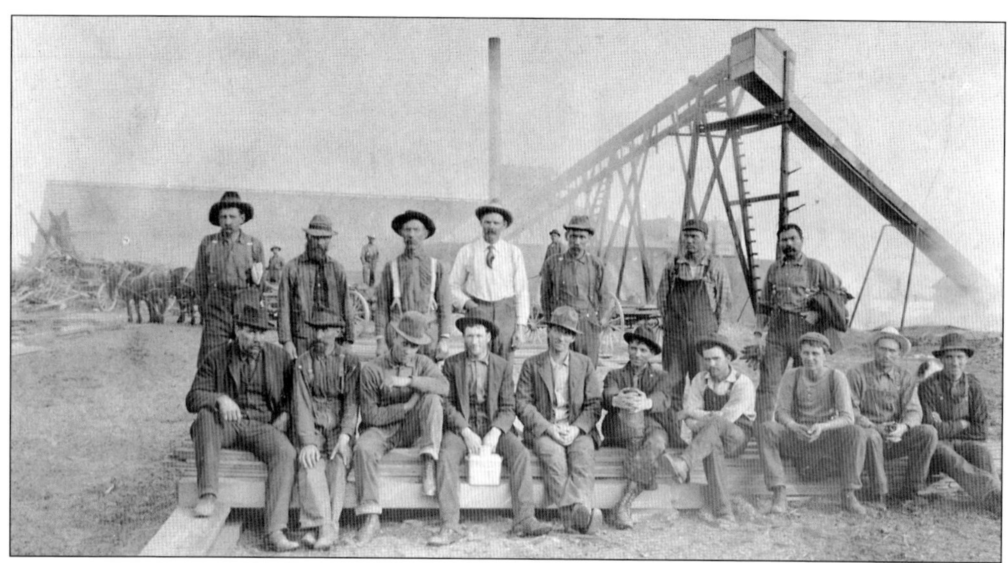

Stanwood Lumber Company Crew. This group portrait includes the early Stanwood Lumber Company crew with owner Albert S. Howard in the back row on the left. Howard died in 1913. David G. Bennie, in the center with white shirt, suspenders, and tie, took over. From then on it was known as "Bennie's mill." Not all the names are known, but John Einarsen, head sawyer, is on the far left in the lower row. Einarsen also worked at the Utsalady Mill in the 1880s.

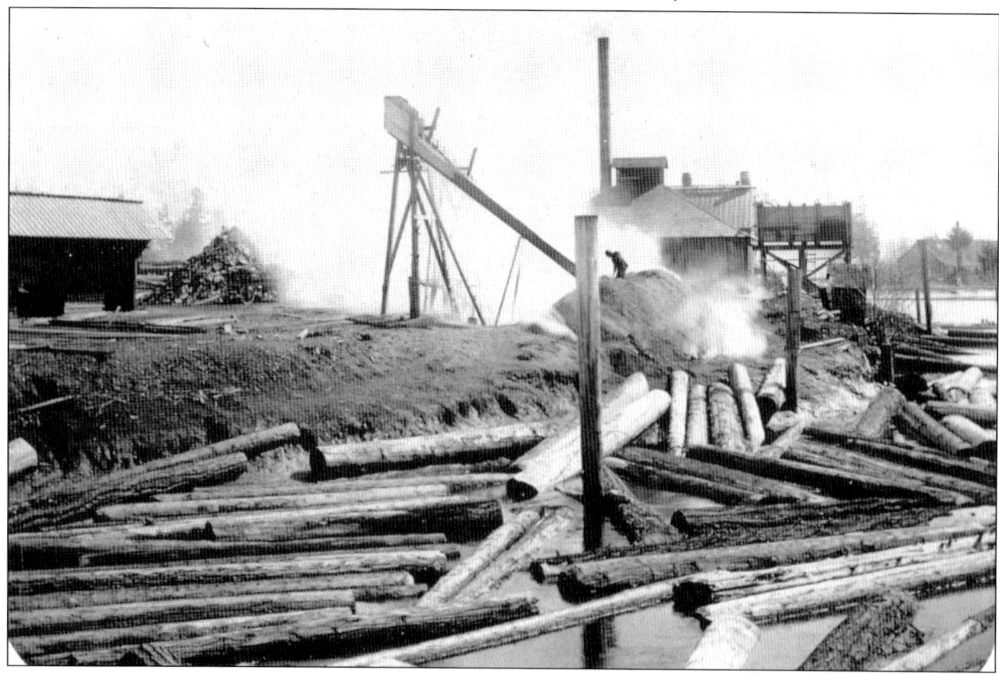

Shoveling Sawdust. Sawdust from the log chute and planer ends can be seen in this east-side view (Douglas, Stillaguamish, and Skagit Sloughs) of the Stanwood Lumber Company before the burner was installed. The logs in the foreground are in the Douglas Slough, which has different names depending on which old map is used. According to an 1876 news article, this slough was big enough to float a craft of 100 tons at high tide through the marsh from the Stillaguamish River to the Skagit River just outside of the dike.

STANWOOD LUMBER COMPANY. The two men on the logs with the pike poles are Nels Olsen (left) and Walt Libby. This dangerous work required cork boots and wits. Nels Olsen and Walt Libby were poling logs for the Stanwood Lumber Company along the Douglas Slough about 1920. Olsen was the mill superintendent as well as the local justice of the peace.

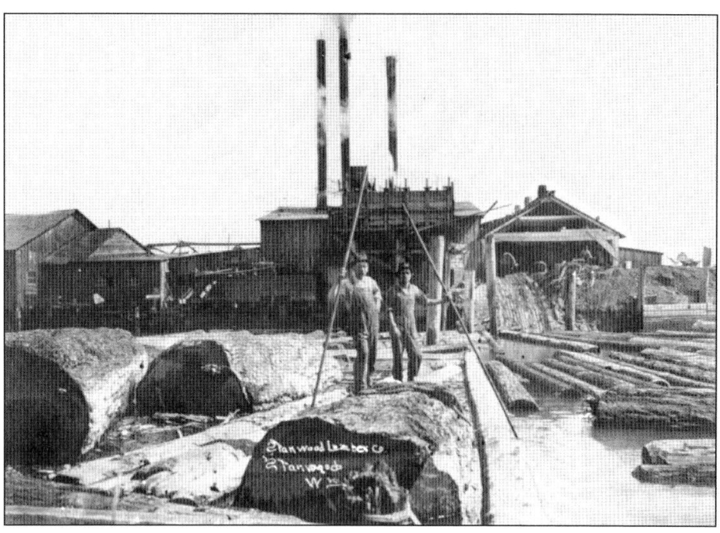

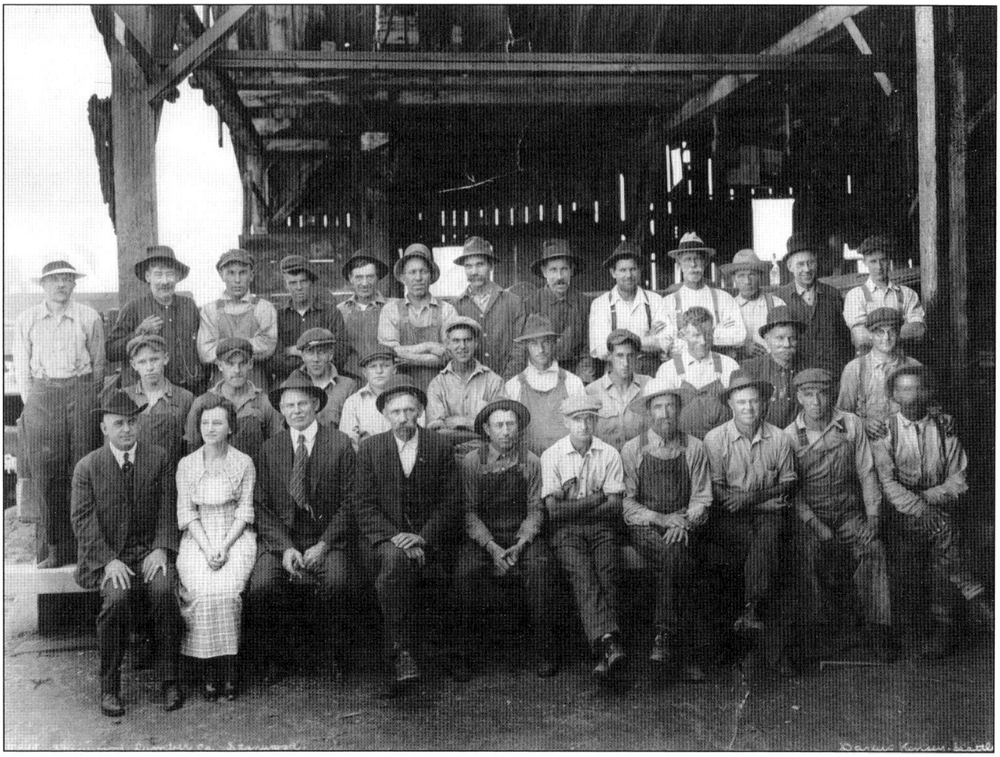

MILL CREW AND OWNERS, THE STANWOOD LUMBER COMPANY. Pictured are (first row) an unidentified lumber salesman, Nina Howard (bookkeeper), David Bennie (manager), Nels Olsen (superintendent), Homer Exelby, Fred Howard, Frank Howard, Roy Olsen, Dan Harvey, and unidentified; (second row) brothers Stanley and Walter Winters, Norman Olson, Edwin Howard, Kenneth Bennie, Chris Tjerne, Leslie Reid, John Einarsen (head sawyer), and unidentified; (third row) Albert Olaussen, Jack Reid, Harold Foss, Rufus Layman, Ralph Savage, Hans Hoganson, C.A. Norlin (superintendent of the planning department), and six unidentified. (Photograph by Darius Kinsey.)

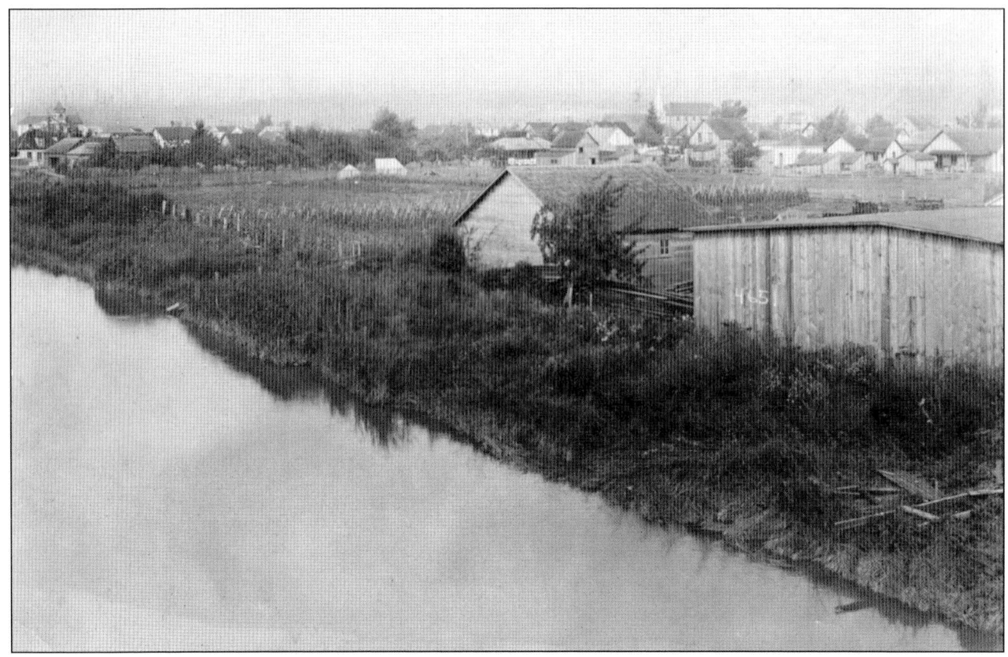

Douglas Slough, Northeast View. This is one of four images taken to create a panoramic view of Stanwood. They are most likely taken from the deck of a boat on the Douglas Slough. The slough is no longer navigable but can still be seen as a ditch at the west end of Stanwood before the bridge to Camano Island. On old maps, it is also known as the Skagit or Stillaguamish Slough. In the distance on the left are the North Street school, the Methodist church steeple, and the International Order of Oddfellows Hall. The D.O. Pearson House is faintly visible.

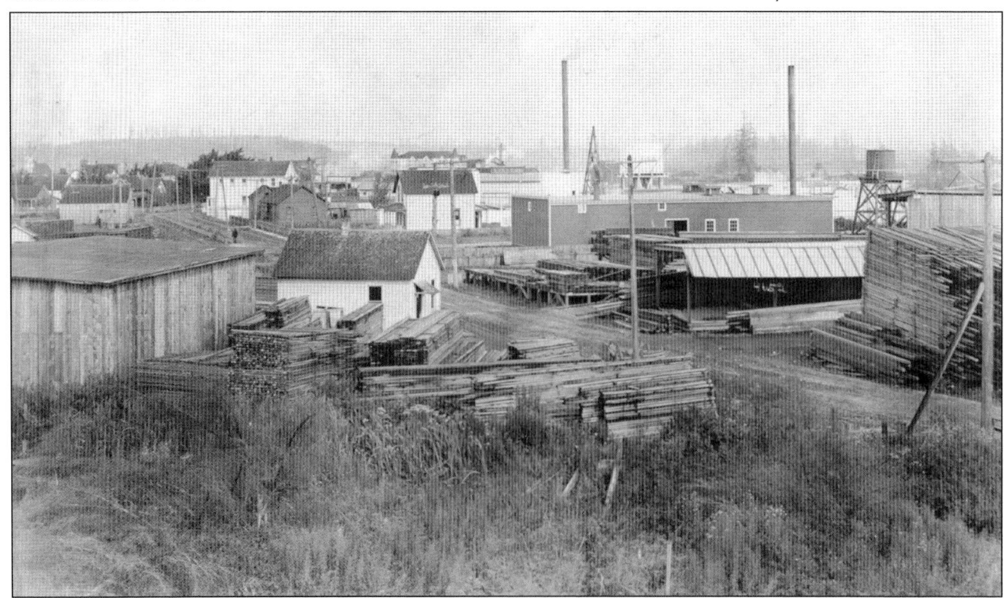

Saratoga Street. This view looks east and shows the road from Stanwood to the Stanwood Lumber Company, known as Saratoga Street. It is difficult to make out, but the tracks of the H&H Railroad can be seen curving toward the mill. In the distance are the Pioneer and Palace Hotel with its towers.

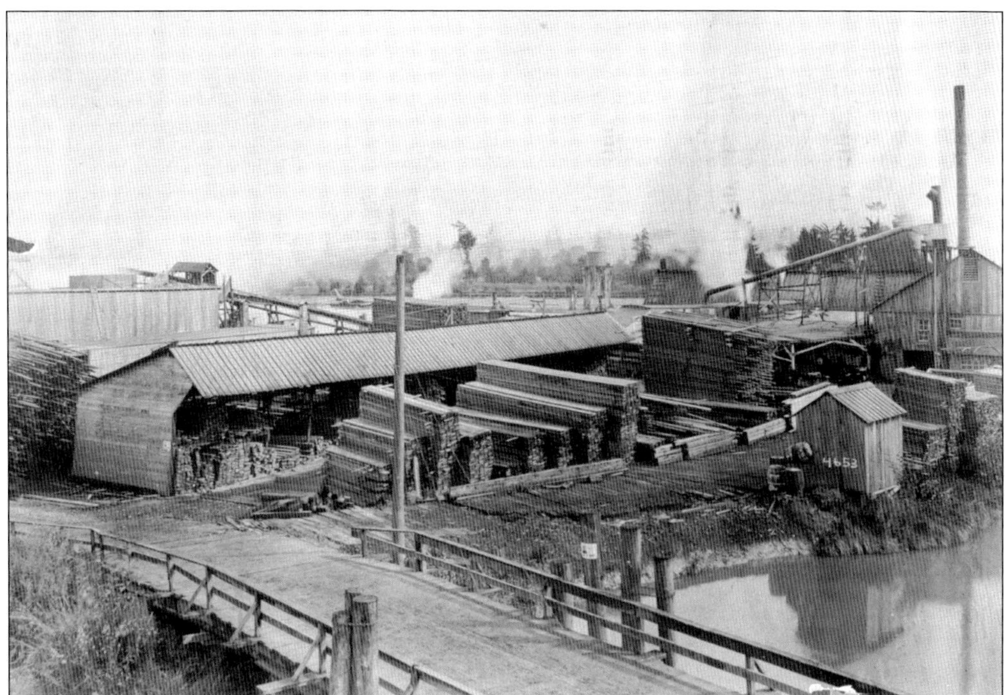

Lumber Stacks, the Stanwood Lumber Company. The photographer took these four photographs from the same location on the deck of a boat or building. This photograph shows the mill buildings of the Stanwood Lumber Company. The bridge in the foreground led to the Ovenell Farm and the ferry crossing. After 1909, it led to the bridge to Leque Island and on to Camano Island over the West Pass.

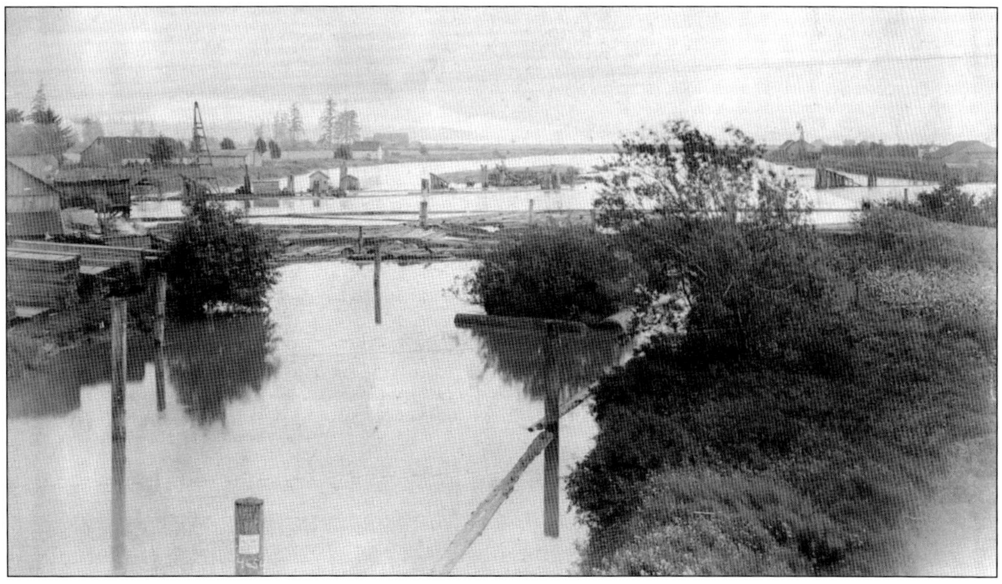

South Pass Saratoga Street Bridge. This view looks south from over the Douglas Slough in the foreground and the South Pass. The South Pass leads to Port Susan, the shallow but extensive bay between Snohomish County and Camano Island. Beyond the mill buildings and the river is the Matterand Farm on Florence Island.

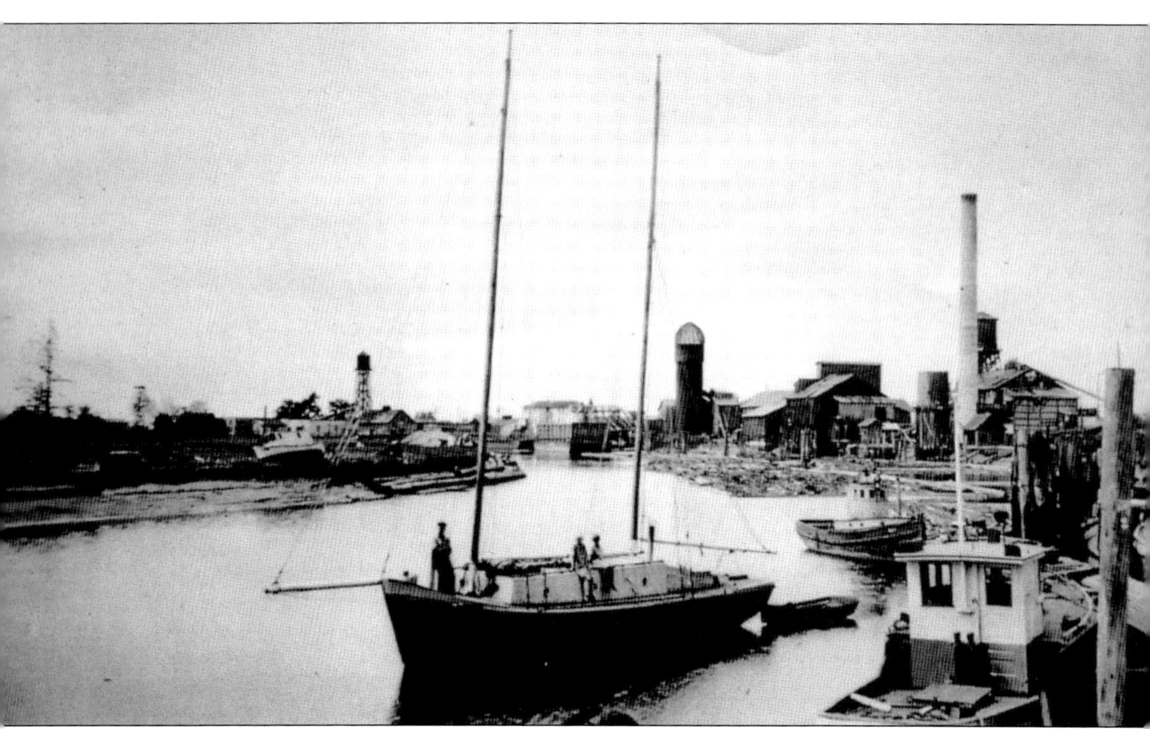

The Lone Sea Rover. This view looks west toward Stanwood's Stillaguamish River waterfront. The *Ladybird* sailboat in the foreground was built by Capt. Thomas Drake in 1930. Doris Matterand MacGregor and Eleanor Matterand Clayton are sitting on the cabin. Capt. Tommy Drake is on the deck of his boat in the foreground. Doris and Eleanor's father, Haakon Matterand, operated a boatyard here for many years. Captain Drake was noted for sailing around the world alone in 1915. He told his tale in his autobiography, *The Log of a Lone Sea Rover*. In the background is the mill, known at the time as the Clough Mill, and its smokestack, which stands today as the Hamilton Stack. (Courtesy of Doris MacGregor and Eleanor Clayton.)

Five

MARKET AND MAIN STREETS

Stanwood was platted in 1889 by William R. and Augusta M. Stockbridge when they bought out Henry Oliver's original claim. The town extended from the waterfront north along Market Street. It was intersected by Broadway and Main Street. Broadway (State Road 532) and Main Street (270th Street) converge and extend eastward toward East Stanwood and the Great Northern Railroad Depot. D.O. Pearson built his third store near his new 1891 home on Market Street (102nd Avenue).

Many of the photographs in this chapter feature the intersection of Market and Main Streets, where John Wagness and other photographers placed their cameras above to capture the activities and events below. For some photographs, he braved the floodwaters featured later in the story. The photographs capture the laying of the bricks needed to avoid the damage of mud and dust. This popular view of Main and Market Streets is repeated many times from the height of the third floor of the Stanwood Hotel.

The Masonic Hall, one of the community's oldest institutions, is seen faintly in the distance of many of the Market Street views. The Camanio Lodge 19 of the Ancient Free and Accepted Masons (F&AM) was chartered in 1872 at Utsalady on Camano Island, where they had a two-story hall built on Utsalady Mill property. It was referred to as the Camanio Lodge for Don Jacinto Caamaño, the Spanish explorer who was the namesake of Camano Island.

Main Street is one of two brick streets remaining in Stanwood. It is one short block of historic bricks that so far has been preserved. The other, Cedarhome Drive NW, is in East Stanwood, where it begins on the east side of what is now Pioneer Highway and heads in the direction of the uplands toward Cedarhome. According to Gustav Joergenson, these were the first county roads with bricks in Snohomish County.

Eastward on Main Street is the original home of the Nels M. Lien family. Nels operated a farm that at one time encompassed land east to the railroad tracks and north to 276th Street. He brought his family from Norway via North Dakota to Stanwood in 1889 and purchased 52 acres of land between Stanwood and the railroad depot. Later he purchased an additional 40 acres. The Liens and the Giards owned significant farms between what became two towns: Stanwood and East Stanwood.

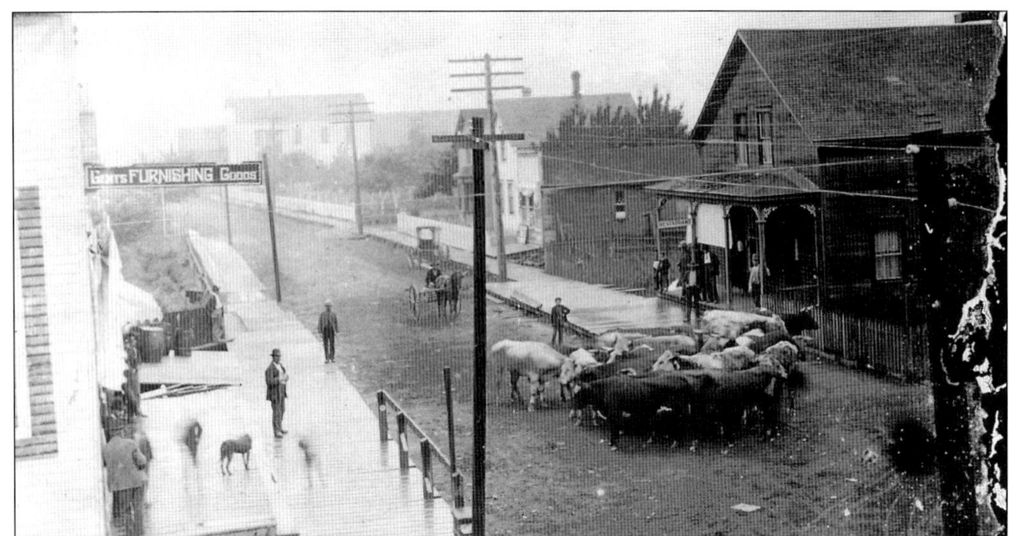

The Bossie Ordinance. In 1904, the new Stanwood Town Council passed Ordinance No. 31, prohibiting the "running of any and all kinds of cattle or cows within the city limits." The guilty owners were charged with a misdemeanor, and the town marshal had to find a place to stockade or corral the cows. Charges were $1 for each cow for up to 10 days. There was a separate Ordinance No. 29 passed to impound horses or mules "running at large." (Photograph by John T. Wagness.)

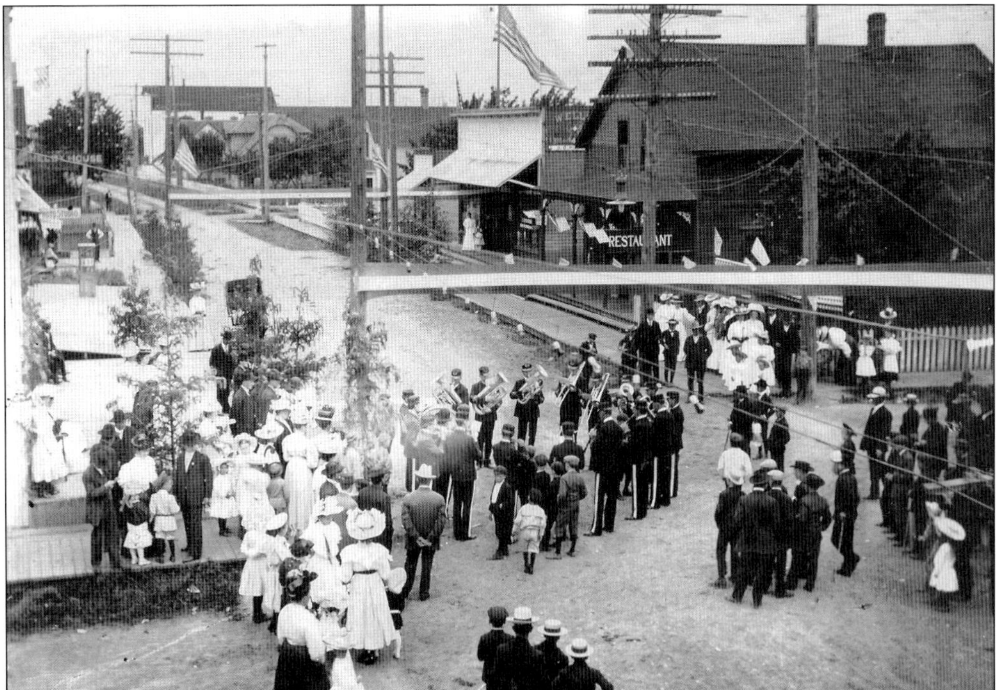

The Stillaguamish Band. This view of the third Pearson Store with its canopy was taken from the Stanwood Hotel. The store was built in 1906. To the right, Main Street intersects with Market Street toward East Stanwood. The Masonic Hall in the distance behind was built in 1895. The second floor was removed and placed next door in 1972. (Photograph by John T. Wagness.)

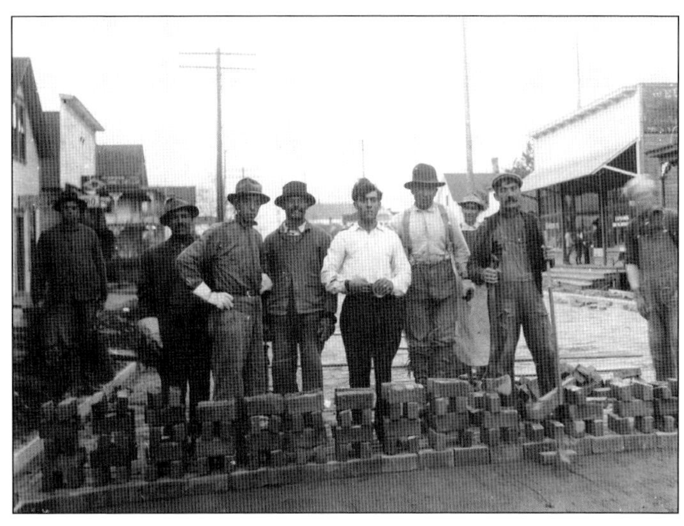

Bricklayers, Market Street. This view shows the bricklayers on Market Street about 1912. The view looks north with the D.O. Pearson Store on the right. With the bricks, the community was no longer a dusty or muddy riverboat stop. This section of the Pacific Highway was soon bypassed from the main highway north past East Stanwood, and it became a more direct drive up the Pacific Highway. (Photograph by John T. Wagness.)

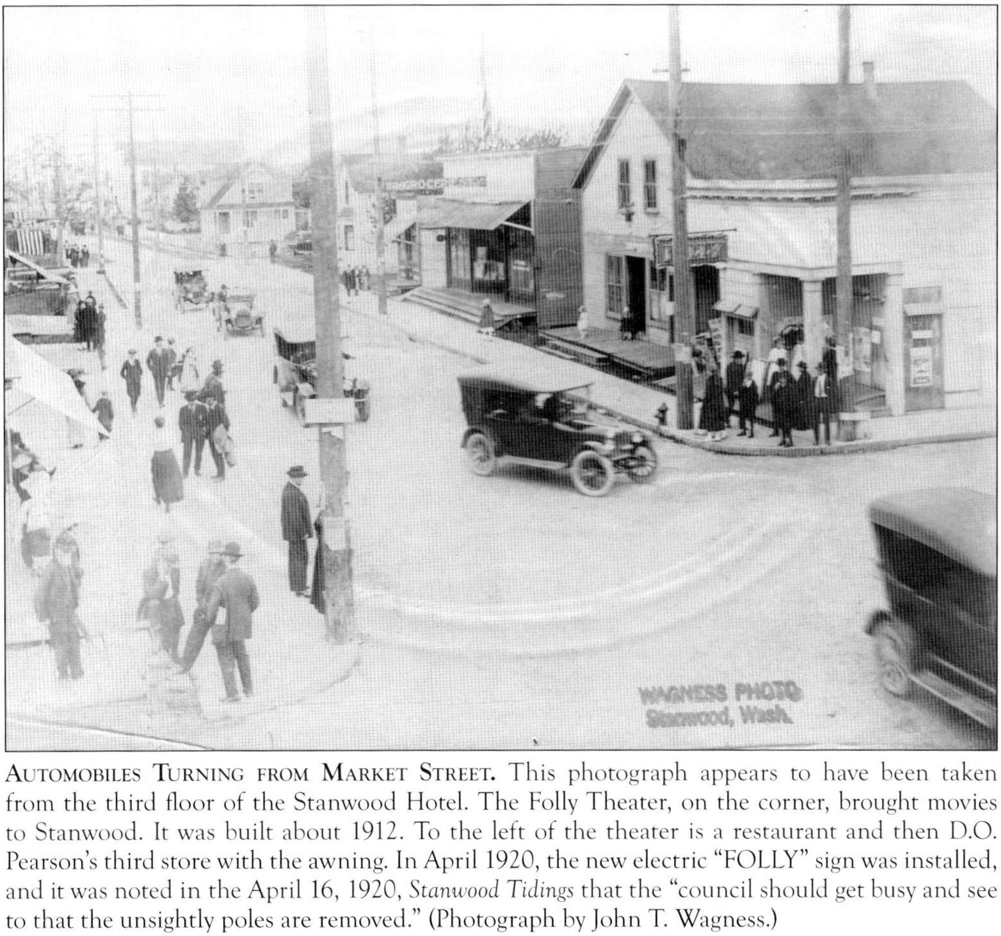

Automobiles Turning from Market Street. This photograph appears to have been taken from the third floor of the Stanwood Hotel. The Folly Theater, on the corner, brought movies to Stanwood. It was built about 1912. To the left of the theater is a restaurant and then D.O. Pearson's third store with the awning. In April 1920, the new electric "FOLLY" sign was installed, and it was noted in the April 16, 1920, *Stanwood Tidings* that the "council should get busy and see to that the unsightly poles are removed." (Photograph by John T. Wagness.)

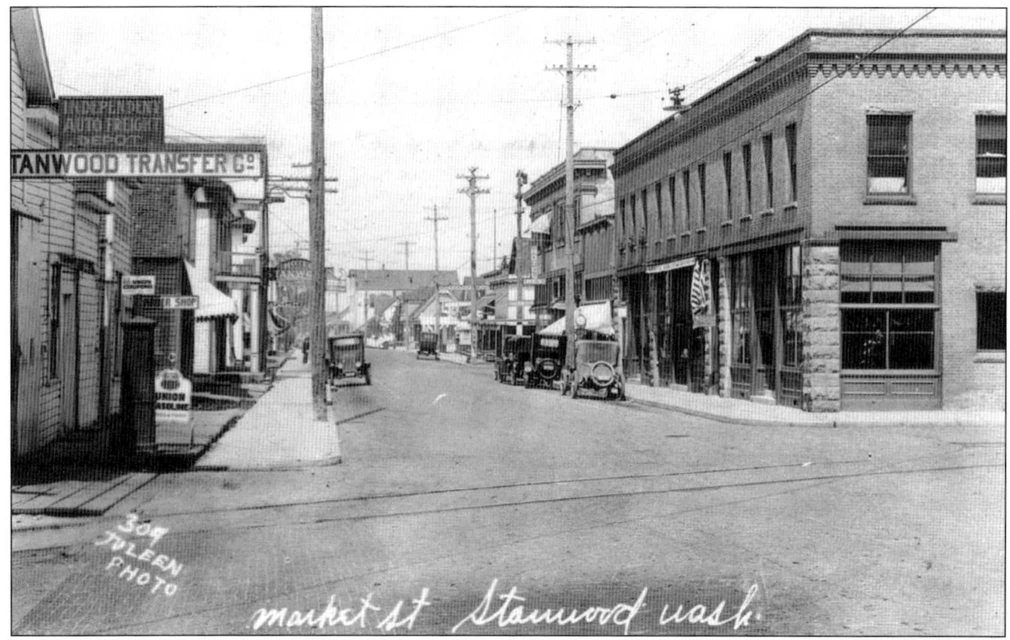

Market Street with Bricks. The H&H Railroad tracks are pictured on Market Street at Broadway. The view shows the new Knudson Building at the corner of Main Street. Knud Knudson came from Norway in 1889, opening a jewelry store. The Stanwood Transfer Company still occupied the corner that soon became the Palace Market. (Photograph by J.A. Juleen.)

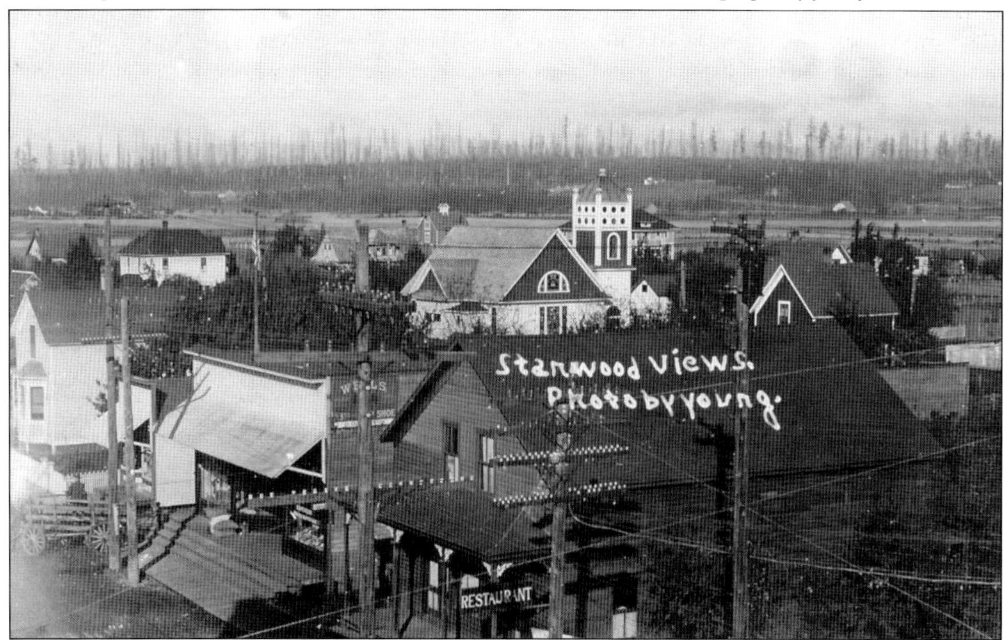

Stanwood Views. The rooftop of the restaurant on Market Street is in the foreground showing the D.O. Pearson Store with a small bicycle shop next door. The Presbyterian church steeple is prominent in the background. The Josephine Sunset Home can be seen just beyond the church steeple. Note the charred trees in the wooded highland beyond. This area was sometimes called "the Burn" for a fire thought to have occurred in the 1860s.

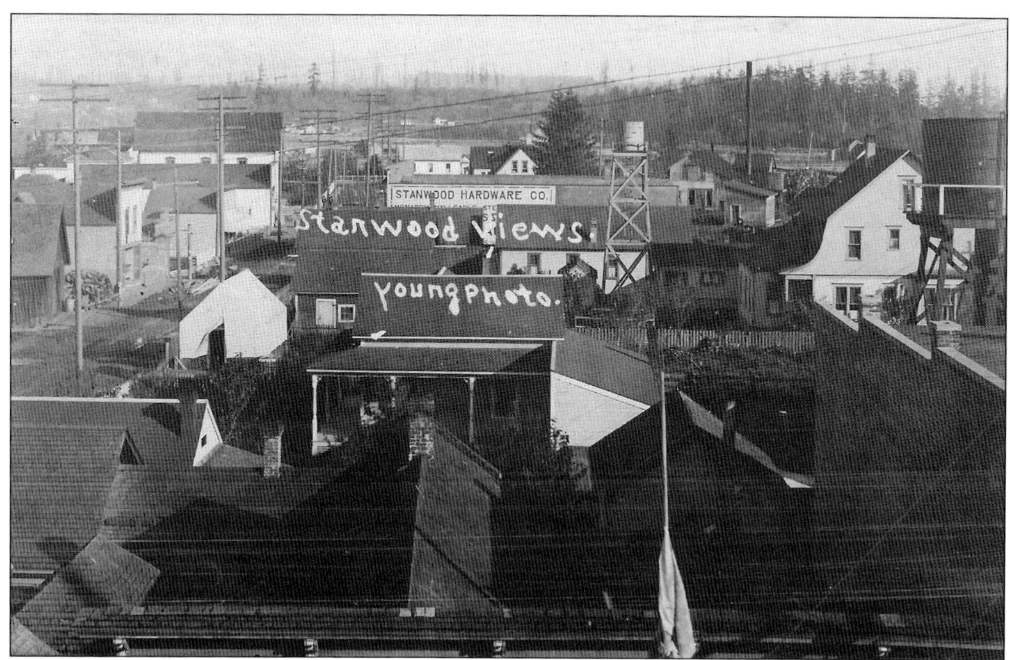

ANOTHER STANWOOD VIEW. This rooftop view looks east toward the uplands. It shows Main Street on the left with the two-story Thompson Store warehouse. The sign for the Stanwood Hardware Company is prominent. It was opened around 1904 by Wellington B. Davis, who operated it until 1926. To the right is the gambrel roofline of the specially designed home of Dr. Orville Reid Allen, which was right next to his hospital on Broadway. The builders were Plett & Paddock, Carpenters & Builders of Stanwood, who erected many of the structures in this neighborhood. (Photograph by Robert Young.)

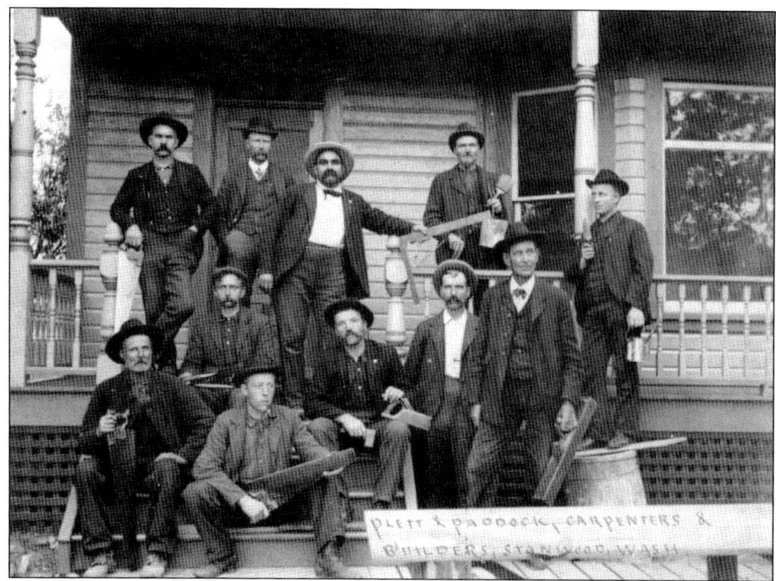

PLETT & PADDOCK, CARPENTERS & BUILDERS. Plett & Paddock, Carpenters & Builders were builders of many of the homes in Stanwood, including the homes of Alfred Ryan and Conrad Lien, as well as the Allen residence and hospital. The hospital had its own water tower.

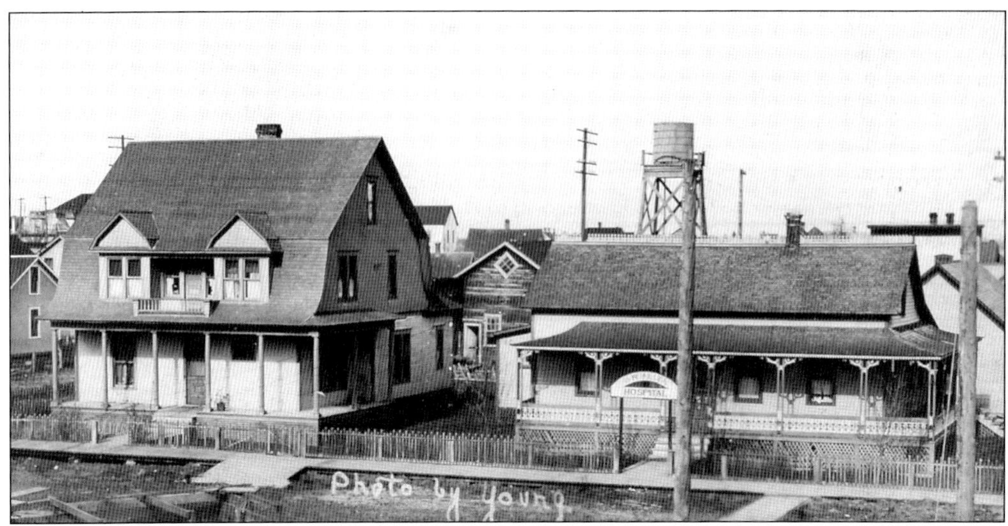

STANWOOD'S HOSPITAL AND DOCTOR'S RESIDENCE. The Stanwood Hospital was established in 1904 by Dr. Orville Reid Allen, who lived in the hospital before his family's two-story home was built in 1905. The hospital, on the right, had a large dining room and a ward to accommodate 10 patients. It was purchased in 1911 by Drs. Leonard H. Jacobsen and Daniel McEacheran. They made many improvements. (Photograph by Robert A. Young.)

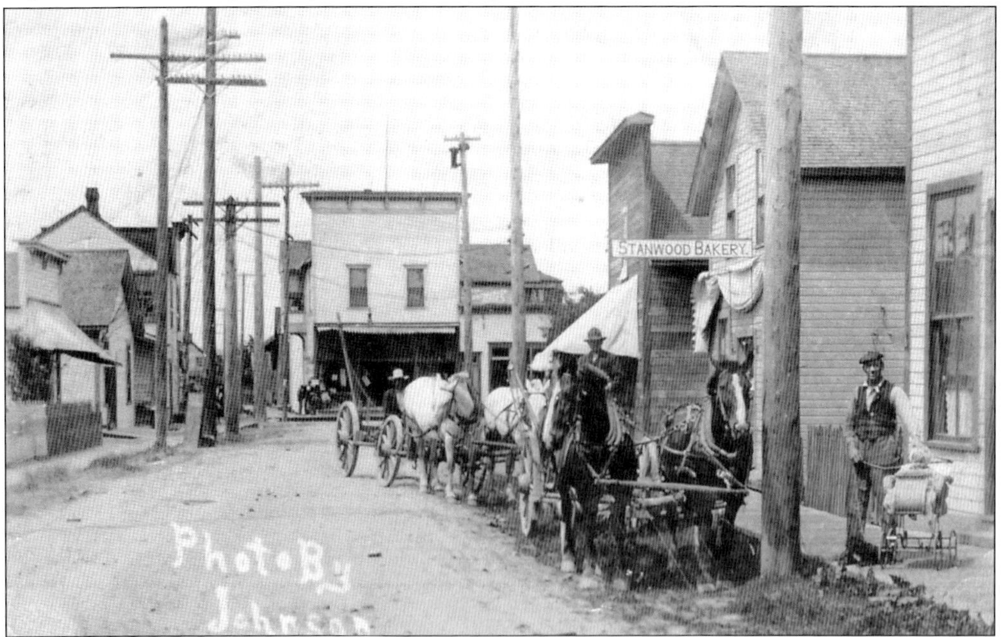

STANWOOD BAKERY ON THE UNPAVED MAIN STREET. The two-story building in the distance at the intersection of Main Street and Market Street was known informally as the Ketchum Store by those who remembered him. Ketchum clerked for D.O. Pearson, and in 1893, Ketchum bought the store built by Louis H. Smith, who had just replaced it after it burned in 1892. He sold it in 1915 to D.W. Alverson. It had many succeeding owners. The Stanwood Bakery sign shows the bakery that was operated by Victor Lilja, who came from Sweden. He moved to Stanwood in 1906. He opened the Stanwood Bakery shortly after that, and it operated until 1926. (Photograph by Edward A. Johnson.)

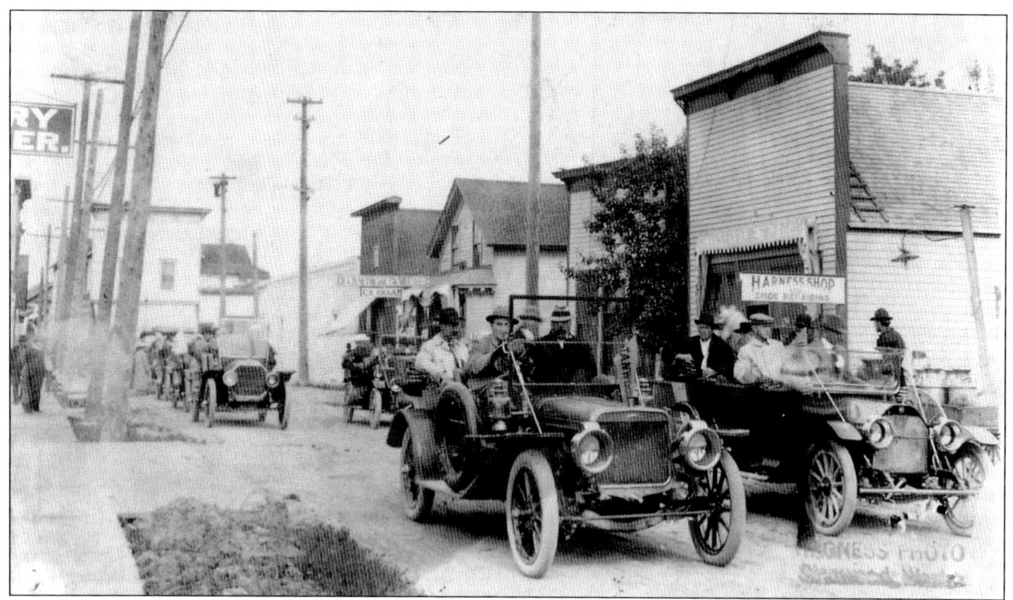

MAIN STREET PARADE OF AUTOMOBILES. The occasion is unknown, but Andrew Klaeboe, the druggist, appears in the front automobile. The harness shop was operated by Andrew Tackstrom, who was on the city council as early as 1904, and later, Andrew Simonson. The Folly Theater is in the distance, and the familiar Ketchum Store is at the end of the street. (Photograph by John T. Wagness.)

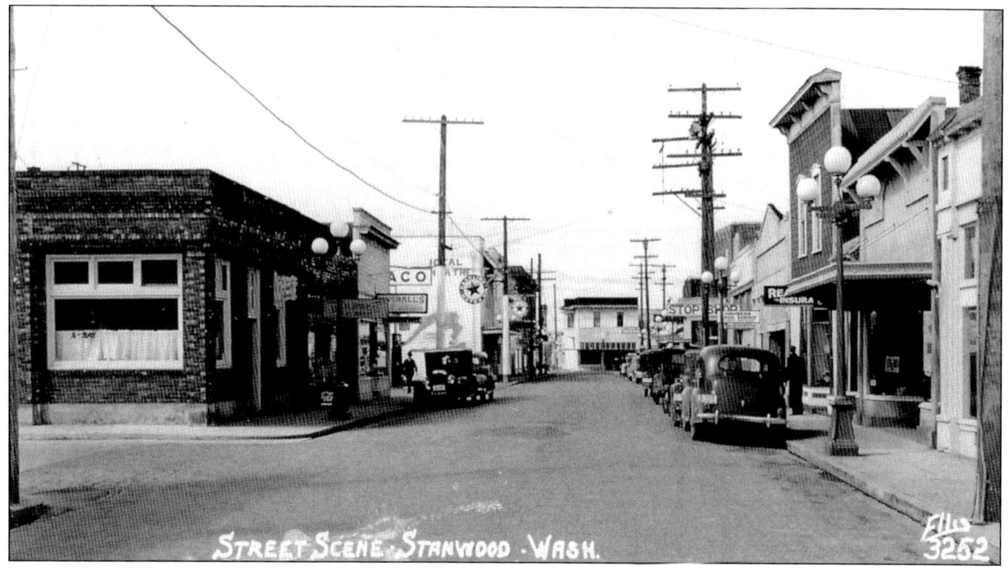

STREET SCENE, STANWOOD, WASH. This view looks west down Main Street toward the Ketchum Store in the 1940s. The brick building on the left was built as the Citizen's State Bank in 1919. It merged with the First National Bank of Stanwood when it moved to the other side of the street. The building became Dr. Ezra G. Wheeler's dentist office, later occupied by Dr. Robert C. Peterson. Signs on the street include the Chic Beauty Shop, Dailifresh Ice Cream with a fountain and lunch counter, the Ideal Theater, Kimball's Variety Store, Texaco Gasoline, and a Camano Island sign. The Rex Hotel and the Central Tavern have taken the place of the Folly Theater. (Photograph by J. Boyd Ellis.)

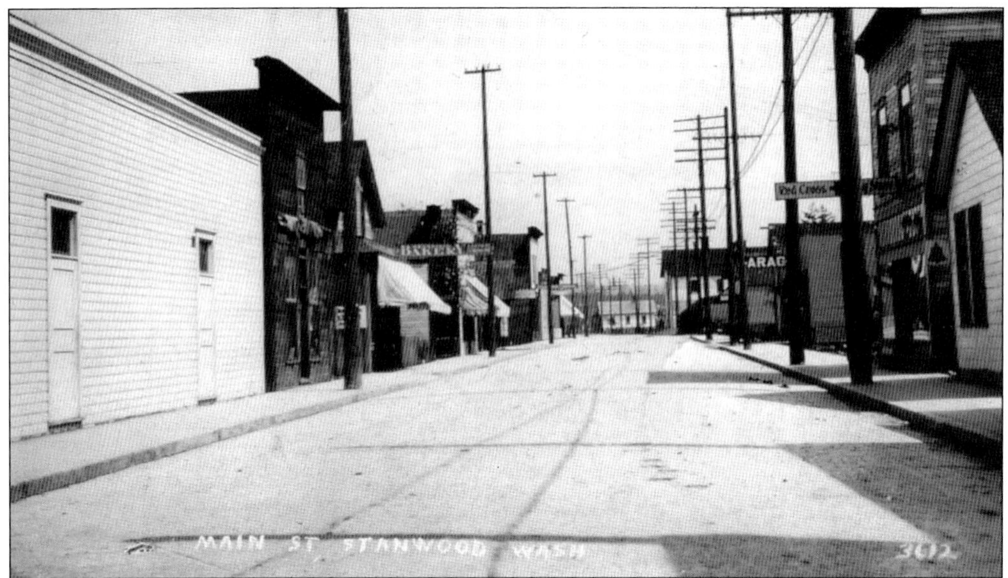

Main Street. This photographic postcard features signs for the Stanwood Bakery, a harness shop, and a garage. On the left is the Folly Theater. The two-story building on the right side of the street is the Red Cross Drug Store. Thompson Hall is the two-story building in the distance on the right after it was moved to become the Sons of Norway Hall. On the far right is the Western Union Telegraph Office. Though now widened, this street is still brick, one of two remaining in Stanwood.

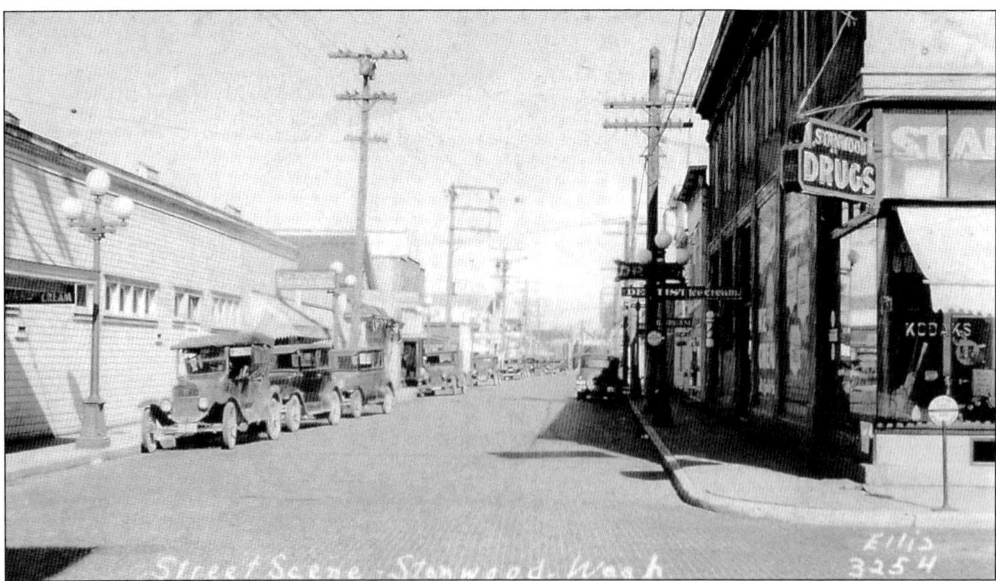

Another Street Scene. This street view looks east down Main Street from the Market Street intersection. The Knudson Building is on the right. Signs for Stanwood Drugs, Cozy Sandwich Shop, Stanwood Bakery, an ice cream shop, and a dentist line the street. In the distance on the left is the Hartney's men's shop, which first opened in July 1909 on Market Street across from the Palace Hotel. In 1923, Jerry Hartney opened his new tile-and-brick building on Main Street. The new two-story First National Bank of Stanwood was built next door on the property of Andrew Simonson, the harness maker and shoe repairer. (Photograph by J. Boyd Ellis.)

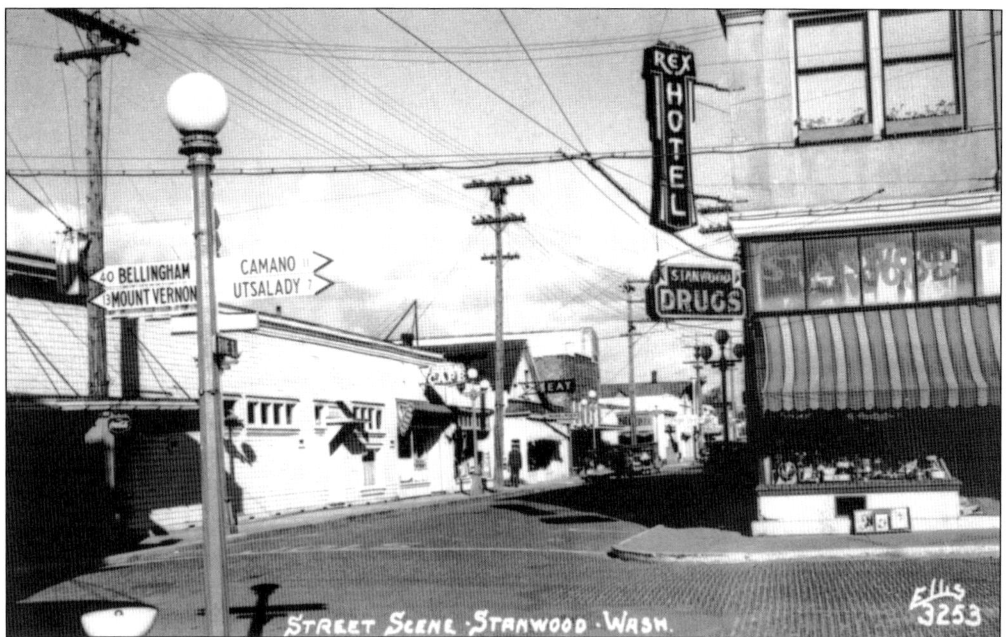

STREET SCENE, 3253. This view looks east from the intersection of Market and Main Streets. Stanwood Drug Store and the Rex Hotel have prominent signs. After Klaeboe sold his Stanwood Drug Store in 1915, it was purchased by William Reeves, followed by E.A. King. In 1926, E.A. King sold the store to Charles Simonson and moved his business to East Stanwood. The Rex Hotel was operated by Charles Dockendorf, mayor of Stanwood. Hartney's clothing store is beyond the "EAT" sign. This photograph can be dated after 1929, when the new First National Bank of Stanwood was built next to Hartney's, replacing the harness shop. (Photograph by J. Boyd Ellis.)

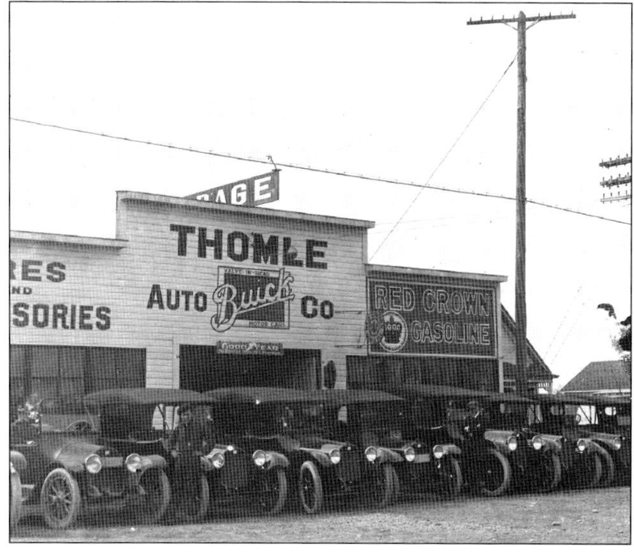

THOMLE BUICK. Magnus Thomle established the Buick dealership in Stanwood in 1913. In this photograph, early-model automobiles are lined up in front on the new brick Main Street. He did not stay in Stanwood long, moving on to Everett to establish other dealerships. This building later became the Bungalow Garage Stanwood Auto Company, started by George Bonser. It was remodeled about 1930 and again in 1964 for new businesses and remains a unique storefront on the brick street. (Photograph by John T. Wagness.)

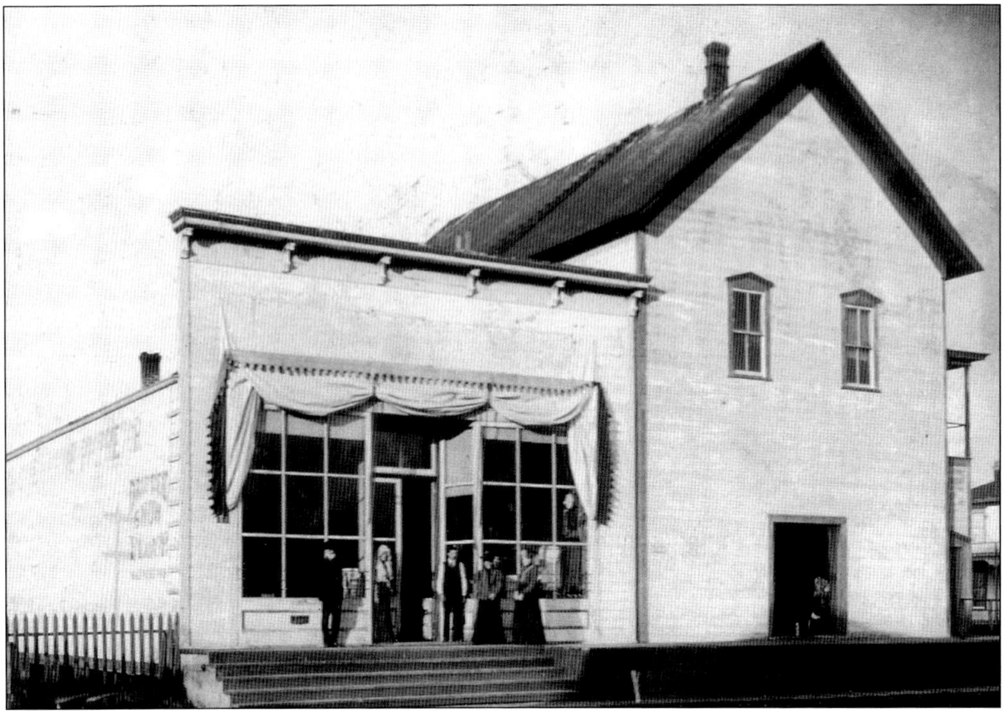

IRVINE STORE. The storefront on the left was moved from the waterfront about 1884 by Jack Irvine. The building on the right was a warehouse. Built in 1879, it had been one of the first trading posts along the Stillaguamish. The S.A. Thompson Company store was enlarged again with a 33-by-114-foot addition in 1938. In 1914, the two-story warehouse section was moved across the street to become the Sons of Norway Hall. Its second story was removed and is still on Main Street.

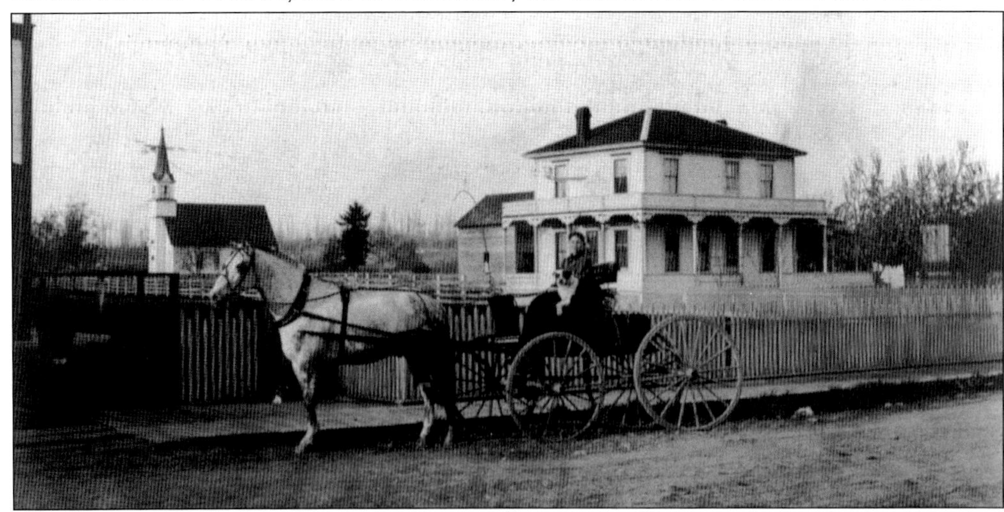

S.A. THOMPSON RESIDENCE. Sven A. Thompson came to Stanwood in about 1888 and took over the Irvine Store in about 1900. Irvine had moved from Stanwood to Seattle about 1896, and the store was taken over by S.A. Thompson with Carl and Alfred Ryan as clerks. In 1936, Thompson remodeled the building. He died in 1937. In 1957, his home became Frances Trusdell's Camano Art Center, which survived for 30 years until 1989. It is still an art center. Note Our Saviour's Lutheran Church in the background. (Photograph by John T. Wagness.)

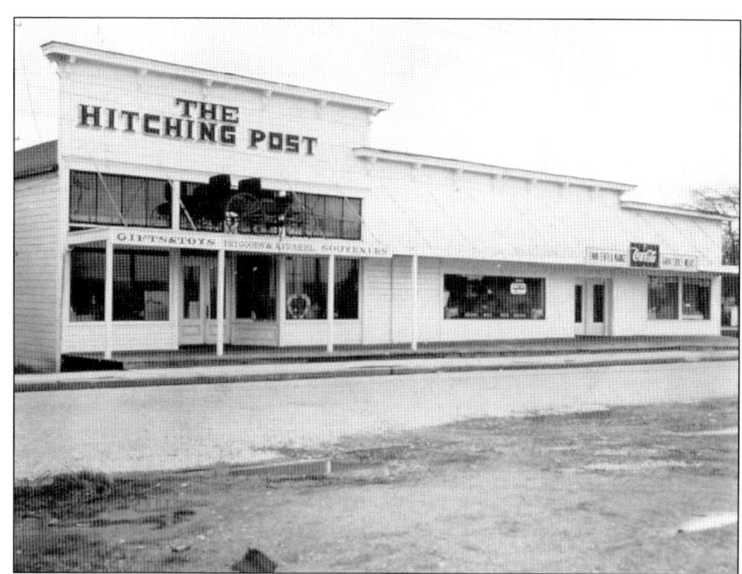

The Hitching Post. In 1949, Earl Clark acquired the building that was once the Thompson Store. Five years later, in 1954, the Hagstroms purchased the property, doing extensive remodeling and changed the name to the Hitching Post, referencing its history. Later, the Heymans of Seattle bought the business and named it Thriftmart. The building burned down in a spectacular fire in 1978.

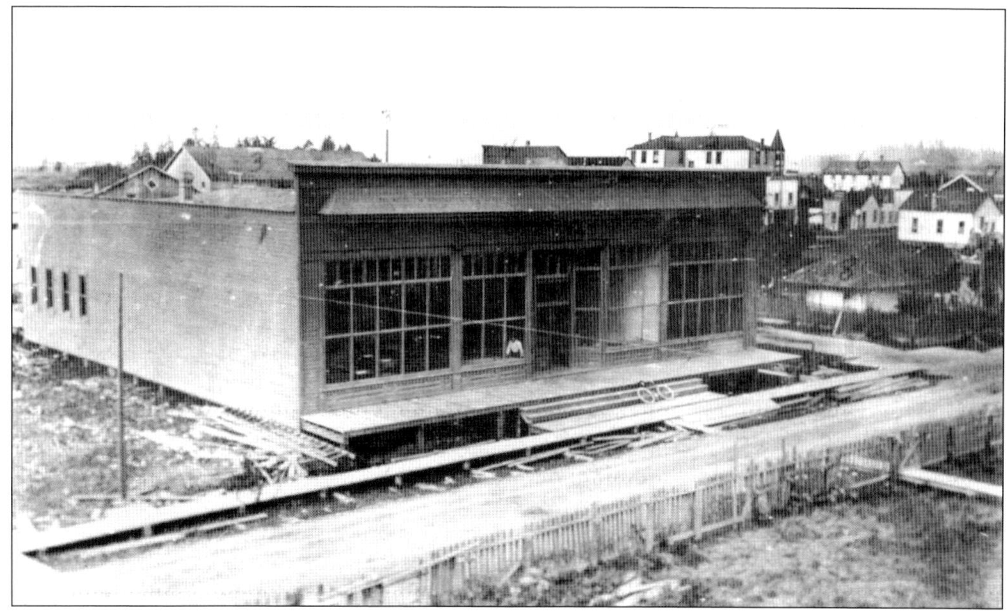

Stanwood Hardware Company. In 1902, a second hardware store was started on Main Street by local investors including Herman Hafstad and Iver Johnson. Wellington B. Davis took it over and operated the hardware from 1906 until 1926. Then a Mount Vernon hardware company, Rafter's, operated it. A 1930 advertisement for Rafter & Co. listed it as "Funeral Directors, Licensed Embalmers with a Lady Assistant." It was purchased by Dick Pusey in 1939. The Pusey family continued to own the property, though the furniture business was sold, and in about 1970, it became the Stanwood Camano Home Center. Future plans for this building include replacement with a new one as an art center with significant investment by the Pusey family descendants and community arts advocates.

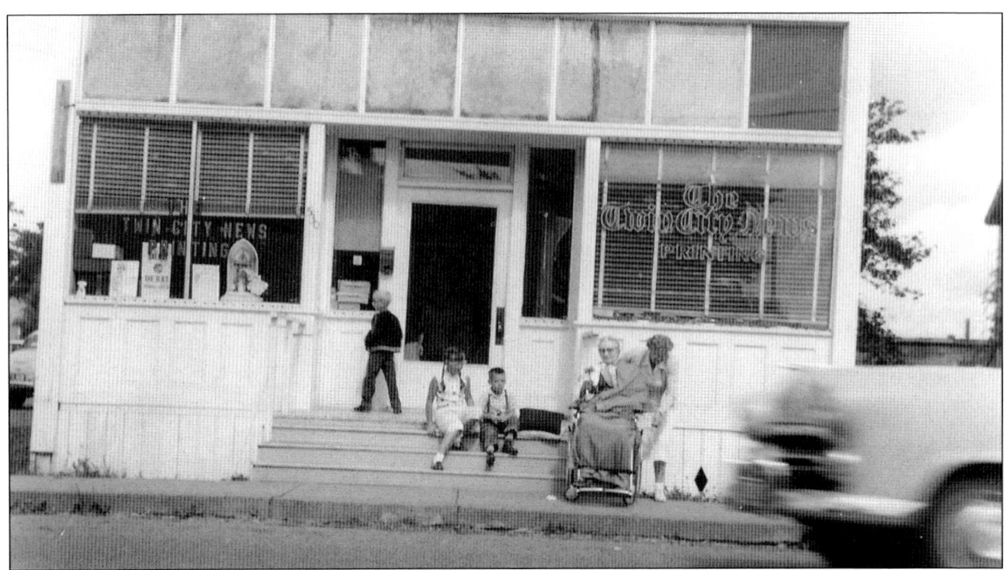

Storefront, Twin City News Printing. This is a snapshot of the news office and printer in Stanwood in the 1950s. The building was erected in about 1910 and served as the news office until 1959. In 1976, the news office moved to the building that had been the East Stanwood Post Office when the new post office was constructed between the two towns. (Photograph by Cliff Danielson.)

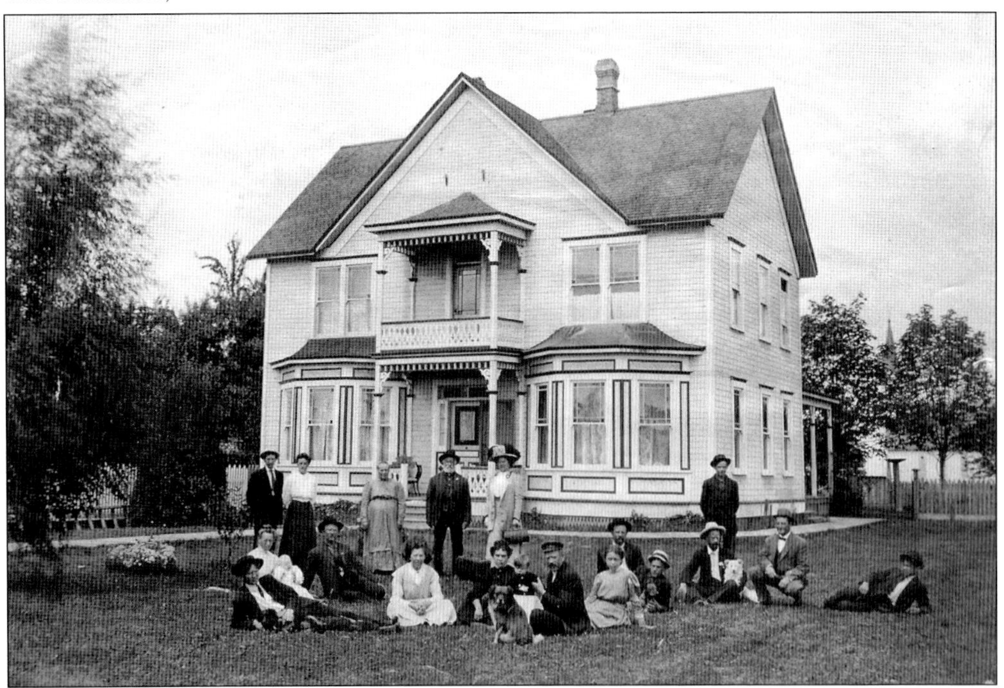

Lien Family and Home. East of the printing office, this home still exists as an apartment house. It was built in 1890, when Nels M. Lien brought his family to Stanwood from Norway through the Midwest. Two of his sons built homes across the street. He had a large farm that extended east to the city limits of East Stanwood. Note the steeple of the Lutheran church in the background of the trees.

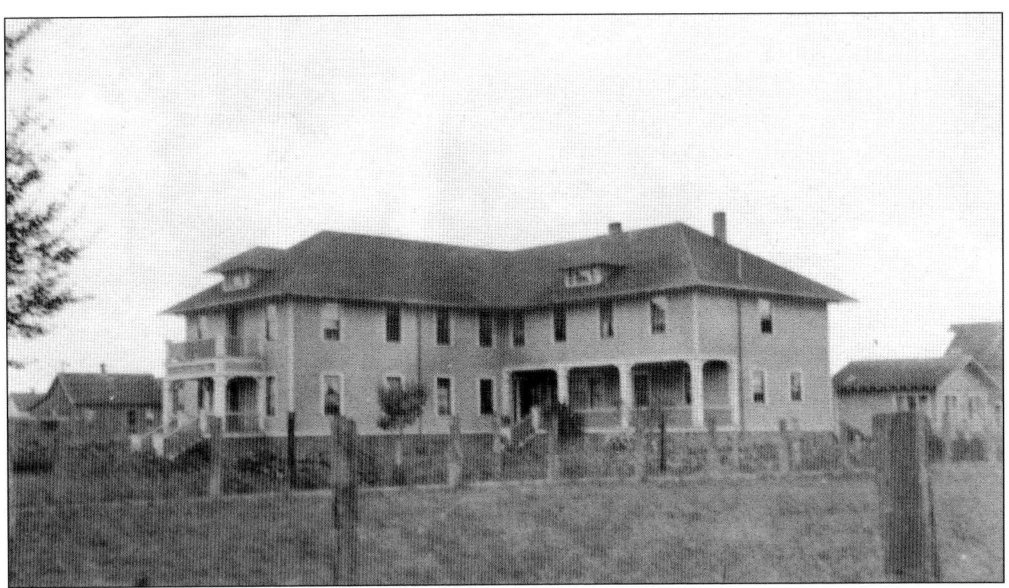

The Josephine Sunset Home. The home for the aged was built by John Hals in memory of his wife, who died in childbirth. Hals owned a large shingle mill that operated near Florence, a community upriver from Stanwood. When John Hals suffered the untimely death of his wife, he turned his tragedy into a gift of 10 acres of land with the original wooden frame building of the Lutheran church. The home for the elderly was built in 1908 at a cost of $10,000. The infirmary addition was completed in 1963, and a new wing was added in 1971. In the earliest days, the home managed its own gardens for food. It is now called the Josephine Caring Community.

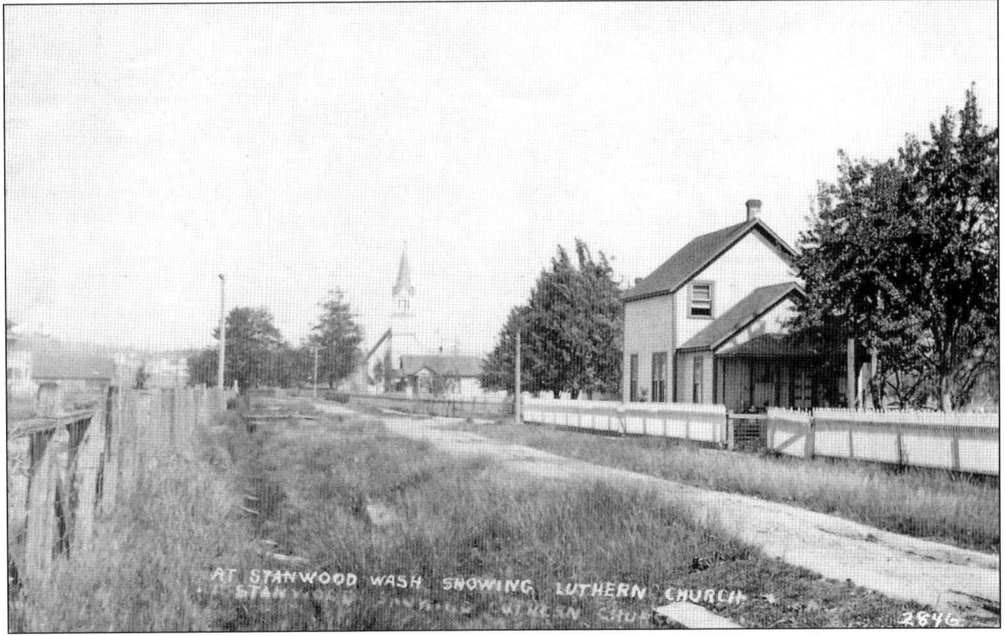

At Stanwood. The buildings at the edge of the image on the left are the Josephine Sunset Home at the intersection of Center and Stillaguamish Streets. In the distance is Our Saviour's Lutheran Church. The home in the distance directly in front of the church is thought to be the John T. Wagness residence.

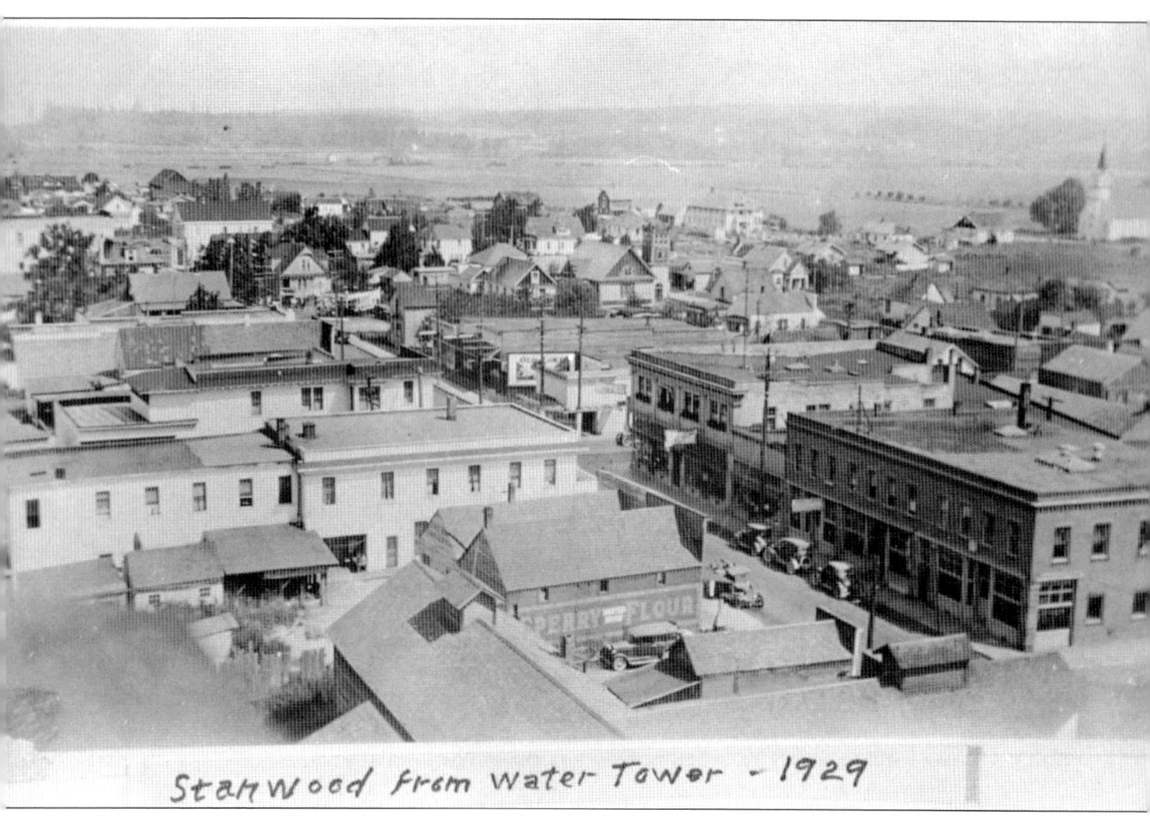

STANWOOD FROM WATER TOWER, 1929. This view looks northeast over Stanwood as it existed just before the Depression. The aerial view shows the Stanwood Hotel with an extended section in the rear. On the east side of the street are the bank building, a storefront, and the Knudson Building. The 1904 bank building held the post office, Ownbey's Variety Store, and West Coast Telephone until the bank and the variety store moved to Main Street at Market Street. No longer a bank from 1930, when the new bank was erected on Main Street, this building held the post office and telephone company. On the second floor was Dr. L.E. Christofferson, who owned and operated the Stanwood General Hospital until it became apartments in 1948. The buildings on this block were demolished in 1965 to construct the new First National Bank of Stanwood, now Bank of America. The water tower was built in 1922 of California redwood and was taken down in 1949. (Photograph by Francis Dannemiller Berg.)

Six

East Stanwood

In 1889, the Scandinavian Trading Union was incorporated to establish a general mercantile. One mile east of Stanwood's original townsite on the river, new businesses were established beginning in 1891 around the depot. Photographs in this chapter feature the railroad over the decades. It is often now considered the main commercial district. But, in the 1980s, a new commercial district formed east of the flats on the highlands with a shopping center and a major grocery store.

In 1922, it was incorporated as a separate town and named East Stanwood. East Stanwood's Commercial Club building was built in 1920 to "function as a social and recreational center to help knit the community in a more closely related spirit of cooperation. Hundreds in the community have attended dances given in the Yankee ballroom—the name given to the dance room," according to the July 28, 1938, *East Stanwood Sun*. It became the East Stanwood City Hall. It burned in July 1938, and the fire was fought by both the East Stanwood and Stanwood Fire Departments.

In 1940, the new Mission-style stucco East Stanwood City Hall and civic center was built. It was planned with a large auditorium and annex for Commercial Club and smaller meetings, a council chamber, a fully equipped modern kitchen, a stage, men's and women's restrooms, cloakrooms, and an entrance lobby. It was built under the direction of the Works Progress Administration (WPA) with a government allotment of $11,775 and a 30-mill levy furnishing the balance for a total of $19,176.

In 1960, the two towns consolidated because of the need to pool funds for a sewage system and other public works. Two years later, the city hall building was sold to the American Legion for $10,500. The hall is still an active community organization known as the Frank Hancock Post No. 92 of the American Legion. This post was officially chartered in 1920 and named in honor of young Frank Hancock, who was killed in action at the Battle of Argonne. Its women's auxiliary was formed soon after in 1921.

The train regularly stopped in Stanwood until April 30, 1971. Soon after, the depot was dismantled. In 2009, it became the Stanwood Station and is now a stop for the Amtrak Cascades route between Vancouver, BC, and Eugene, Oregon, with a connection to the Empire Builder from Everett, Washington, east to Chicago.

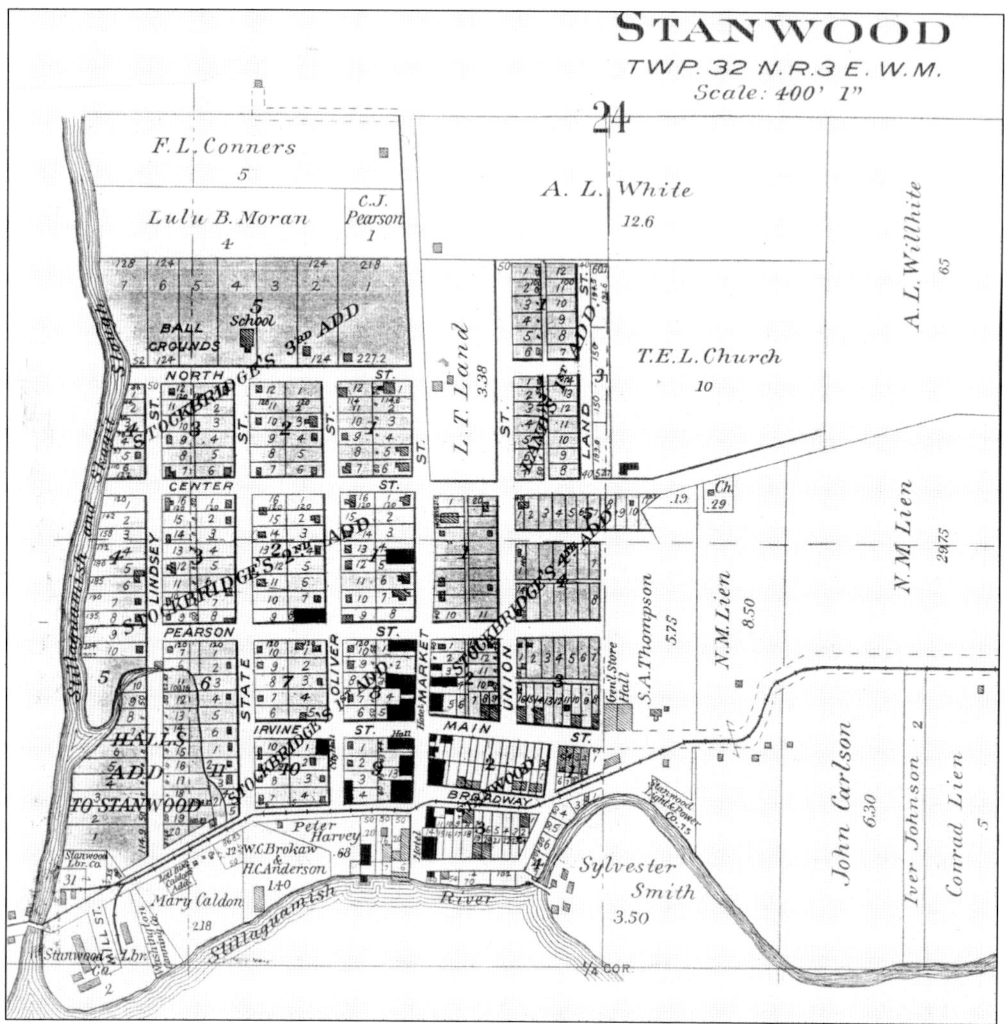

Plat Map of Stanwood, 1910. This plat map shows Stanwood in 1910. It helps to illustrate the winding of the river and the Irvine Slough, which flowed into it until decades later when it was straightened to flow more directly near the Hamilton Stack. The river curves again south toward Florence. It also shows how Broadway proceeded west toward a small bridge that led to the Ovenell Farm and the West Pass crossing to Camano Island. The map also shows the route of the H&H Railroad tracks between the Stanwood Lumber Mill and the Great Northern Railroad connection. The view on the next page shows the Catholic church but not the railroad depot building. The Stillaguamish and Skagit Slough on the left (west) side of town has been filled in and is now a drainage ditch; it was also known as the Douglas Slough. The street on the lower left was originally named for Jack Irvine, but it is now a continuation of 270th Street. The original names of the north-south streets on the Stockbridge 1889 plat map were Lindsey, Oliver, State, Market, and Union. The east-west streets were Broadway, Main, Pearson, Center, and North. Broadway turns and becomes Saratoga Street.

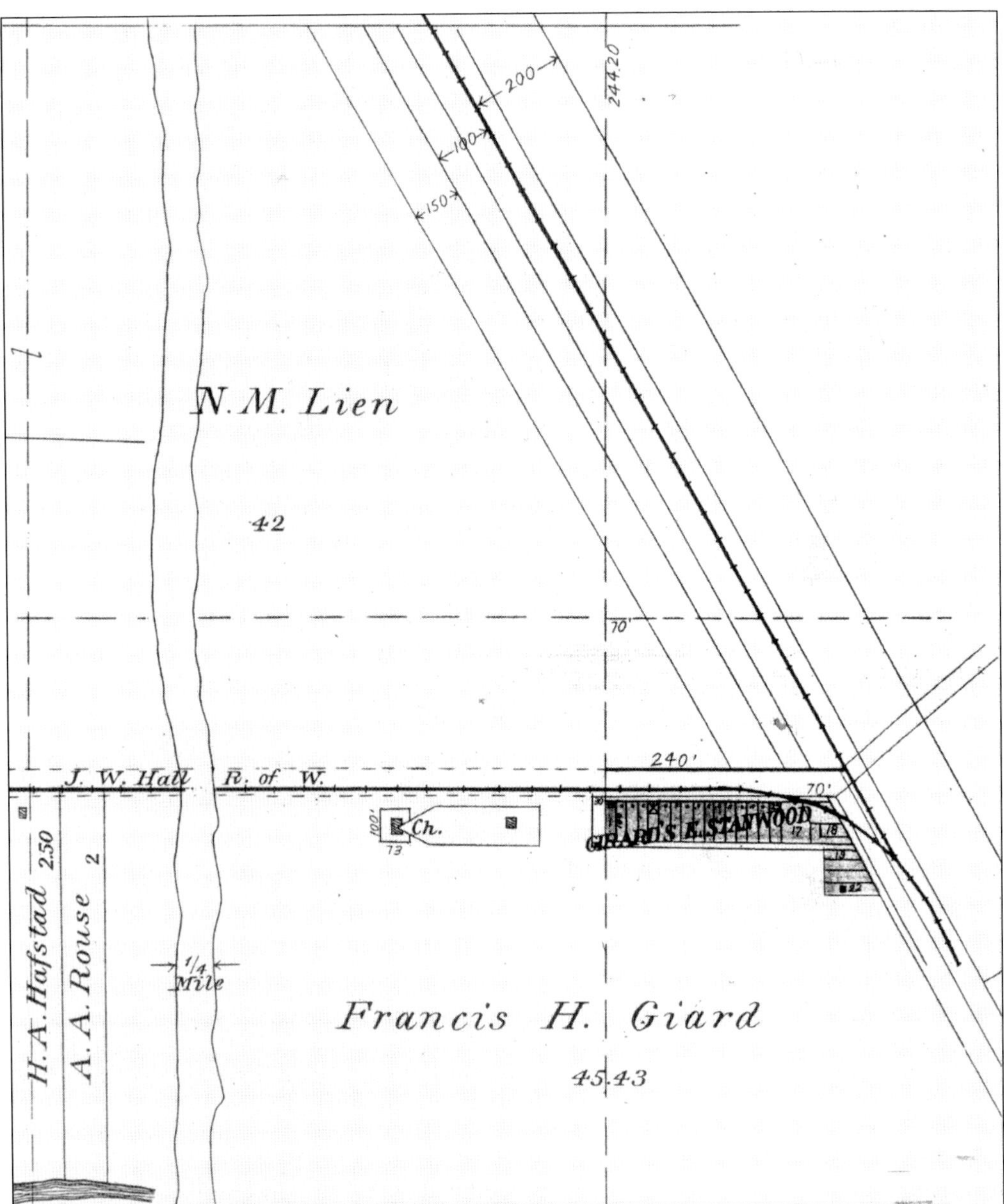

Plat Map of East Stanwood, 1910. This map shows the first plat of East Stanwood where the depot was located a mile east of the waterfront. Two large farms occupied the land in between what became two cities, Stanwood on the waterfront and East Stanwood near the depot. The map leaves out a quarter mile of open land between the two towns that was owned by Francis Giard and Nels M. Lien. Upon his return from gold mining in 1904, Francis Giard (1872–1956) bought his farm east of Stanwood and south of State Street (271st Street) and grew fruit and berries. In 1906, Giard registered the plat of East Stanwood adjacent to the depot and just east of his large farm. In 1922, East Stanwood became an incorporated town with a vote of 88 for and 22 against. Francis Giard was its first mayor. He was also an early partner of the Bank of Stanwood.

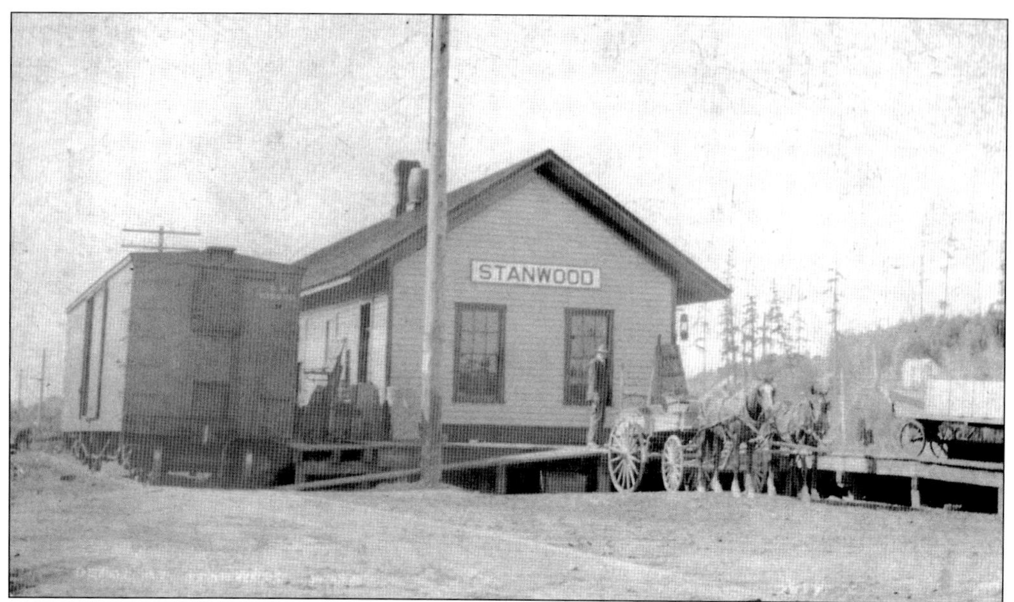

EAST STANWOOD DEPOT. This photographic postcard is one of the first of the Stanwood Depot. There was a telegraph office operated by Ben T. Willard in the 1920s under the training of Harry E. Parsons, the station agent who learned telegraphy as a young boy. He came to Stanwood in 1909 and worked for the railroad for 26 years.

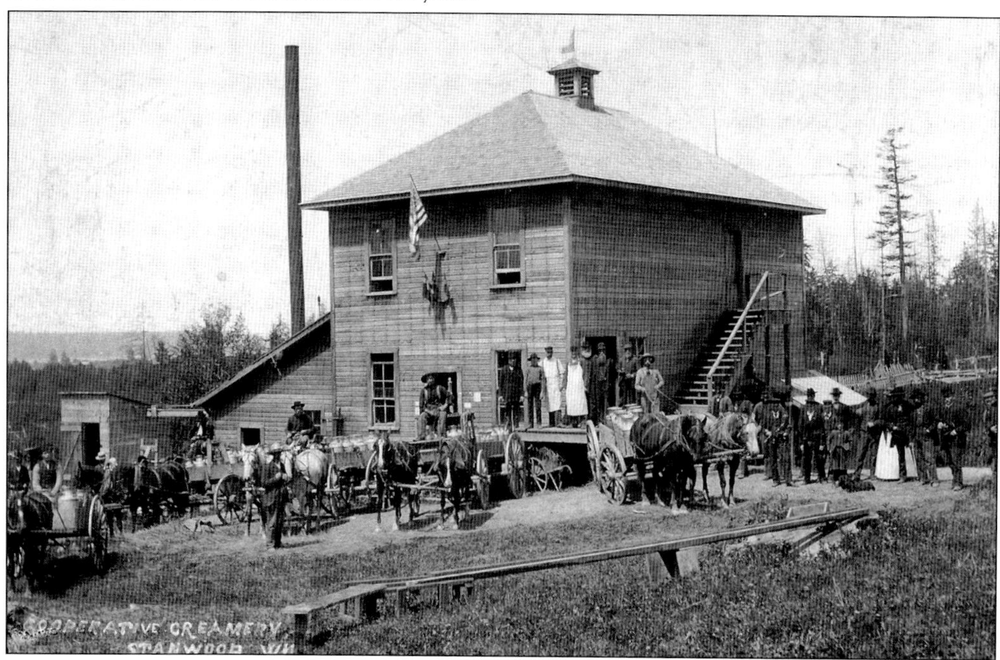

COOPERATIVE CREAMERY. The Cooperative Creamery was incorporated in 1895 in East Stanwood east of the depot. A few years later, the loading dock was extended, and a roof was built over the dock. The operation started with a capital stock investment of $1,500 by Rev. Christian Joergenson, A.J. Brue, and E.P. Hansen and was debt-free within a few years. It won several prizes for its products. It operated as a creamery for many years and later was a cheese factory. (Photograph by Herman Siewert.)

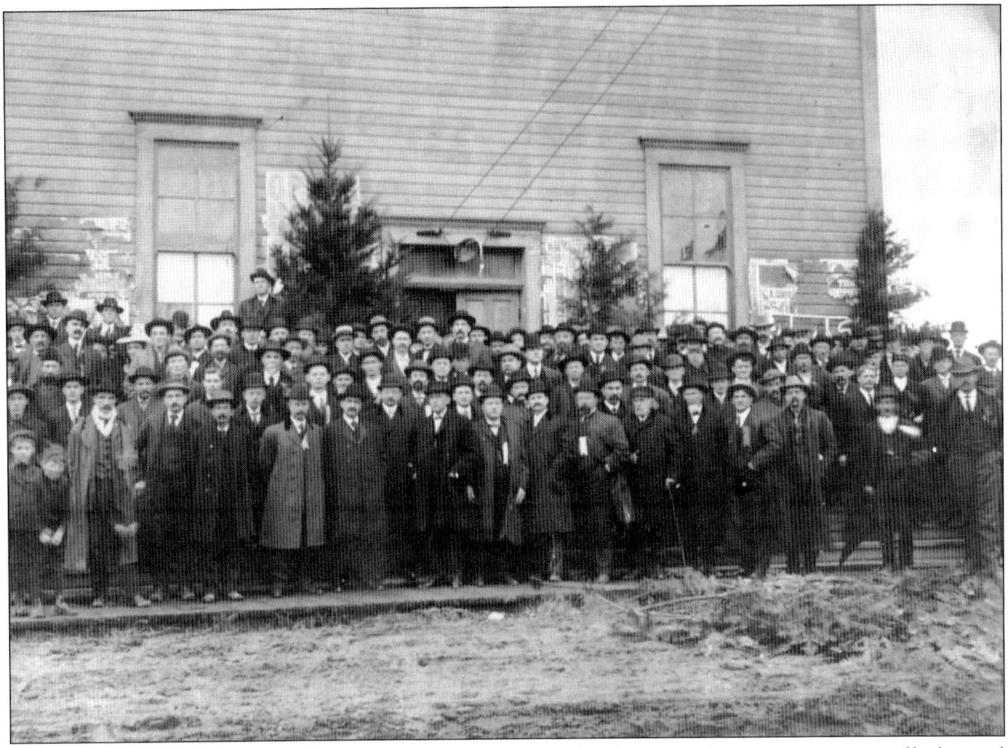

WASHINGTON STATE DAIRYMAN'S ASSOCIATION, 1907. The Stanwood community proudly hosted the state dairymen at the International Order of Oddfellows Hall (now known as the Floyd Norgaard Cultural Center.). The dairy farmers formed the Washington State Dairy Federation in 1892. This was said to be the first dairy trade association in the nation.

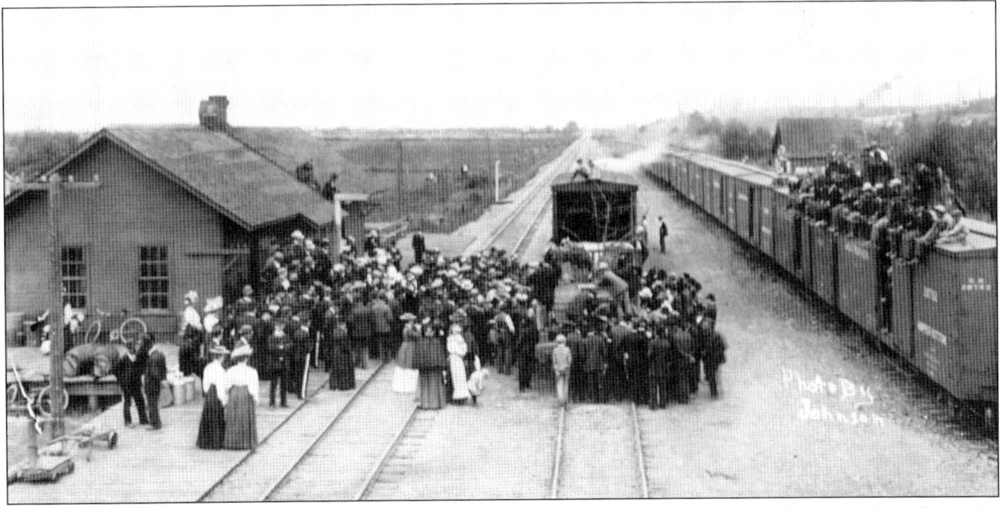

DEMONSTRATION TRAIN. This is the view of the Great Northern (now Burlington, Northern & Sante Fe) Railroad Station at East Stanwood. The tracks were completed in 1891. This is thought to be a farming demonstration train for the Washington State College agricultural extension on September 13, 1910. This dramatic photograph looks north from the depot in East Stanwood and shows a crowd gathered around railcars for the latest scientific information on crops for local farmers. (Photograph by Edward A. Johnson.)

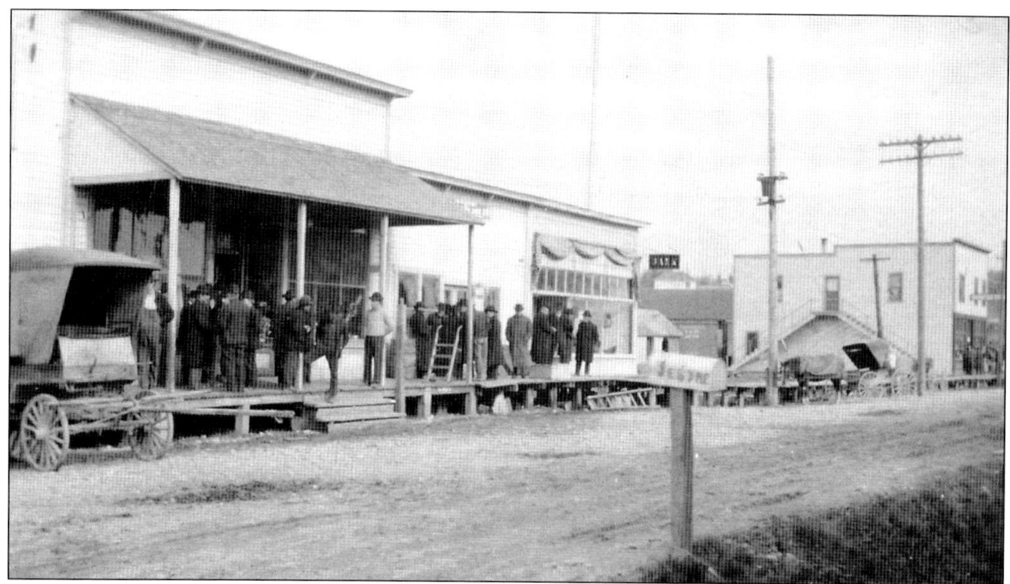

People's Union, East Stanwood. The People's Union was incorporated in East Stanwood in April 1903. There had been a Scandinavian Trading Union incorporated in 1889, and because several names of officers are the same, it is possible that the earlier organization became the People's Union. Its hall and warehouse were dedicated in October 1904. Its original store is the one with the awning.

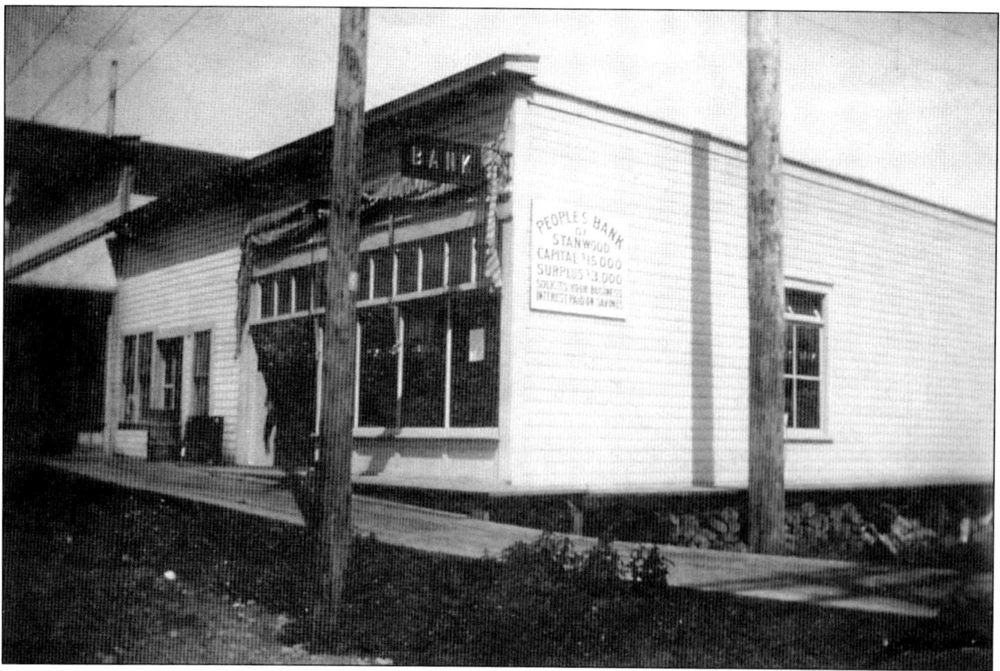

People's Bank of Stanwood. The People's Bank was established through the People's Union in 1910. Its first officers were Carl J. Gunderson, president; Thomas K. Logen, vice president; Halvor P. Husby, secretary; and Haakon Vognild, cashier. In 1914, the bank's name was changed to the State Bank of East Stanwood, and in 1930, it became the National Bank of East Stanwood. In 1947, its third building was erected, which currently serves as the Stanwood Police Station.

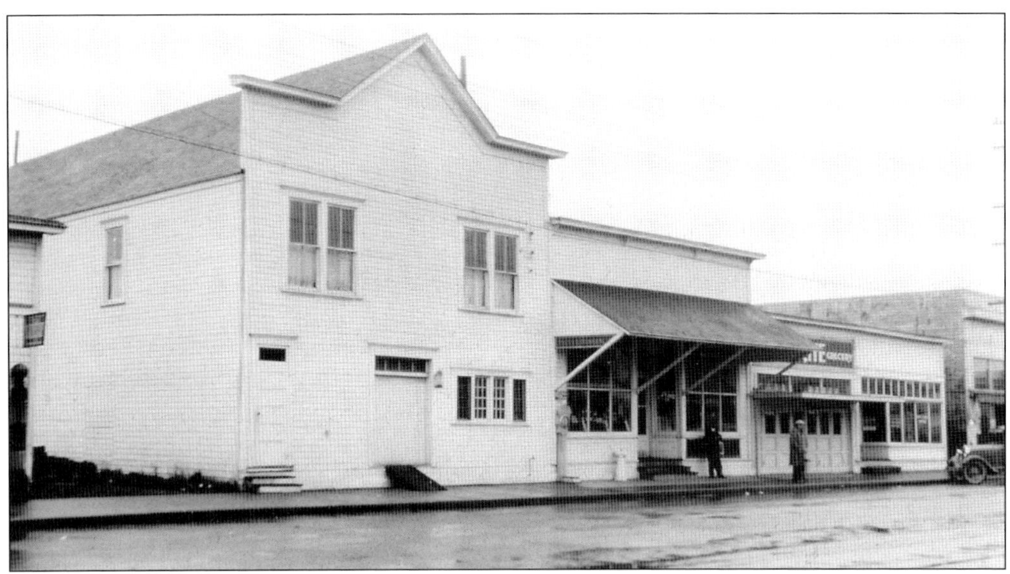

People's Union Warehouse Building. This is a later photograph of the People's Union warehouse next to the People's Union building. Ellen Yngve was the last of a succession of ownership from 1921 to 1923. She and James J. Hansen then purchased the merchandise and formed a partnership. The partnership rented the building until 1930, when they purchased the building too and became the sole owners of the entire interest of the People's Union Cooperative. In 1942, Otto Gilbertson opened Gilbertson Hardware in the People's Union building. Harold Moe took it over in 1964.

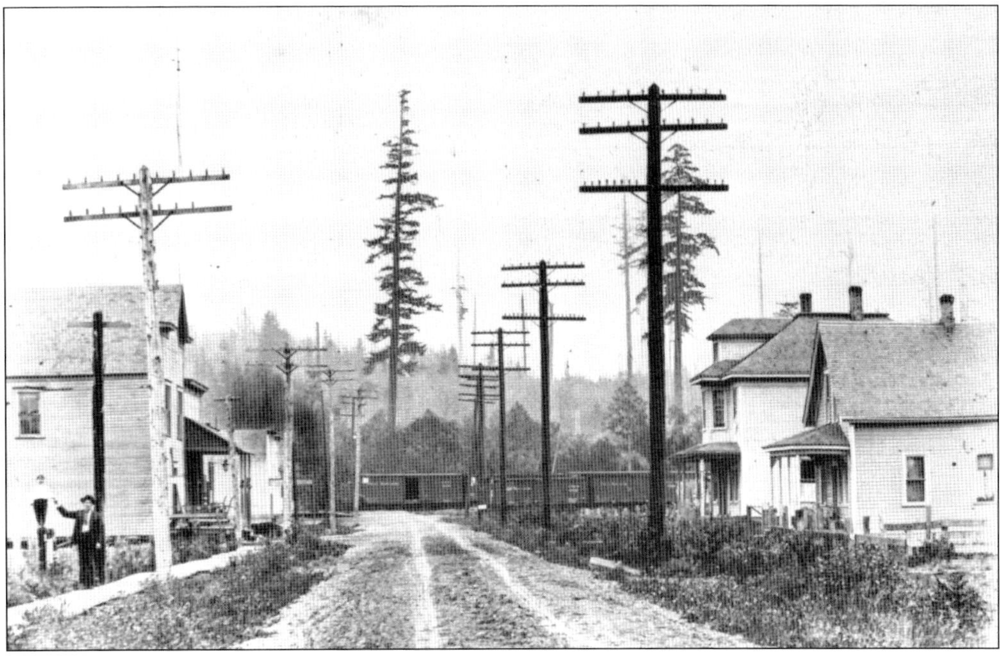

Early East Stanwood View Looking East. This view of wagon tracks leading to the railroad crossing shows very few buildings except for the side view of the People's Union on the left. On the right is an early three-story apartment building that still exists in Stanwood, though it was moved to Eighty-Eighth Avenue NW. It is still an apartment building.

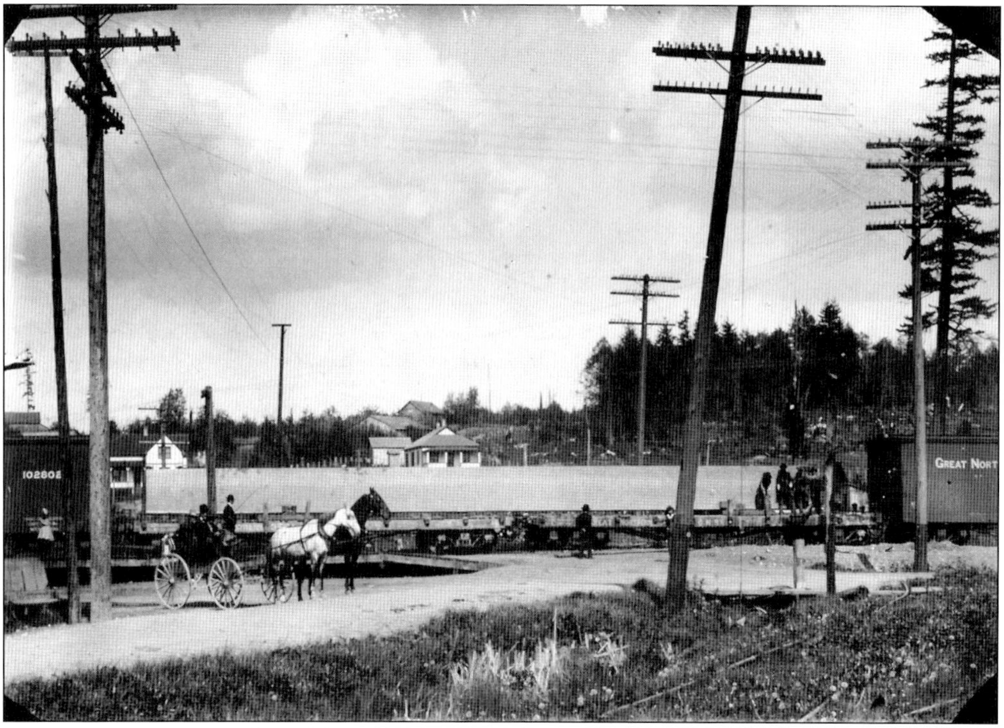

72-Foot Sawn Timber. This timber, the length of two railroad cars, was switching at East Stanwood in 1909 according to handwriting on the photograph received by Carl Gunderson through Alf Willard. Details are limited, but there is a note that this timber might have been logged by the English Logging Company, though where it was sawn is not known. (Photograph by Hellick Aas.)

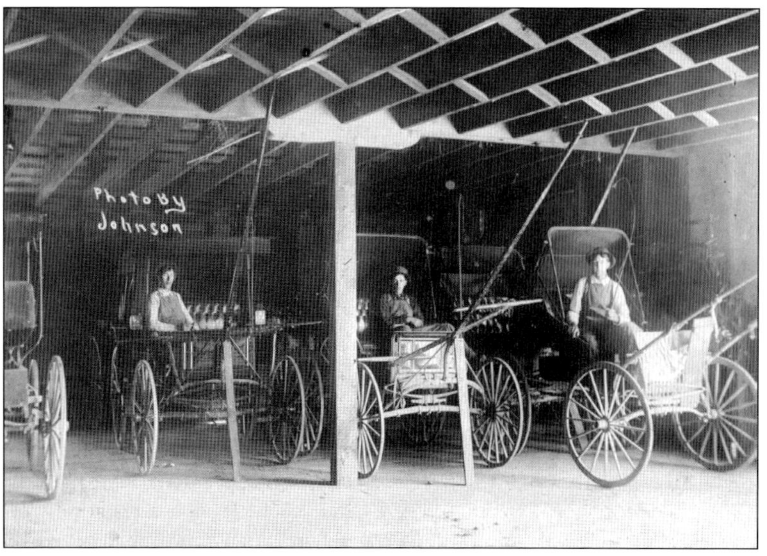

Montana Livery Stable. The Montana Livery Stable was operated by Enoch Peterson and possibly Olav Furuheim and had other operators over the years. In 1921, the Rygg brothers purchased the building from Enoch Peterson and remodeled it into the modern home dairy. (Photograph by Edward A. Johnson.)

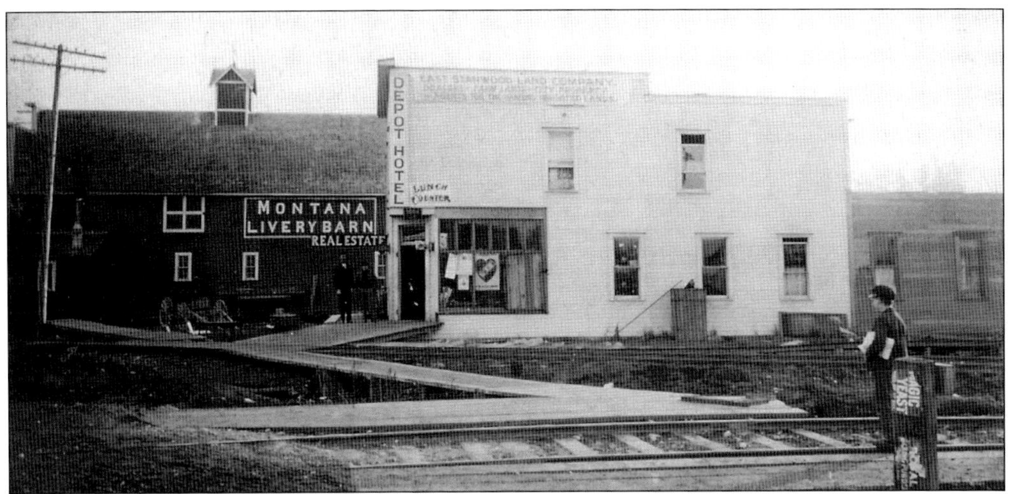

Depot Hotel and the Montana Livery Barn. The hotel and livery were across the road south of the depot. The railroad tracks served the H&H Railroad to transfer lumber or logs to rail cars. The Depot Hotel and restaurant changed to a home bakery and lunchroom in 1915. It was sometimes called the Masterson building before it became part of the Hotel Bartz. It also sold fresh fruit, candy, ice cream, and cigars and tobacco. It was purchased by Isaac Rygg in 1921. He moved the business to Everett in 1929 to expand but purchased the Dairyland Cheese Company from George Monson in 1932 with his brother Oscar Rygg.

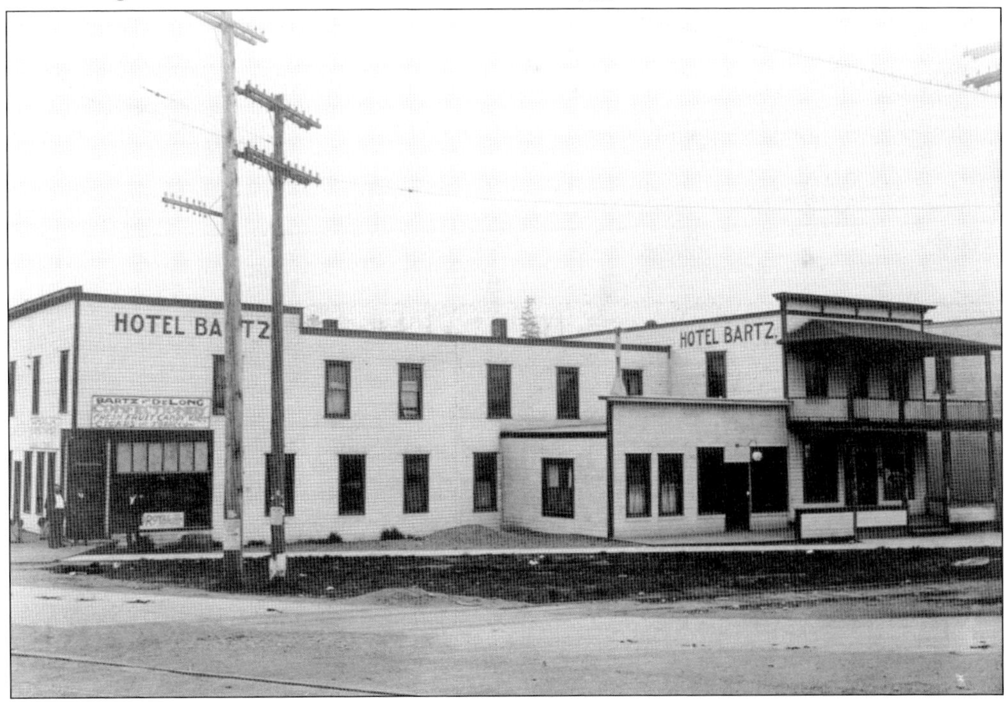

Hotel Bartz. The Hotel Bartz was opened in 1911 by Allen Bartz, who had briefly owned the Stanwood Hotel. In 1937, the Hotel Bartz was remodeled by Idan Gilbertson. The entire front of the Hotel Bartz was changed, and the upper porches were enclosed as improvements were made to accommodate a store. Next to the storefront out of view is the Pastime Café, now a restaurant. In 1942, a Gilmore Gasoline service station was built on the property in front of the old Hotel Bartz.

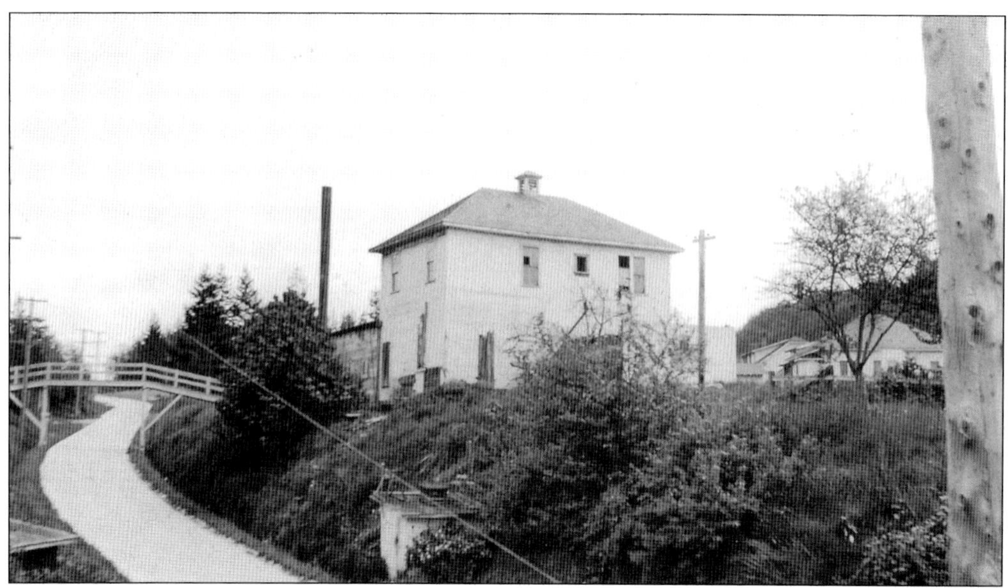

STANWOOD COOPERATIVE CREAMERY. Einar Juel of the Stanwood Cooperative Creamery Association arranged to purchase used equipment from the Snohomish creamery, went on a scow and sternwheeler up to Snohomish, and loaded the steamer with the machinery. Juel paid for the machinery, and when he reached Stanwood the next morning, 25 farmers were there to get the machinery from the waterfront up to the building on the hill. The 1895 creamery building stood on the hill east of the railroad tracks until 1989, when the lumber was recycled.

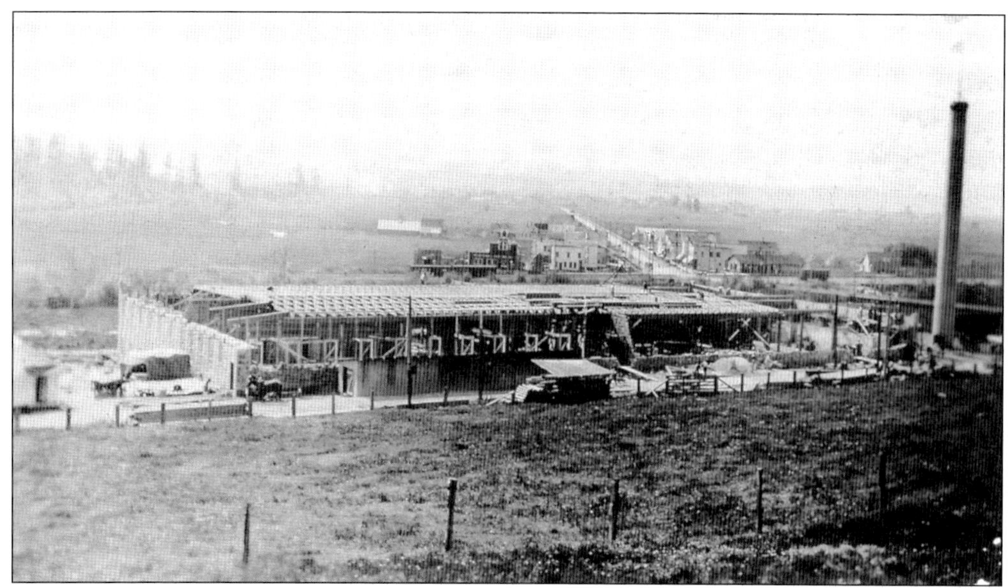

THE PACIFIC COAST CONDENSED MILK COMPANY UNDER CONSTRUCTION. The new modern condensery came to Stanwood as the Pacific Coast Condensed Milk Company, one of many built in Washington since 1889. Other plants were also in Monroe, Kent, Mount Vernon, and Carnation. According to one source, this became one of the bases of rivalry between the two towns.

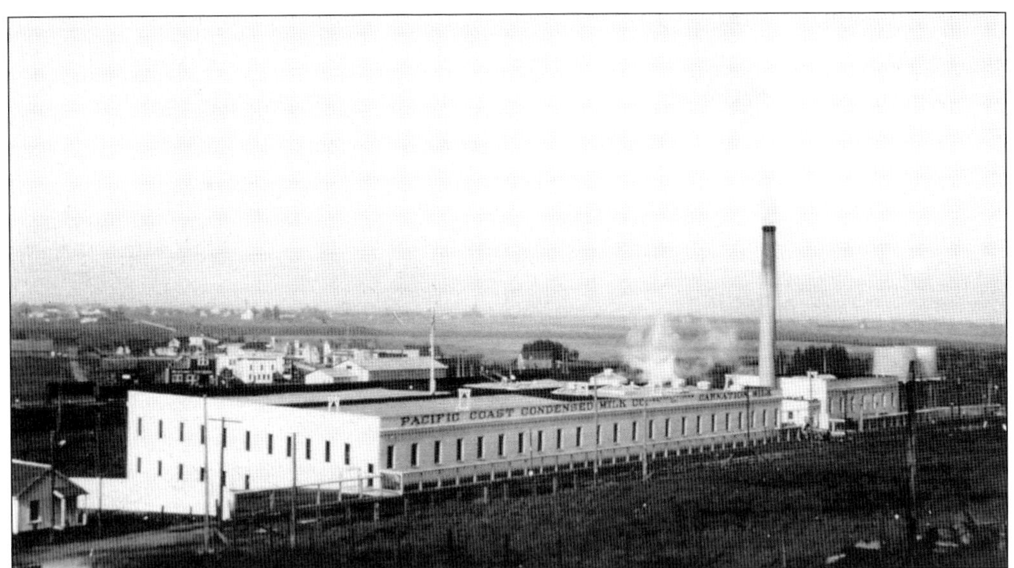

The Pacific Coast Condensed Mill Company. The Pacific Coast Milk Products Company tried to build its first milk processing building on the waterfront, but it was difficult to get there. After a search for a better location, it built the large white building as a condensery in 1914. It became part of the Carnation Company in 1916. During its heyday, it processed 200,000 pounds of milk daily from 7,000 cows. The factory covered 36,000 square feet and had a holding tank 103 feet high.

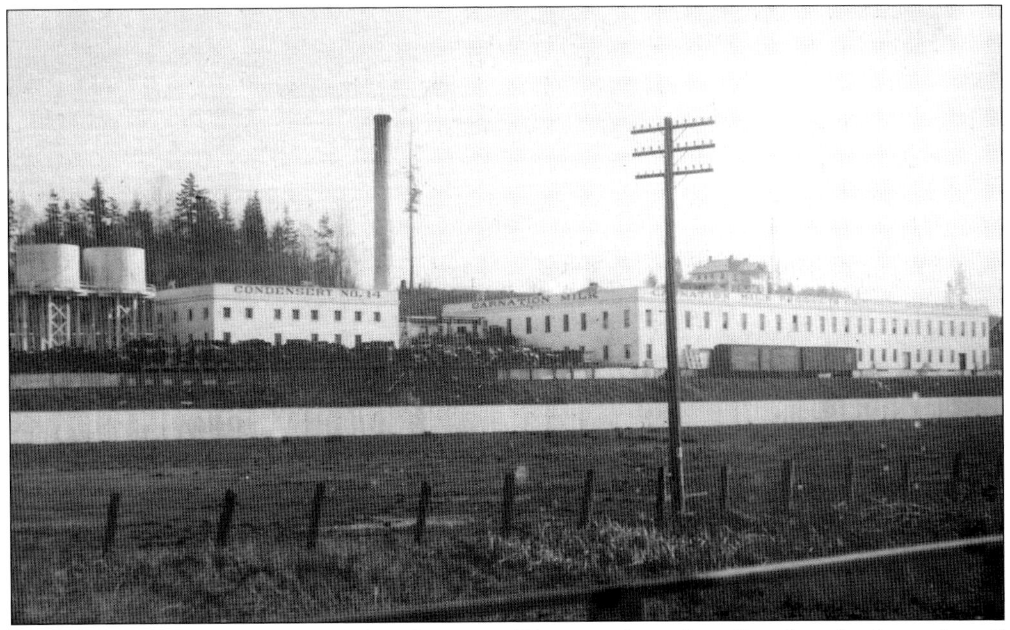

Condensery No. 14, Carnation Milk Company. This view from the railroad tracks shows the rail sidings that served the milk company in East Stanwood. In 1933, the Bozeman Canning Company of Mount Vernon took over the vacant building and converted it to a pea cannery. It later became a vegetable processing plant under the names of Stokely, Van Camp, and Pictsweet. The buildings are currently occupied by a cold storage company. Above the building is the Klondike Mansion. The smokestack, built in 1914, was dismantled due to a crack in the cement structure in 1986.

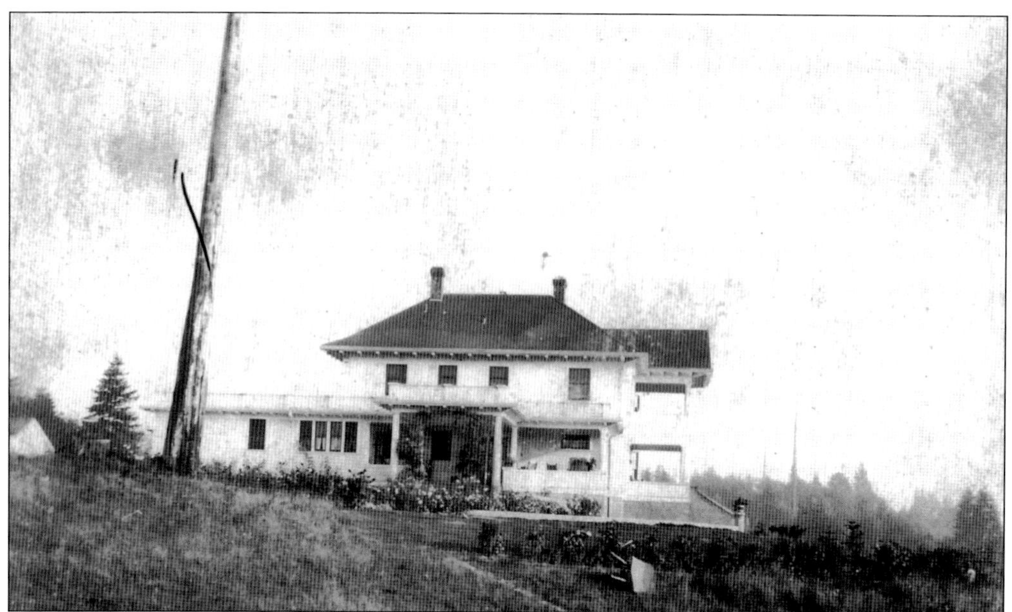

Henry C. "H.C." Anderson's Klondike Mansion. This is a side view of Henry C. Anderson's large mansion, which still exists. H.C. Anderson built the white mansion situated on the east hill overlooking Stanwood. He made his fortune in the goldfields of Alaska. He married Ida Iverson in 1906. Ida died in 1913 of starvation because she followed a "fasting cure" diet. Her death greatly affected H.C. From his mansion on the hill, he was alone to view the town and his vast holdings from his Klondike success. He lived in the mansion for less than a year and died at the age of 49 on August 6, 1914. He left a fortune to his daughter, Agnes.

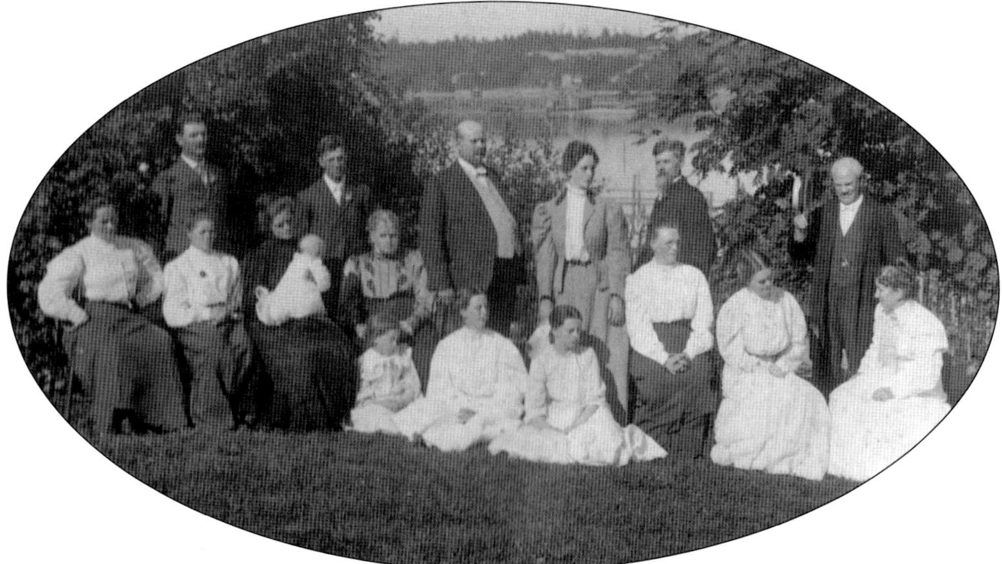

Iverson Family Portrait. The occasion of this family portrait is unknown. Henry C. Anderson is in the center, and to the right of him is his wife, Ida Iverson. To the right of her is Oliver B. "O.B." Iverson. O.B. Iverson was an early surveyor from Norway via South Dakota who wrote early observations of the territory's landscapes, most relevantly the area around the Stillaguamish River delta. He was also a territorial legislator in 1876 and 1877 representing Snohomish County.

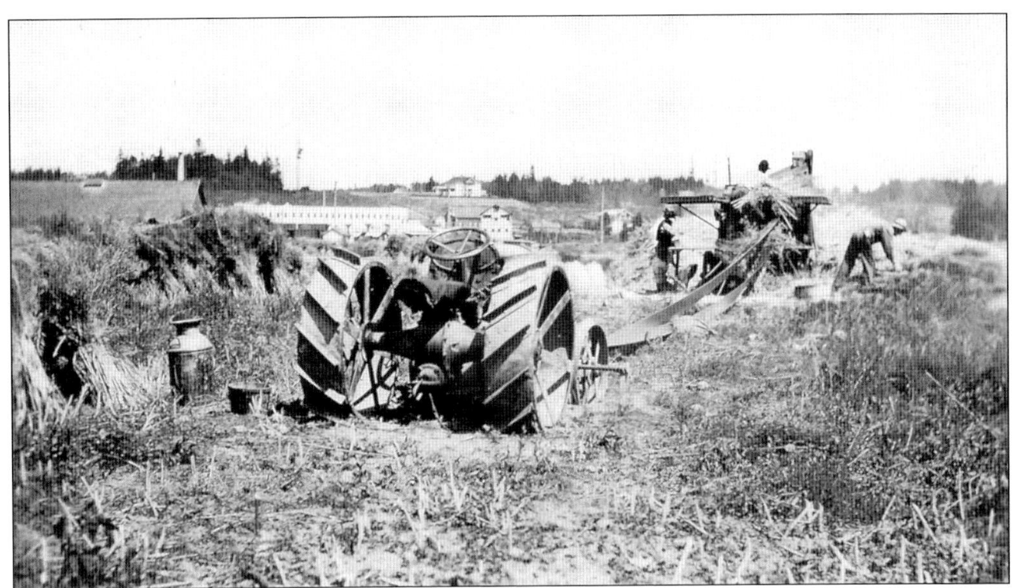

Threshing between Towns. This photograph shows the threshing on the Giard Farm. Francis Giard was the first mayor of East Stanwood. In the distance are the condensery and, on the hill, H.C. Anderson's Klondike Mansion, which is still prominent in the skyline. The Francis Giard Farm was located south of 271st Street and west of Eighty-Eighth Avenue NW. Both Anderson and Giard made significant fortunes in Alaska during the Klondike Gold Rush and returned to invest in their hometown as bankers and farmers.

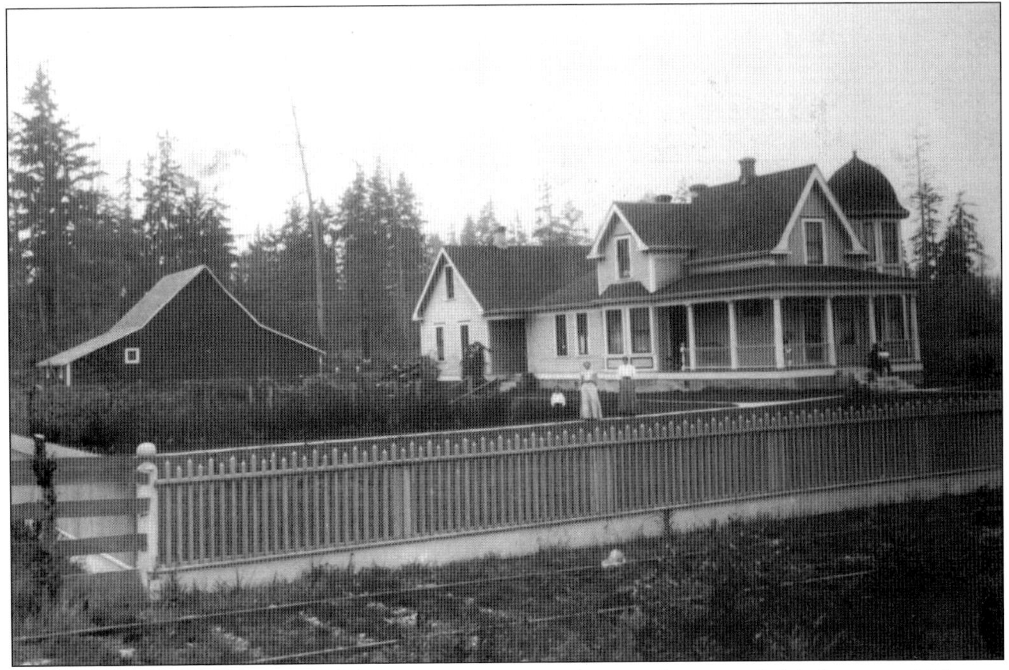

The Giard Farmhouse. The elaborate tower was a distinct feature of this home, which was demolished in 1964. The trees in the background are long gone, and his farm field where the Irvine Slough begins is now a shopping center and State Route 532. Note the H&H Railroad tracks just in front of the fence.

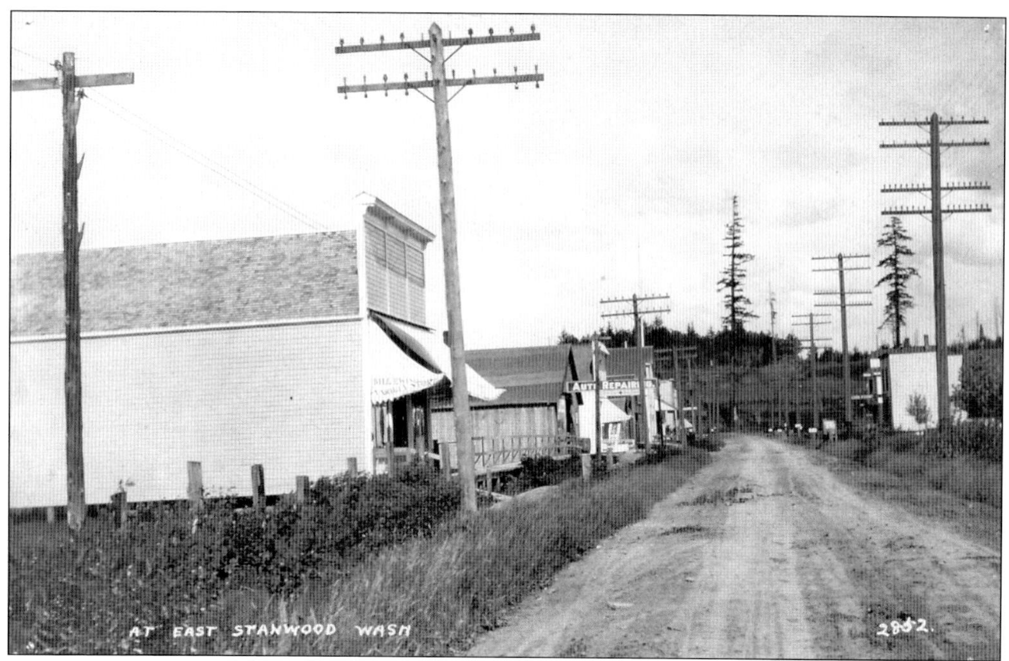

AT EAST STANWOOD. This view is thought to be from around 1906, about the time the area was platted by Francis Giard. The railroad went through in 1891. One of the canopies reads "Bill Ewing's Variety Store." Other business signs include an auto repair. Gunderson's Star Furniture is in the foreground on the right.

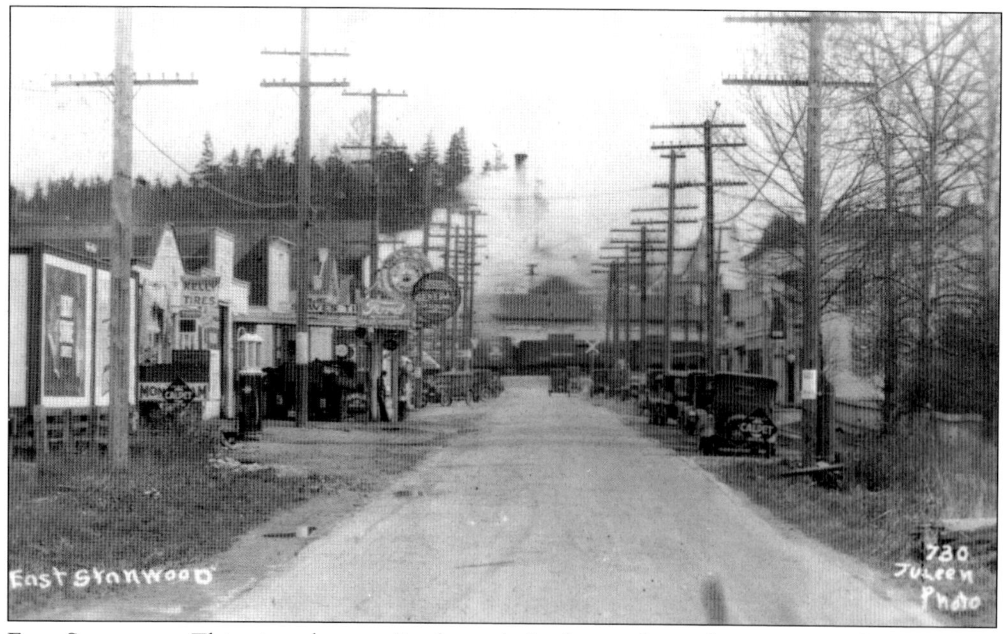

EAST STANWOOD. This view shows a Ford car dealership with gasoline pumps. The Stanwood Grain Company is in the distance behind the railroad cars. This was the old Pacific Highway complete with billboards before Highway 530, first known as SSH (Secondary State Highway) I-E, and the viaduct bypassed Stanwood. Prior to this time, the highway wound to the west toward Stanwood and turned at Market Street north to Skagit County. (Photograph by J.A. Juleen.)

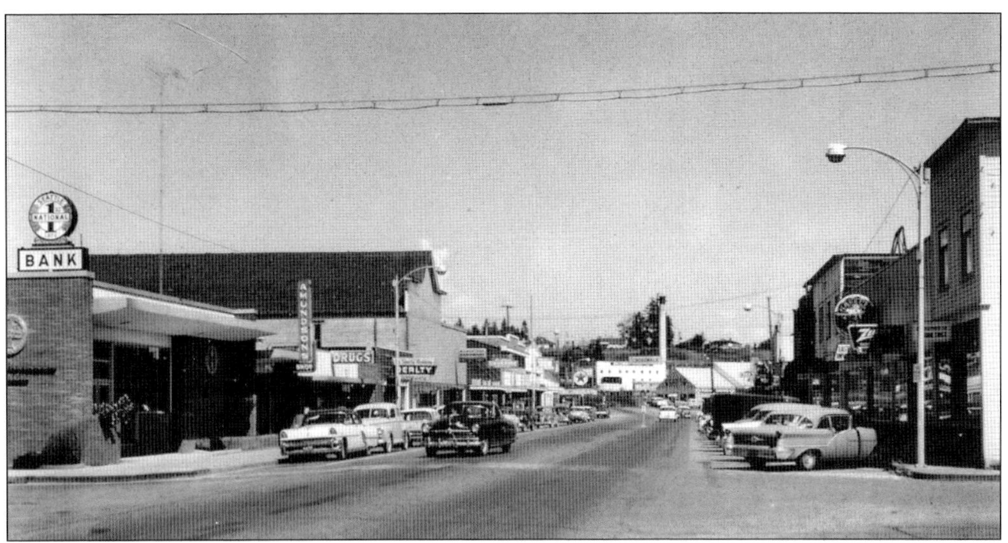

East Stanwood Street View. This is a 1950s view looking east toward the food processing plant (formerly the condensery). The Seattle First National Bank is on the left at the intersection of 271st Street and Eighty-Eighth Avenue NW. The view also includes Amundson's and partial views of signs for "DRUGS," Ira Shorty Ordwing Real Estate, Gilbertson Hardware, Shurfine, East Stanwood Investments, and Dr. Josephson, Optometrist.

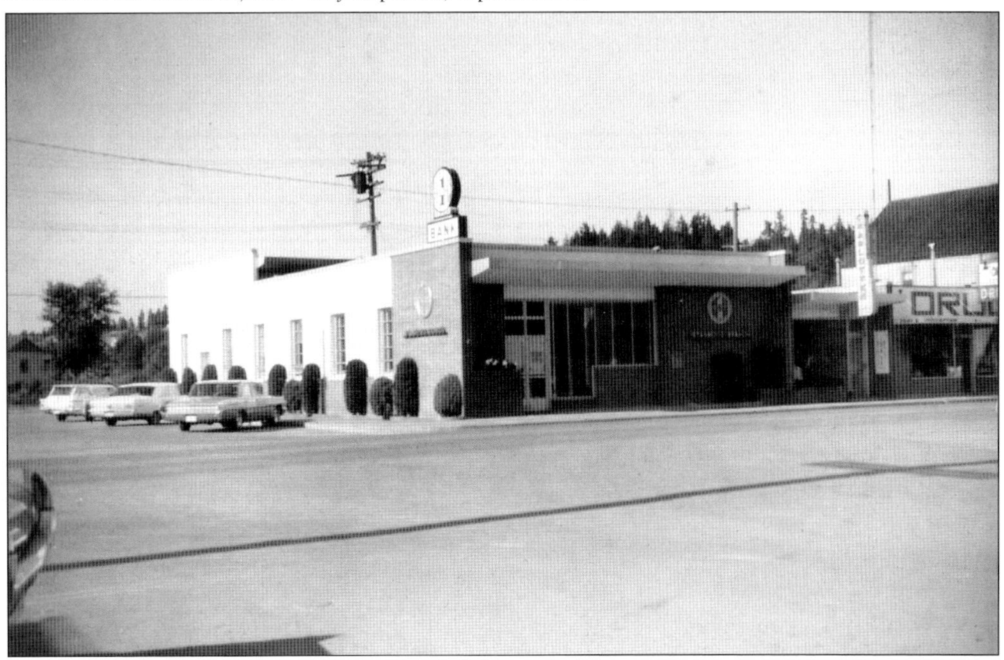

First National Bank of East Stanwood. The Seattle First National Bank was constructed in 1948 as the State Bank of East Stanwood, which was established when the People's Bank erected its original Neoclassical bank in 1913. Later, in 1930, it became the National Bank of East Stanwood. In 1907, a relative newcomer, Carl J. Gunderson (1876–1976), had arrived. After a couple of years in Cedarhome, he became manager of the People's Union Store. He was instrumental in establishing the People's Bank in 1910. In 1956, it was acquired by Seattle First National Bank. It became the Stanwood Police Station some time after the banks merged in 1992.

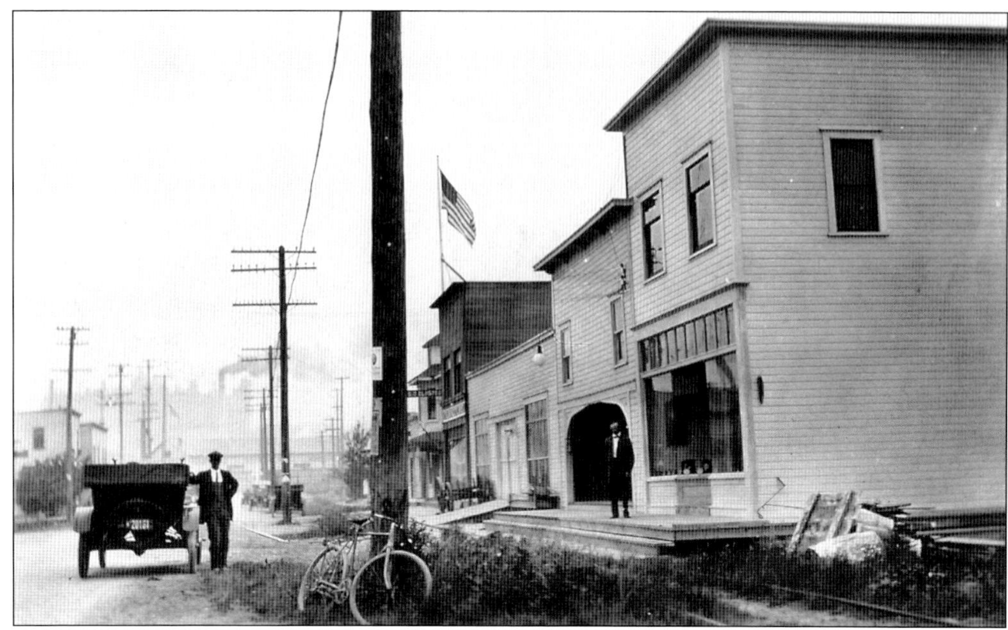

East Stanwood Street View, about 1928. This view looks east down 271st Street with the H&H Railroad tracks along the storefronts. East Stanwood's Liberty Theater opened with its arched entryway in 1917. On its right is Paul Loe's jewelry store. On its left is Star Furniture, owned by Carl Gunderson. The East Stanwood Post Office was located in the building he named Gunderson Hardware, Furniture, and Implement Company for several years. In 1929, Gunderson built his new brick building with his furniture store, mortuary, and chapel on the first floor and office and apartment space on the second floor. The building still exists. In the 1930s, Dr. Harold J. Greer was on the second floor of the building.

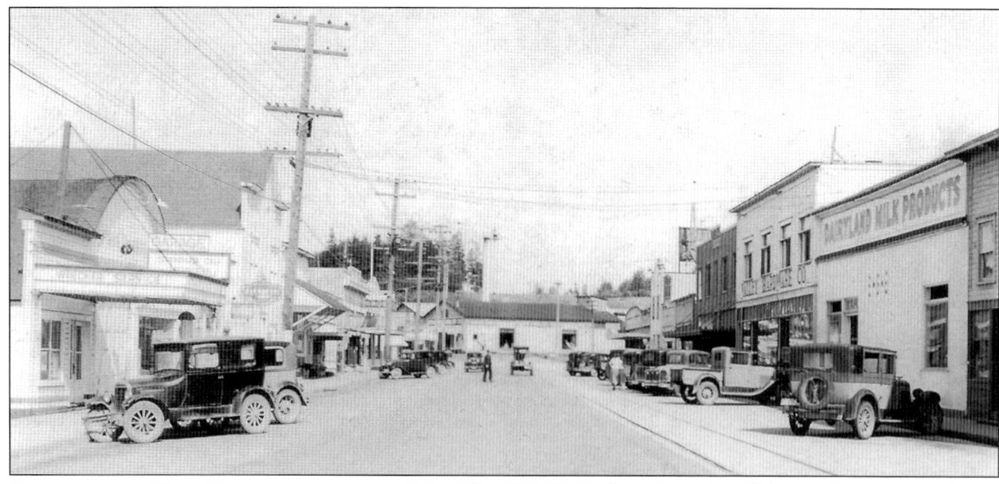

Storefronts, East Stanwood, about 1932. The H&H Railroad track still lines the streets of East Stanwood, making it difficult for automobiles to park. Note the Stangeland Garage, Dairyland Milk Products, and Valley Hardware. In the distance is the Stanwood Grain Company. In 1930, East Stanwood was required to vacate a strip of 12 feet next to the pavement from the depot to Giard's property. The town was then able to pave the old and new rights of way with cement, telephone poles were removed from the alley, and parking on the south side of the street was easier for customers of businesses. (Photograph by J. Boyd Ellis.)

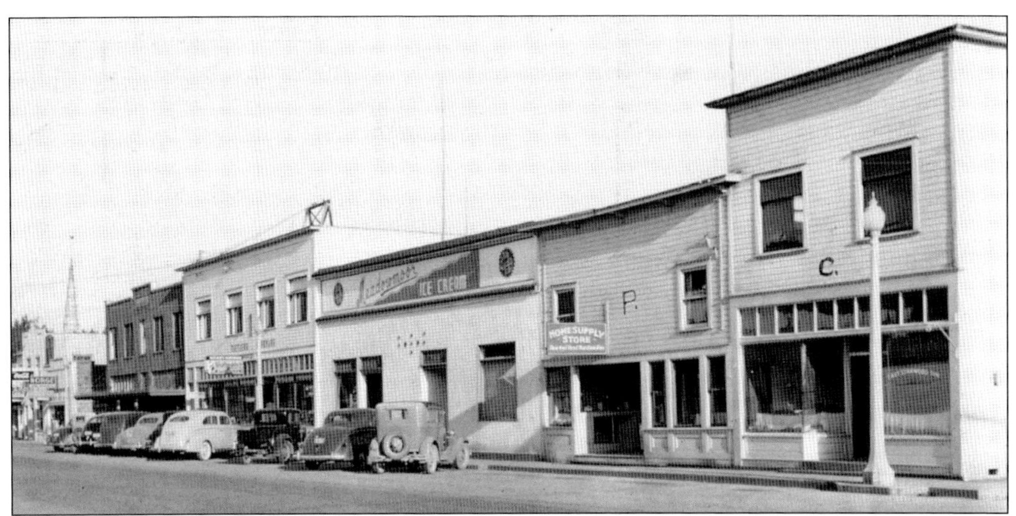

Storefronts, 1941. In this photograph, the Dairyland Milk Products building is now the Meadowmoor ice cream building. Isaac Rygg purchased the Daisy Meat Market in Stanwood and then purchased the Home Meat Market in East Stanwood. In 1920, the Daisy Meat Market advertised "homemade sausage and lard." Other signs are for the Tietjens's Hardware, the Home Supply Store, and the *East Stanwood Sun* newspaper office. In 1942, the *East Stanwood Sun* (in the building on the right) reported it was quitting business because items were hard to procure, presumably because of World War II. The *East Stanwood Sun* was published from about 1938 until its last issue on July 30, 1942. Carl and Mabel Christensen were the publishers. These first four buildings were demolished in 1965.

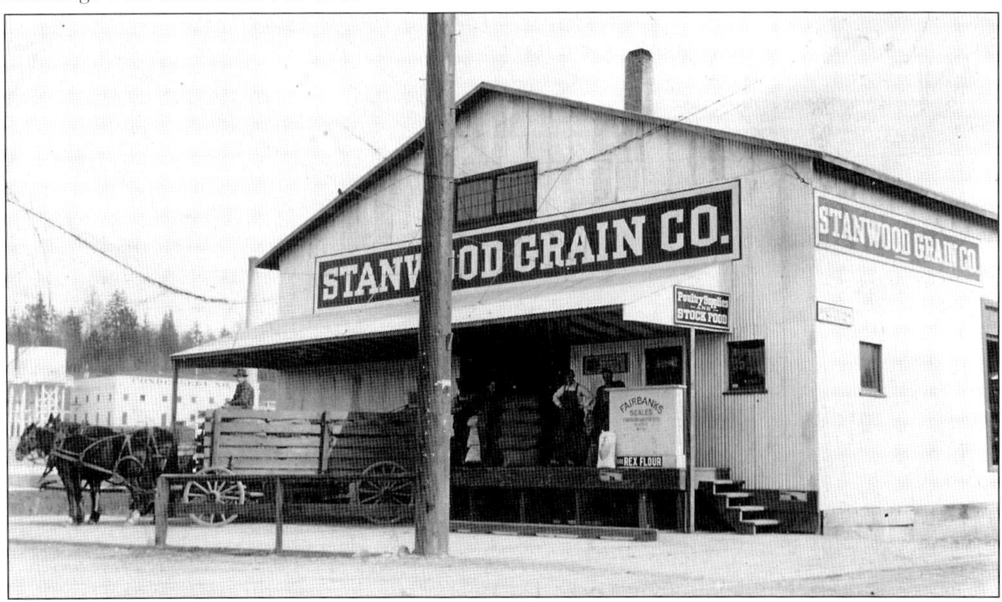

Stanwood Grain Company. The Stanwood Grain Company was moved from the waterfront to just east of the railroad tracks in East Stanwood in 1914. About 1941, the name of the company changed to Twin City Grain. It burned in October 1954 but was quickly rebuilt. In 1957, the name was changed to Stanwood Feed and Farm Supply. The business featured custom grinding with a full line of ready-mixed feed, including pet food. Later, it was purchased and operated by Monroe's Wolfkill Company.

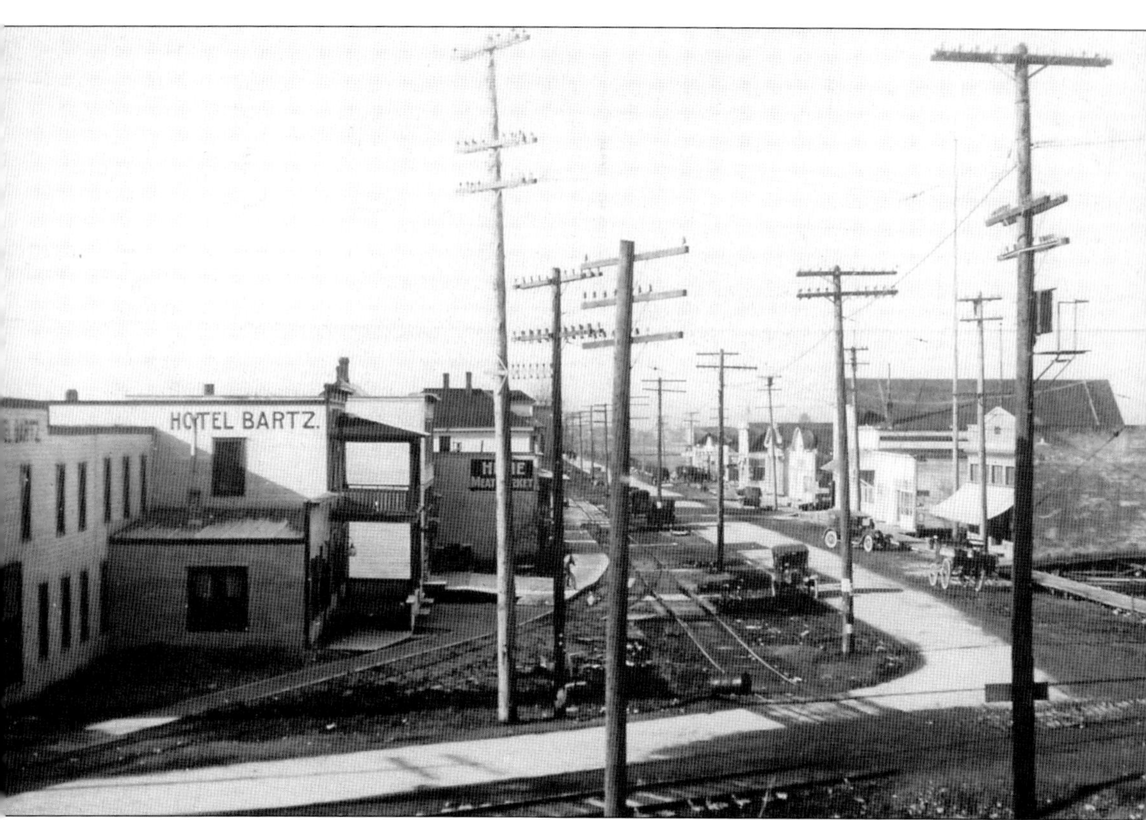

Hotel Bartz and the H&H Railroad Tracks. This 1918 photographic postcard of East Stanwood looks west toward the track of the H&H Railroad and its connection with the Great Northern Railroad. From left to right are the Hotel Bartz, Pastime Confectionery, and the first Home Meat Market building. On the north side of the street are the People's Union, a garage, and a bank building. Behind the building with the Home Meat Market sign is the Peterson apartment building, which was later moved to a nearby street. On the right is the Frederickson & Stubb Mercantile, built in 1918.

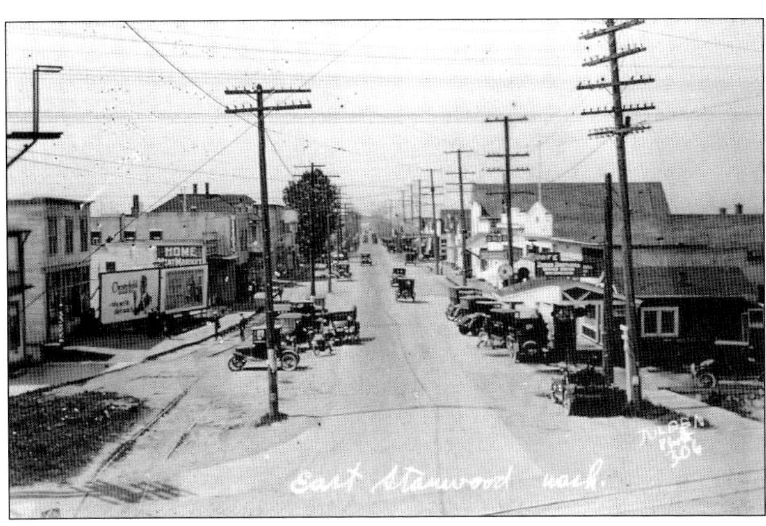

East Stanwood. The billboard on the left covers the lot where the Rygg Building was erected in 1927. On the north side of the street is the new N.V. King Building with the drugstore sign, which is barely visible. The Dodge Brothers Service Station appears to be quite busy. (Photograph by J.A. Juleen.)

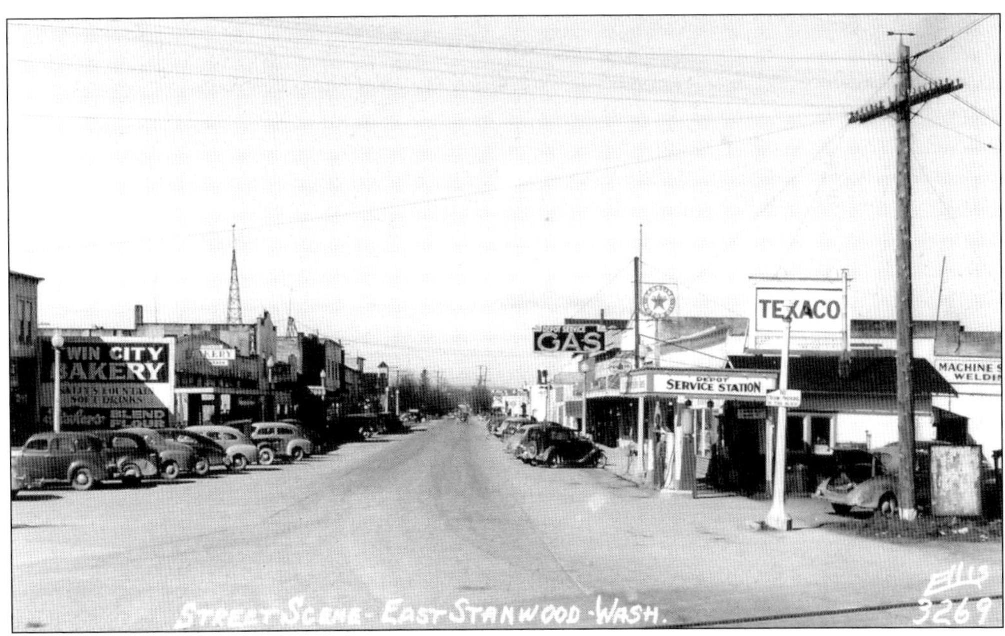

An East Stanwood Street Scene. The Dodge Brothers station is now the East Stanwood Busy Corner. In 1921, the Rygg Brothers Creamery began making Meadowmoor ice cream. Isaac Rygg expanded to Everett and began the Dairyland Cheese Company of East Stanwood. Oscar Rygg sold the meat business in East Stanwood in 1948. On the left is a later-era Twin City Bakery in the Rygg Building, which had been a meat market with freezer lockers and a restaurant and bakery. There was also a refrigeration business there. This became the Scandia Bakery and Lefze Factory in 1971. (Photograph by J. Boyd Ellis.)

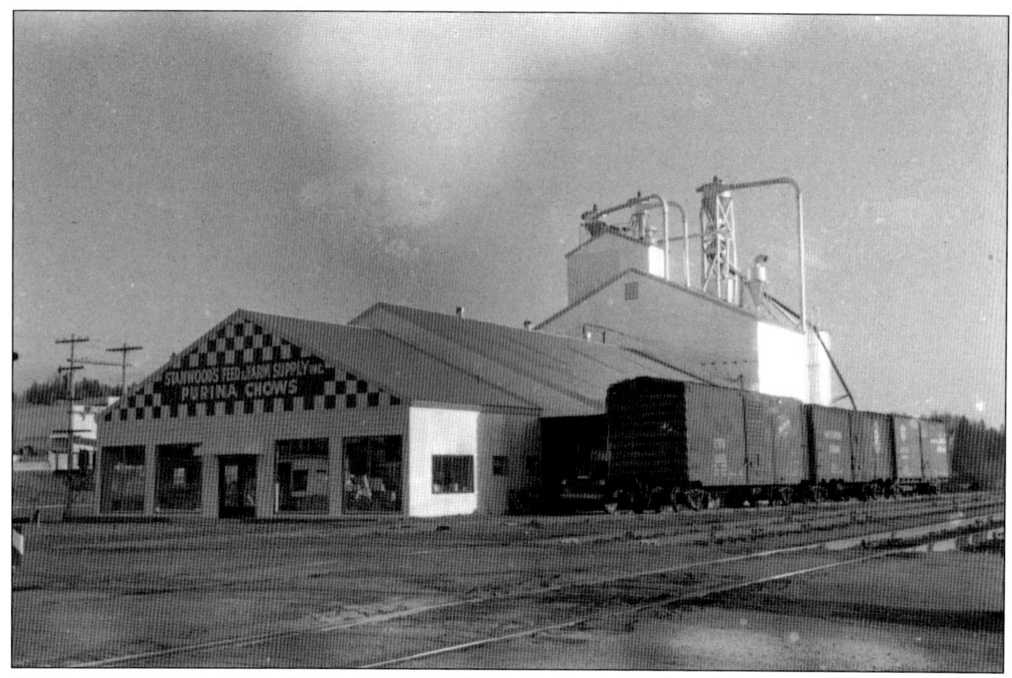

Stanwood Feed & Grain Supply. Prior to Wolfkill, Skagit Feed and Grain Supply took over the Stanwood/Twin City Grain business. Wolfkill sold its feed business to Cargill in 2012, and these buildings were demolished in 2013.

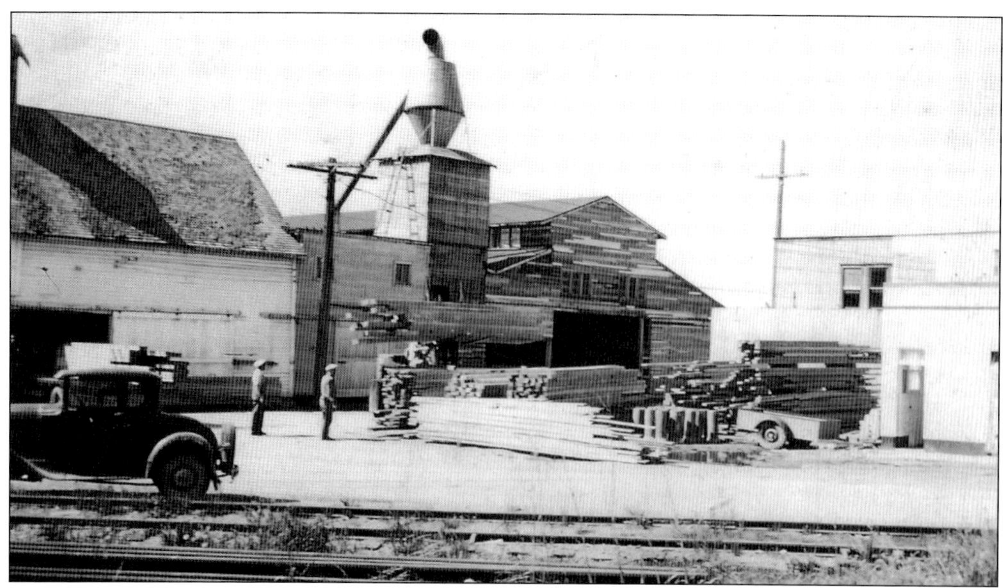

Eilertson's Lumber Company, East Stanwood. The Eilertson Lumber Company opened in the old livery barn on Florence Road in 1934. There were many enlargements, a warehouse, and a planer on the west side and another on the east side of the road. It became Twin City Building Supplies in 1959. It was sold to Copeland Lumber in 1979.

Seven

Floods and Freezes

Being at the mouth of a river creates numerous obstacles. Every few years, floods threatened the comforts of hearth and home in the winters and springs. Occasional snowstorms and freezes also caused problems. For those from New England, the northern Midwest, and the Scandinavian countries, the Western Washington winters seemed mild, but floods were everywhere.

Among the photographs in this chapter are those taken by John T. Wagness of the west side of Stanwood and Albert J. Palmquist, who was a druggist in East Stanwood from 1921 until 1923. He captured some unique views of East Stanwood and the local business buildings, especially during the floods. Palmquist worked for and then purchased the Rex Drug Store of East Stanwood, which provided photograph-developing services. His store was in the N.V. King Building. The N.V. King Building was built by the druggist E.A. King and was named for his wife, Nina V. King. In 1939, Mr. and Mrs. Kenneth Murray took over the operation of the variety and 10¢ store. It was sold again in 1942, and the name was changed to Nelson's Variety about 1960 with new owners.

The local newspaper reported flooding in 1886–1887, 1906, 1909, December 1917, December 1921, February and November 1932, January 1935, October 1947, and December 1949. The most devastating were the 1951 and 1959 floods. In the following years, less extensive flooding occurred in 1960, 1965, 1966, 1972, 1974 through 1977, 1979, 1980, 1982, 1983, 1985, 1987, 1989, 1990, and 1991. Since then, flooding in low spots occurred in 2002, 2019, and 2023.

The city dikes have held in recent years, and threats from the Skagit River to the north have been minimal. Zoning and planning have been effective to some degree. The author of a 1963 flood plain information study includes the recognition that floods are a normal part of a river's life: "Valley residents should never lose sight of the fact that the flood plain can only be borrowed; basically it belongs to the river."

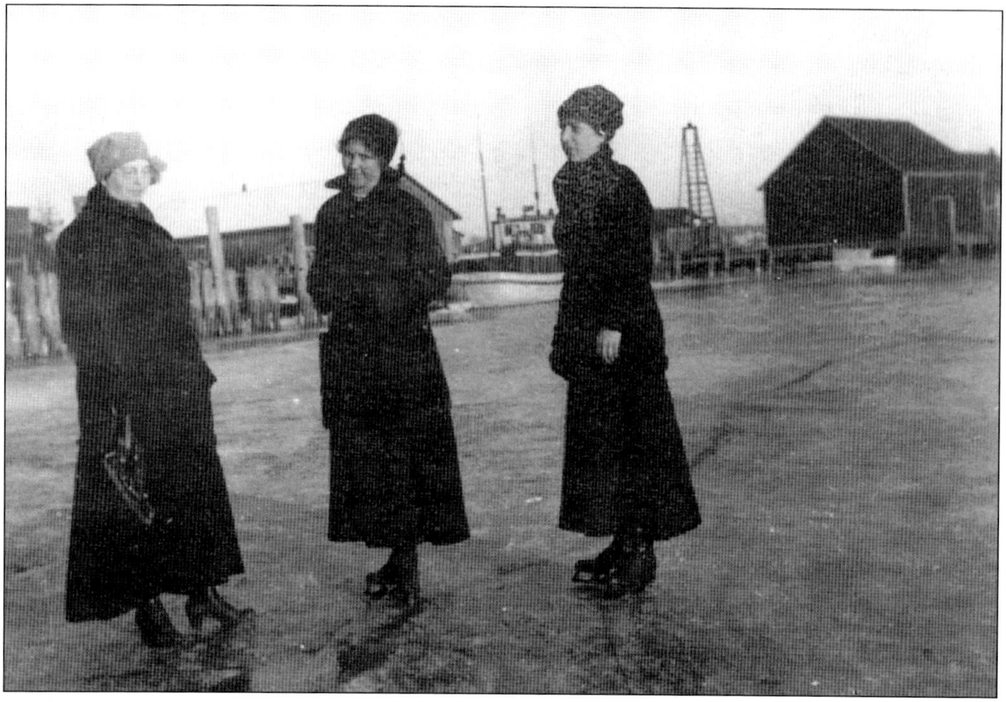

ICE SKATING, THE STILLAGUAMISH RIVER. Two of the women are wearing skates to glide over the Stillaguamish River. In 1916, the freeze lasted for the month of January, allowing people, including Ole Eide, to skate on the river. The big freeze lasted for one month, and on February 1, Eide remembered waking up to three feet of wet snow. Eide, who became the local game warden, noted that ice skating now seems to be a thing of the past.

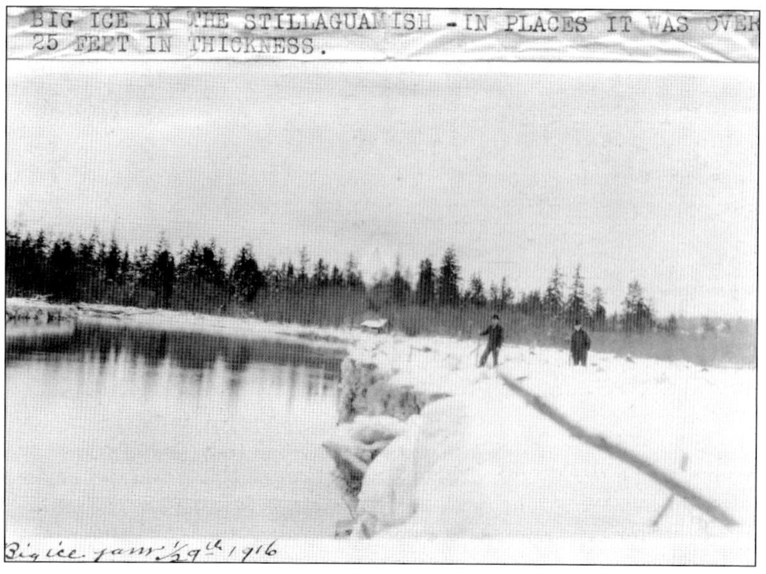

BIG ICE JAM, 1916. This snowstorm is well represented in photographs and news reports in every town in Western Washington at the time. This view looks north along the snow-laden banks of the Stillaguamish River. In the picture are Adolph and Herman Joergenson on their family farm south of East Stanwood.

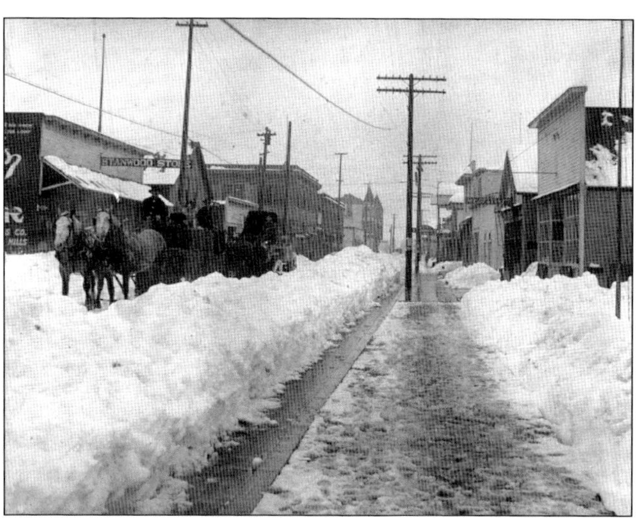

Market Street with Snow. In January 1916, ice also closed the lower Columbia River to navigation by river steamers. John A. Juleen, a local photographer, advertised postcards of snow scenes for sale in his Everett studio. Businesses in the photograph are, on the right, the Independent Meat Market, the flour and grain business, the Ketchum Store, and the three-story Hotel Stanwood. On the left is the Pearson's Stanwood Store, the Folly Theater, and the Knudson Building. (Photograph by John T. Wagness.)

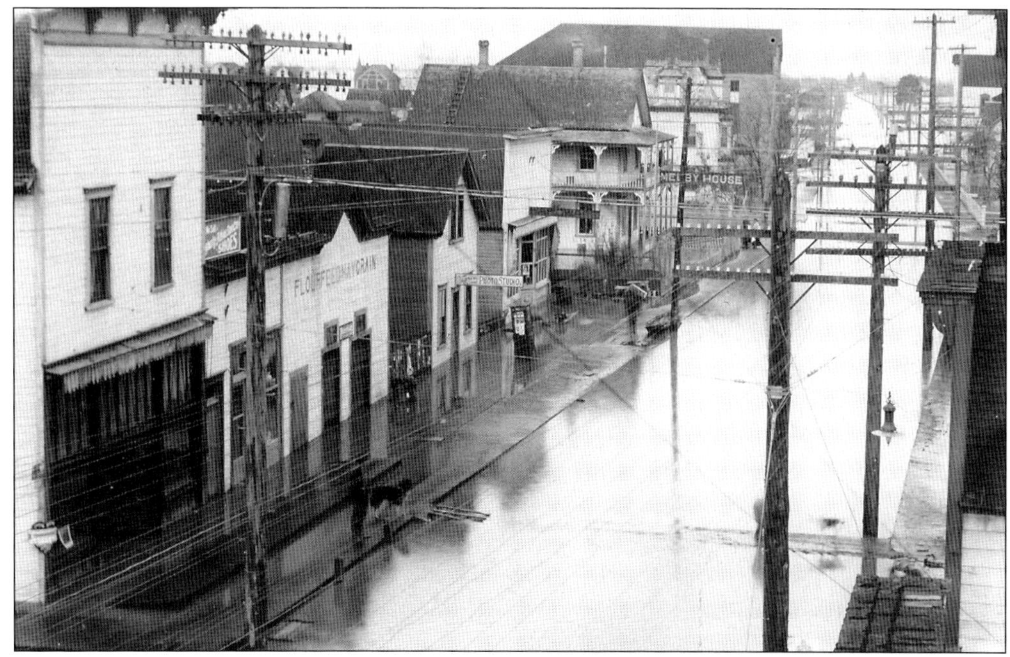

Flooded Market Street. This second-story view looking north provides a clear view of the Ketchum Grocery Store on the left. The next building is one small storefront and a flour feed and grain business. Beyond that building is the Wagness Photo Studio, Hafstad Hardware, and a more elaborate and remodeled Melby Hotel. In 1933, Ed and Marie Bryant took over the hardware store, remodeled it, and established Bryant Hardware. The water's reflection provides a distant look down 102nd Avenue NW, also known as Old Pacific Highway. (Photograph by John T. Wagness.)

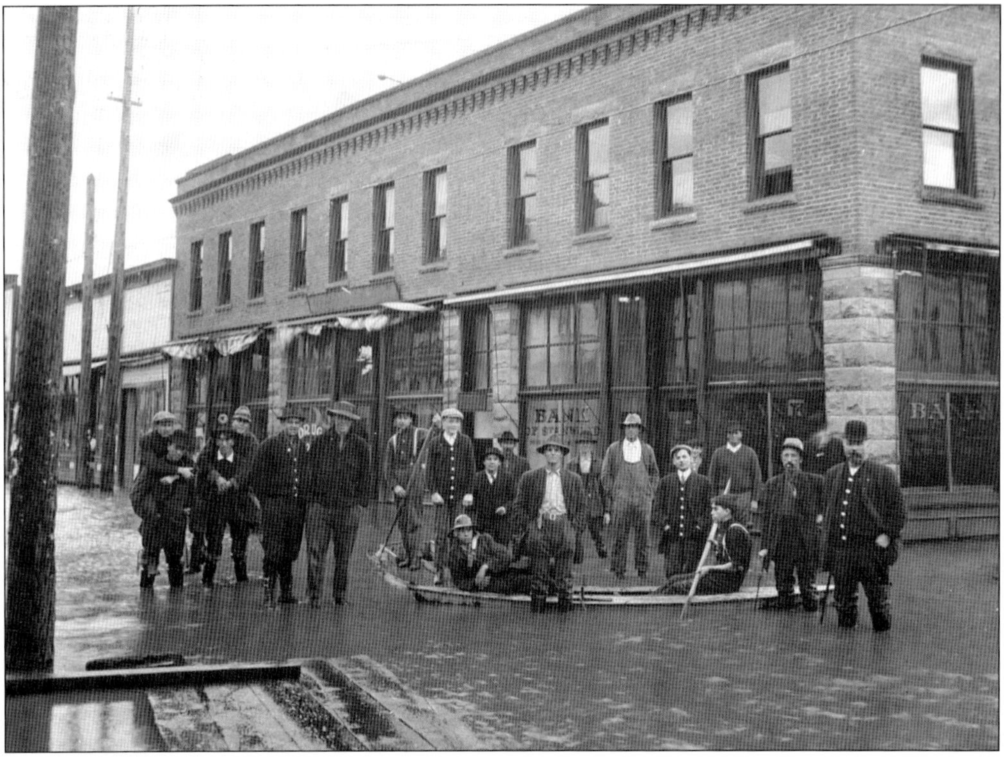

Messing About in Boats. The men standing in floodwaters in Market Street in front of the Bank of Stanwood (the two-story brick building) include Andrew B. Klaeboe, Herman A. Hafstad, Mr. Husby, George Hancock, Leo Dannemiller, and Harry Gippel. The winter months would bring storms and flooding to the Stillaguamish Valley, and the farmers took it in stride. (Photograph by John T. Wagness.)

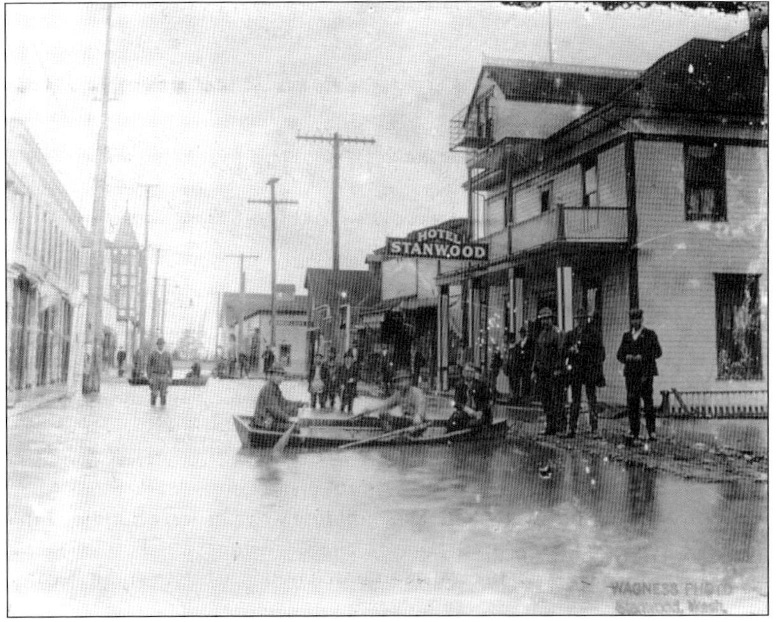

Hotel Stanwood and Floodwaters. Flooding events in Stanwood often brought out small boats or rowboats on Market Street. The view shows the Hotel Stanwood, which still stands. This is thought to be the 1909 flood. (Photograph by John T. Wagness.)

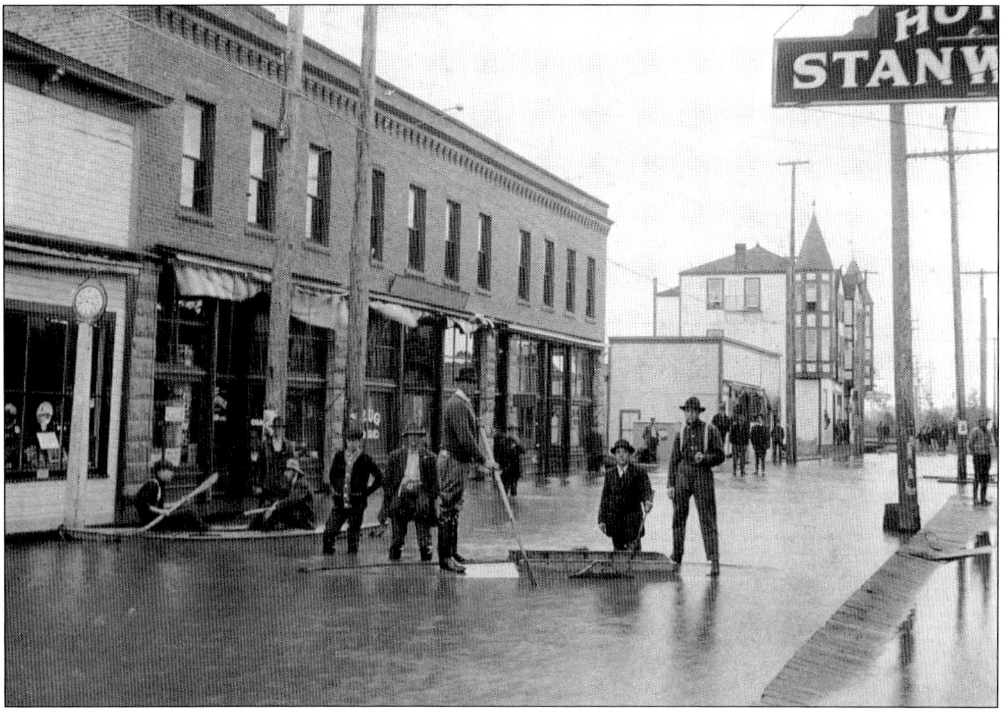

LOOKING SOUTH TOWARD THE RIVER. This view looks south from Main and Market Streets in this same flood. The Knud Knudson's Jewelers street clock is on the left in front of his store. The Palace Hotel is in the background. In 1937, the bank building was sold to William Bailey, and it was known as the Bailey Building for many years. (Photograph by John T. Wagness.)

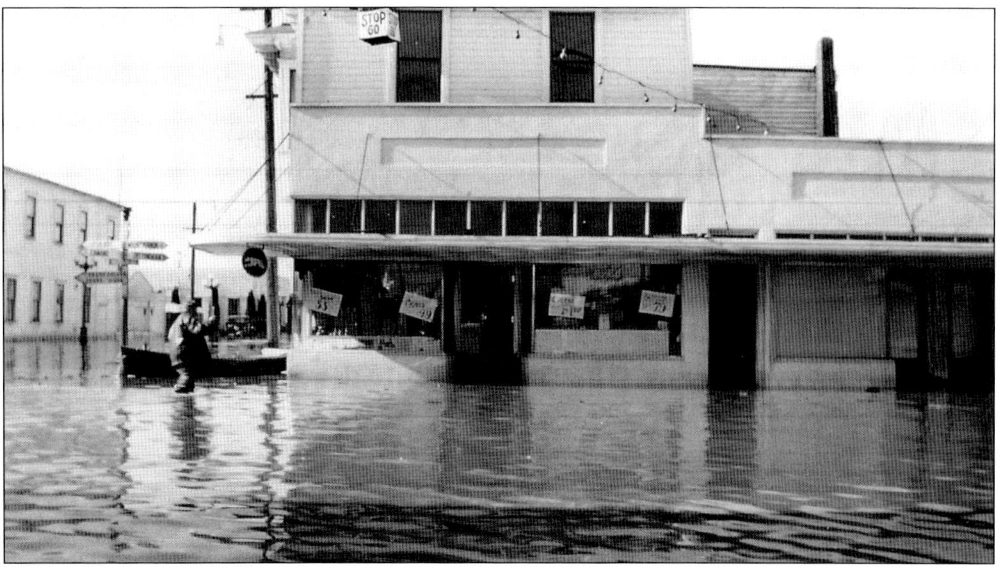

FLOOD SURROUNDING LOCAL GROCERY, 1951. This is the west intersection of Market and Main Streets. The rear of the Hotel Stanwood is on the left. This building was a grocery building built soon after the 1892 fire. There were several interim owners, including George Ketchum, before it was purchased by Ernest A. Rosser in 1939. Allan Anderson purchased it in 1940, and it became Allan's Cash Grocery until 1967. It is now a restaurant after many owners and businesses since.

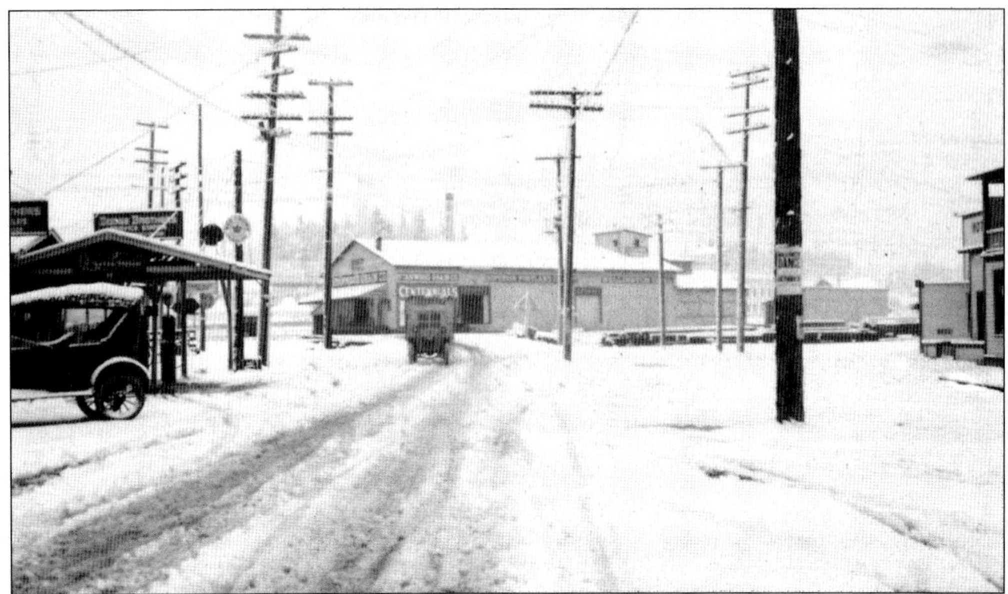

Snowstorm, East Stanwood. This view looks east toward the railroad tracks and the Stanwood Grain Company. This snowfall is thought to be the 1916 snowstorm. The Dodge Brothers Service Station was established on the Pacific Coast Highway, as seen in earlier pages.

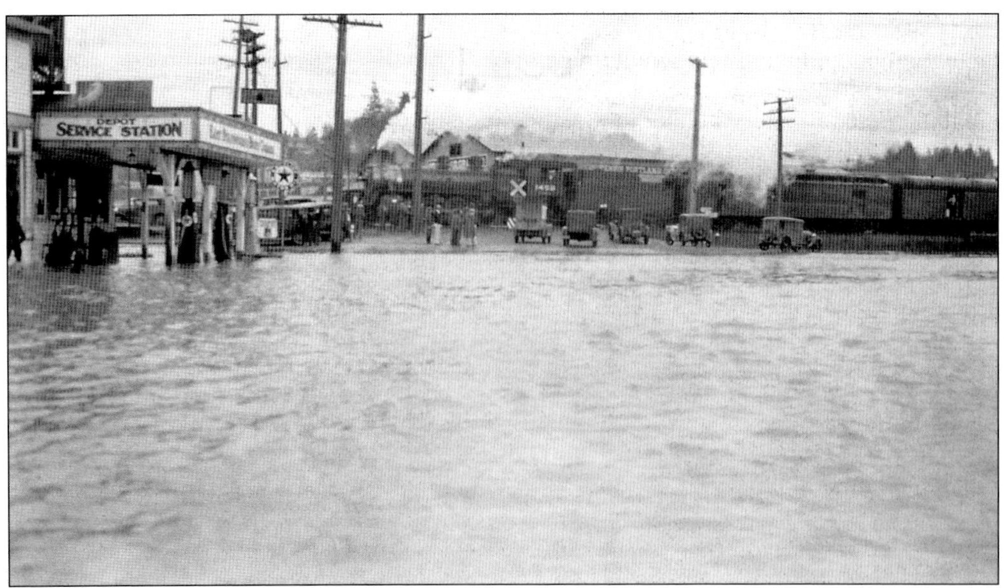

Floodwaters, East Stanwood. This view looks eastward, showing waters almost covering the Great Northern Railroad tracks as the train is presumably moving slowly, about to stop for passengers. The East Stanwood Busy Corner canopy shelters the gas pumps of the Depot Service Station.

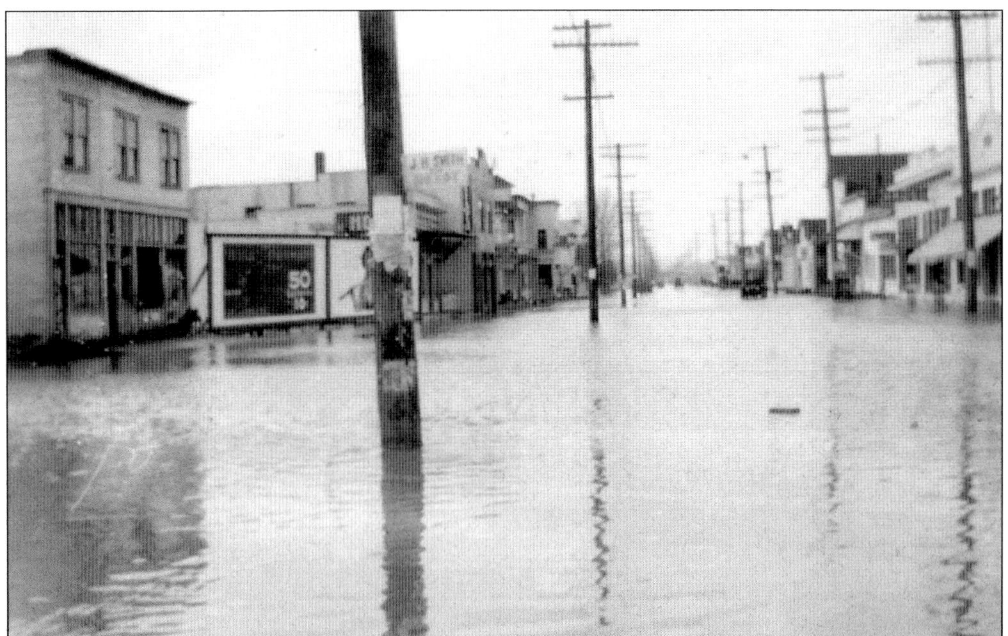

East Stanwood Flood, 1921(?). This view shows the Pastime Confectionery on the left; it was also a pool hall. The building was constructed in 1907 and sold cigars, tobacco, fruits, soft drinks, ice cream, candles, and other sundries. There was a barbershop on the east side of the building. In later years, after Prohibition, it became a succession of taverns, and it is now a well-established restaurant since 2001. (Photograph by Albert Palmquist.)

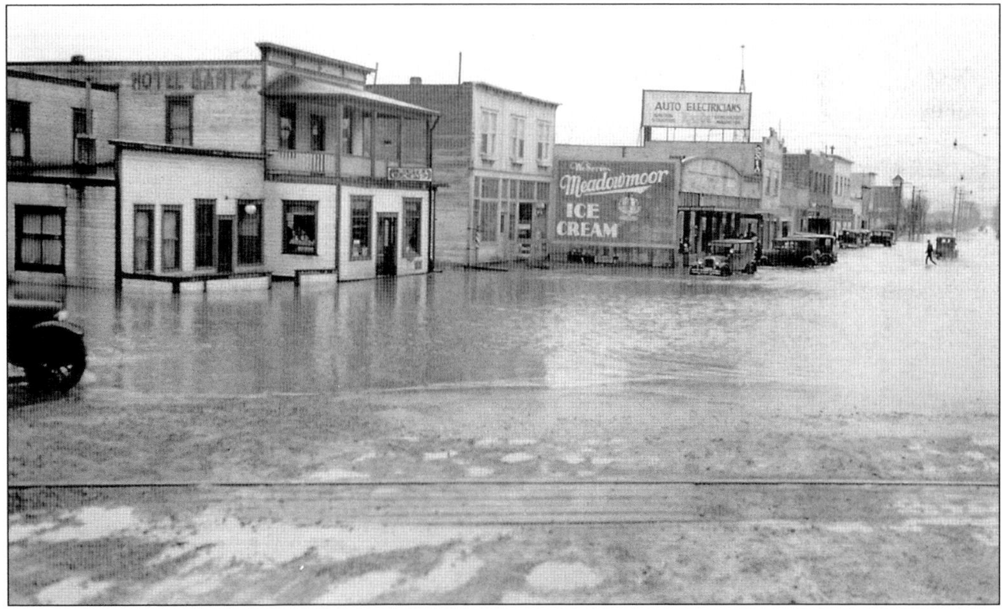

The Hotel Bartz and Café. The Hotel Bartz (on the left) was built in 1911. The storefront section was later remodeled and became known as the Pure Foods Market until the 1960s. Next to the Meadowmoor sign is the Pastime Café. In 1927, Isaac Rygg erected the Rygg Building with an arched front. One of its first renters was the Chaffee's Clothing store, featuring "Correct Apparel for Women," in October 1927.

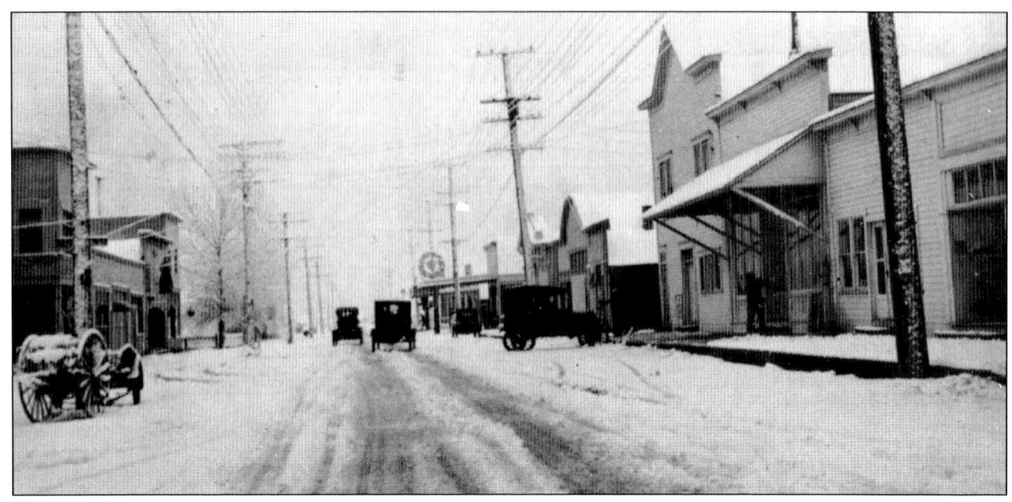

Driving West in the Snow. This street view shows the snow in East Stanwood in 1916. The view looks east with the People's Union on the right. Snow tires were not yet available, but there was a patent in 1904 for "Grip Tread for Pneumatic Tires" by New York inventor Harry D. Weed, who sold the patent in 1912 to the American Chain and Cable Company in Detroit. (Photograph by Albert Palmquist.)

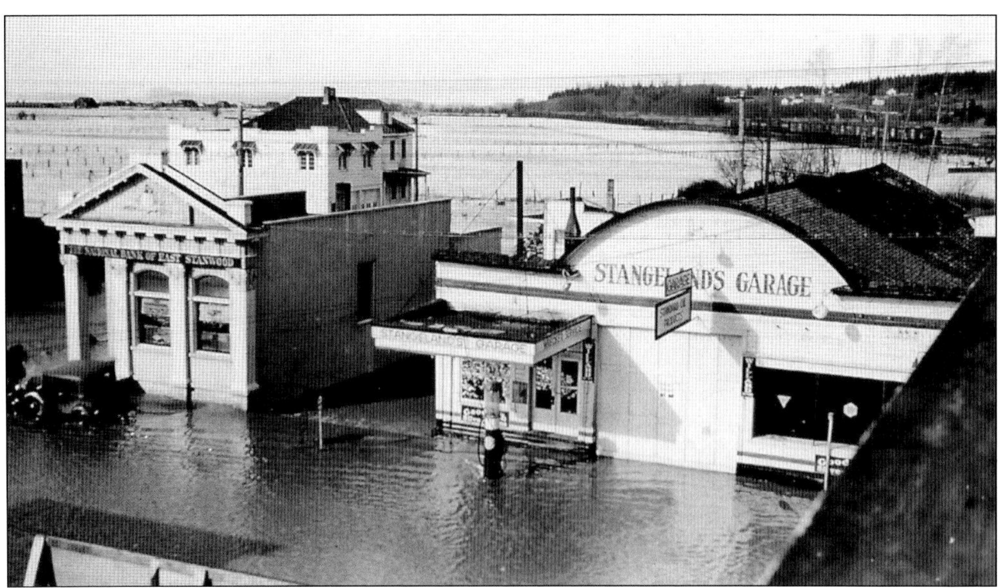

Rooftop View Looking Northwest. This view looks north down on the north side of 271st Avenue NW during a 1920s flood. In the distance is a train on the Great Northern Railroad tracks the flooding barely missed. In the background are the rooftops of the East Stanwood Fire Department building and the Peterson apartment building, which had been moved from Main Street and is shown in many earlier photographs on the south side of Main Street. The unusual Greek Revival–style building was the State Bank of East Stanwood. (Photograph by Albert Palmquist.)

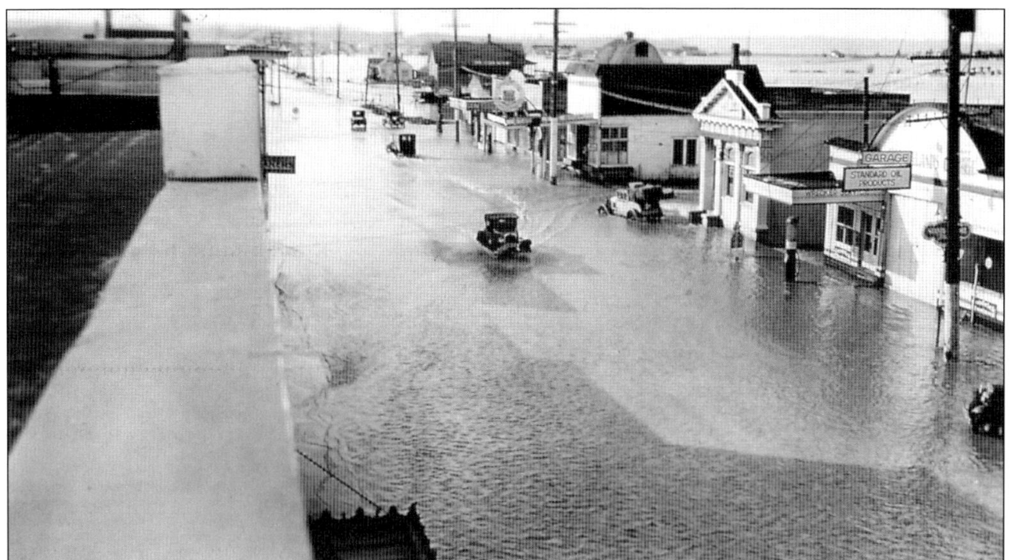

FLOODING ON MAIN STREET. The Lien Barn and one of the family homes are in the distance in this photograph, taken around 1921. The First National Bank of East Stanwood had an interesting Greek Revival design. It was built in 1913 as the State Bank of East Stanwood. Little is known of Stangeland's Garage next door. The bank began as People's Bank in 1910 in a storefront next to the People's Union (now the granary). By 1930, it was the National Bank of East Stanwood. The existing modern brick building was constructed in 1948. In 1956, it was bought out by Seattle First National Bank (later Seafirst), which eventually became part of the Bank of America in 1998. It now serves as the Stanwood Police Station. (Photograph by Albert Palmquist.)

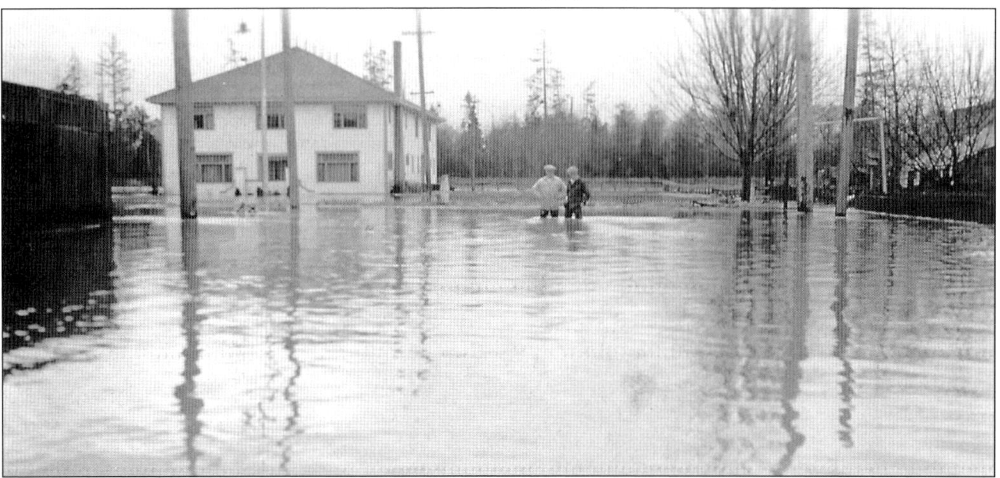

EAST STANWOOD'S ORIGINAL CITY HALL. Floodwater engulfed East Stanwood, and this view shows the Giard property in the distance southward. On the right outside of the photograph's frame is the Giard home. On the left, the East Stanwood Commercial Club building was erected in 1920. The two-story East Stanwood Commercial Club building on that site burned in July 1938. The fire was fought by both the East Stanwood and Stanwood Fire Departments. It was rebuilt in 1940 with WPA funds and had an unusual stucco Mission architectural style. In 1962, the city hall building was sold to the American Legion for $10,500. The hall is still an active community organization known as the Frank Hancock Post No. 92 of the American Legion. The Frank Hancock Post was chartered in 1920.

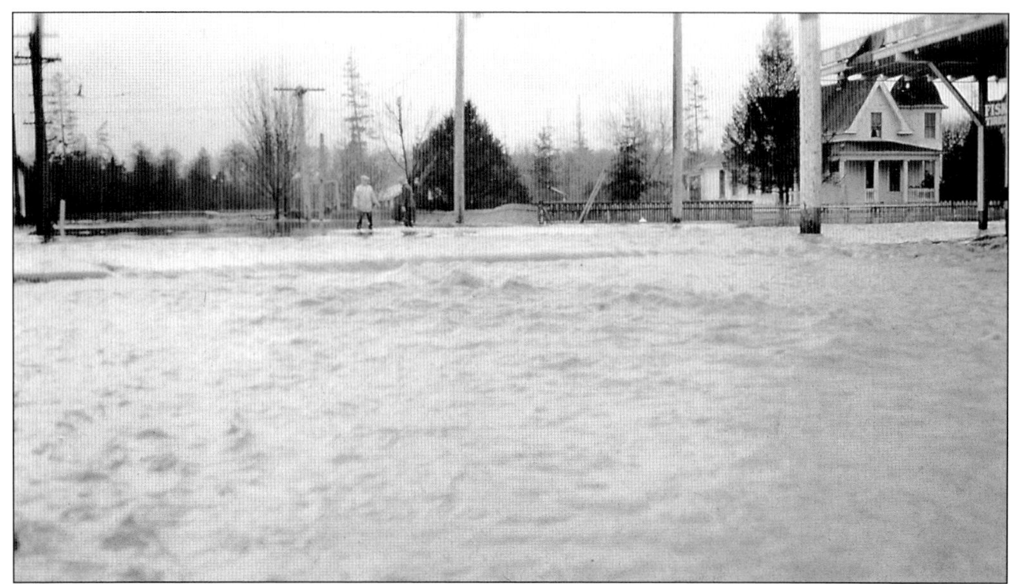

Floodwaters, Main and Giard Streets. The beautiful towered Giard home was built in 1905 by Francis H. Giard, who platted East Stanwood in 1906 and became its first mayor when it was incorporated in 1922. The house was located at the southwest corner of Eighty-Eighth Avenue and 271st Street in the heart of East Stanwood and was demolished in 1964. The railroad tracks in front of the house were those of the H&H Railroad. The Irvine Slough originated from these farm fields south of East Stanwood near Viking Village.

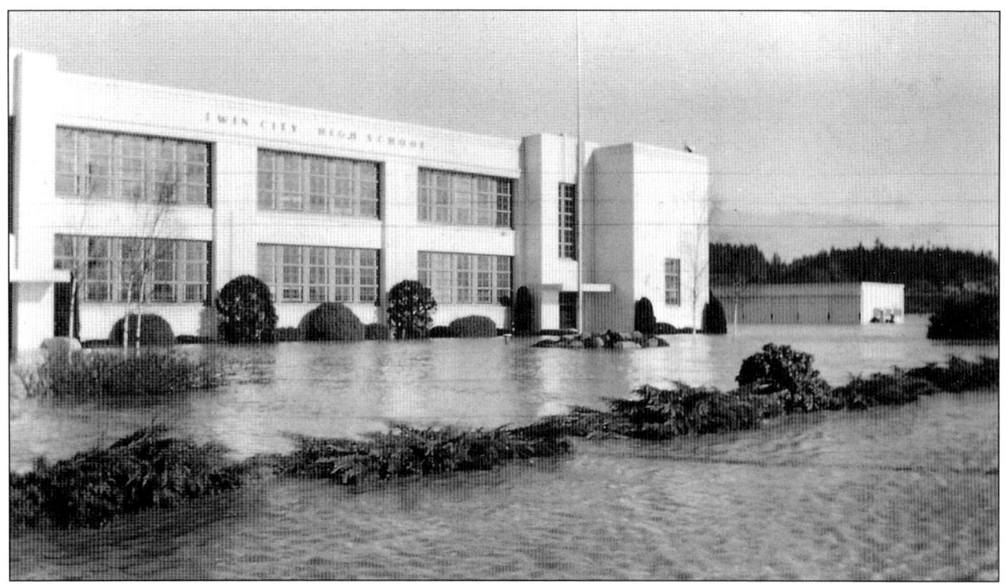

Twin City High School. Between the two towns, the 1951 flood of the Twin City High School was the largest flood on the Stillaguamish River to date. Flooding, along with siltation, dramatically contributed to the changing of the course of the river and its sloughs over the years.

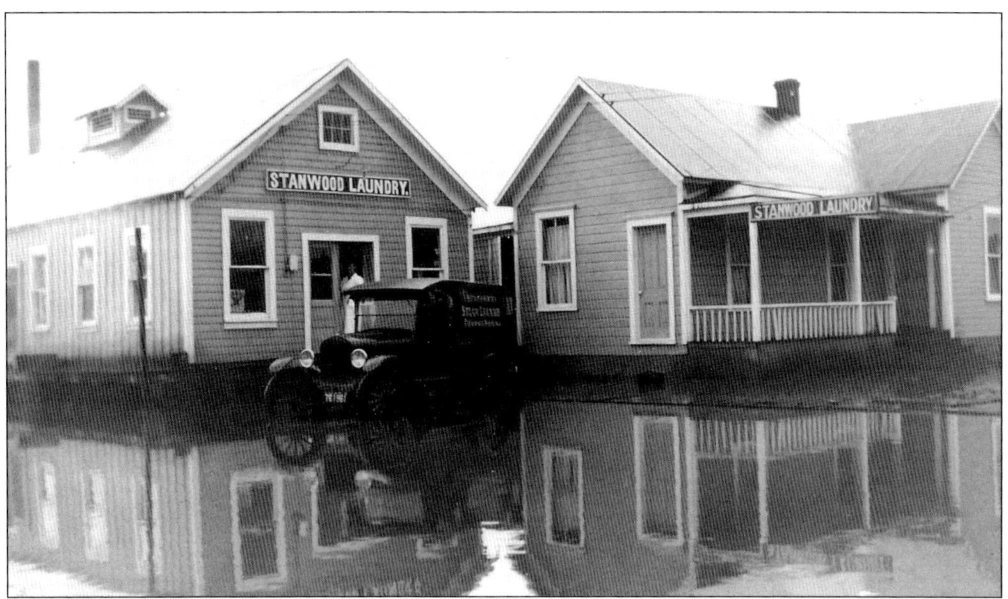

Stanwood's Laundry, Broadway. The Stanwood Steam Laundry buildings are seen here during the 1932 flood. The two buildings are surrounded by flooded streets with a vintage delivery vehicle. Stanwood Laundry, operated by the Crandall family, added a large boiler to add efficiency. The family operated it until 1920, when it was sold to Henry Matthew Babington. In 1923, it was purchased by Karl Schmidt, who operated it with his wife, Maria, until 1944, when it was taken over by Forrest Johnson.

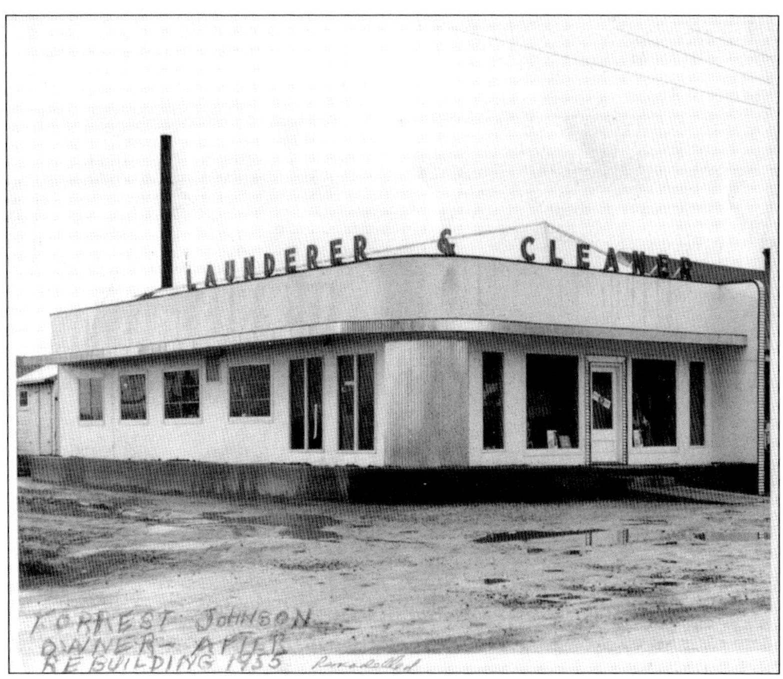

Launderer & Cleaner. Forrest Johnson took over the laundry in 1944 and remodeled it in 1955 and then again in 1962. The building with its 20th-century metal siding was demolished a year later, and the business was moved to the River Road and Main Street. (Photograph by Forrest Johnson.)

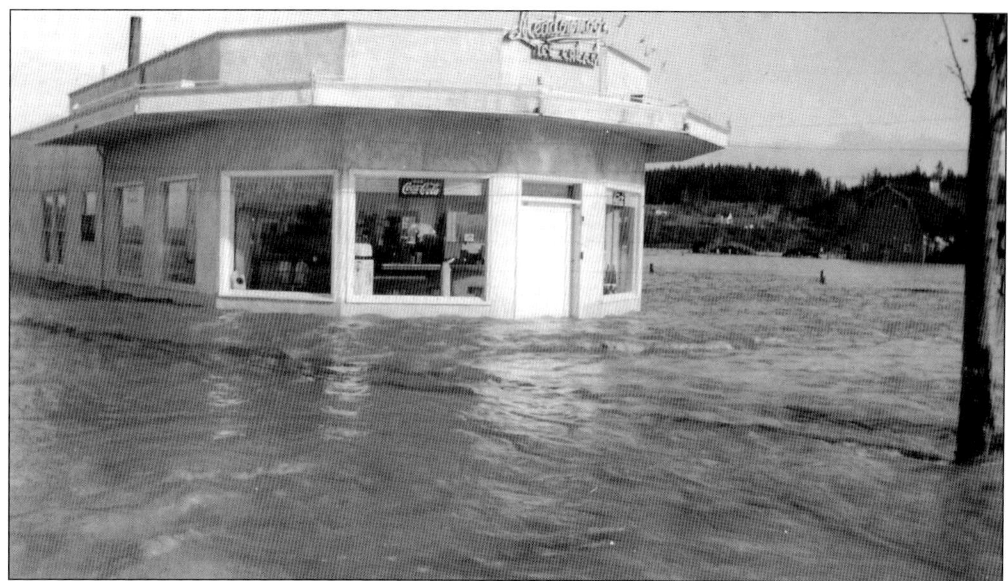

Milky Lane Drive Inn. The 1951 flood inundated an early hamburger and milkshake drive-in. The flood was perhaps the reason for it being redecorated in 1953. Note the Meadowmoor milk sign. The drive-in was located across the street from the 1959 Twin City Lanes. In 1954, it became Adair Motor Parts near what is now K-Pro Auto.

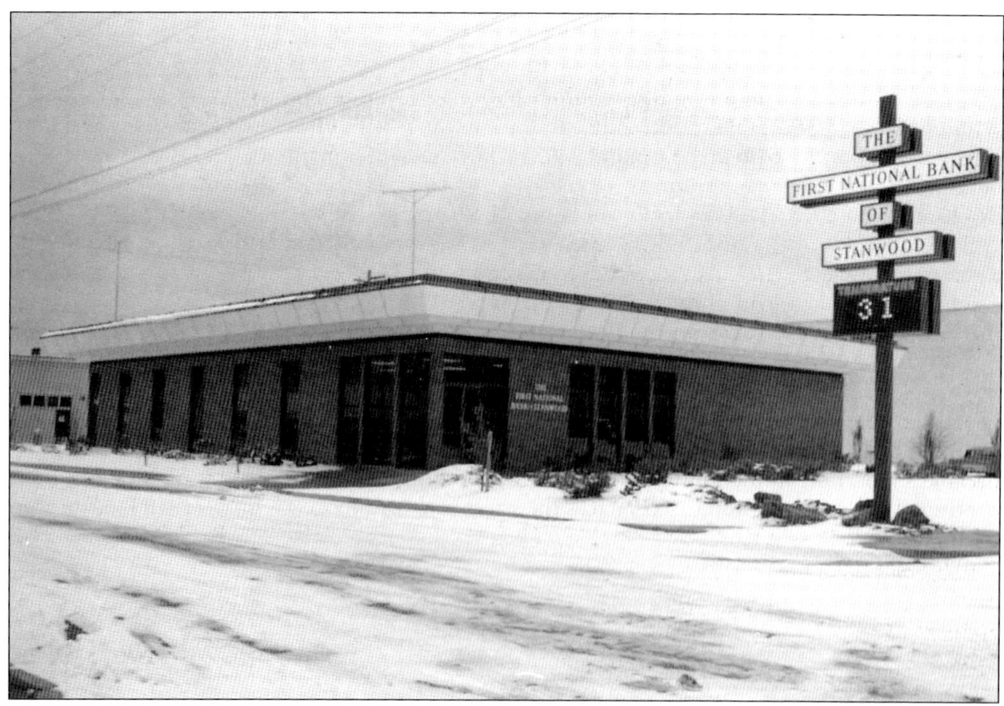

The First National Bank of Stanwood. The original Bank of Stanwood survived until 1964, when all of the buildings on that corner were displaced by this new single-story bank. The First National Bank of Stanwood was acquired by Bank of America after several local mergers and acquisitions. This photograph was taken in January 1968.

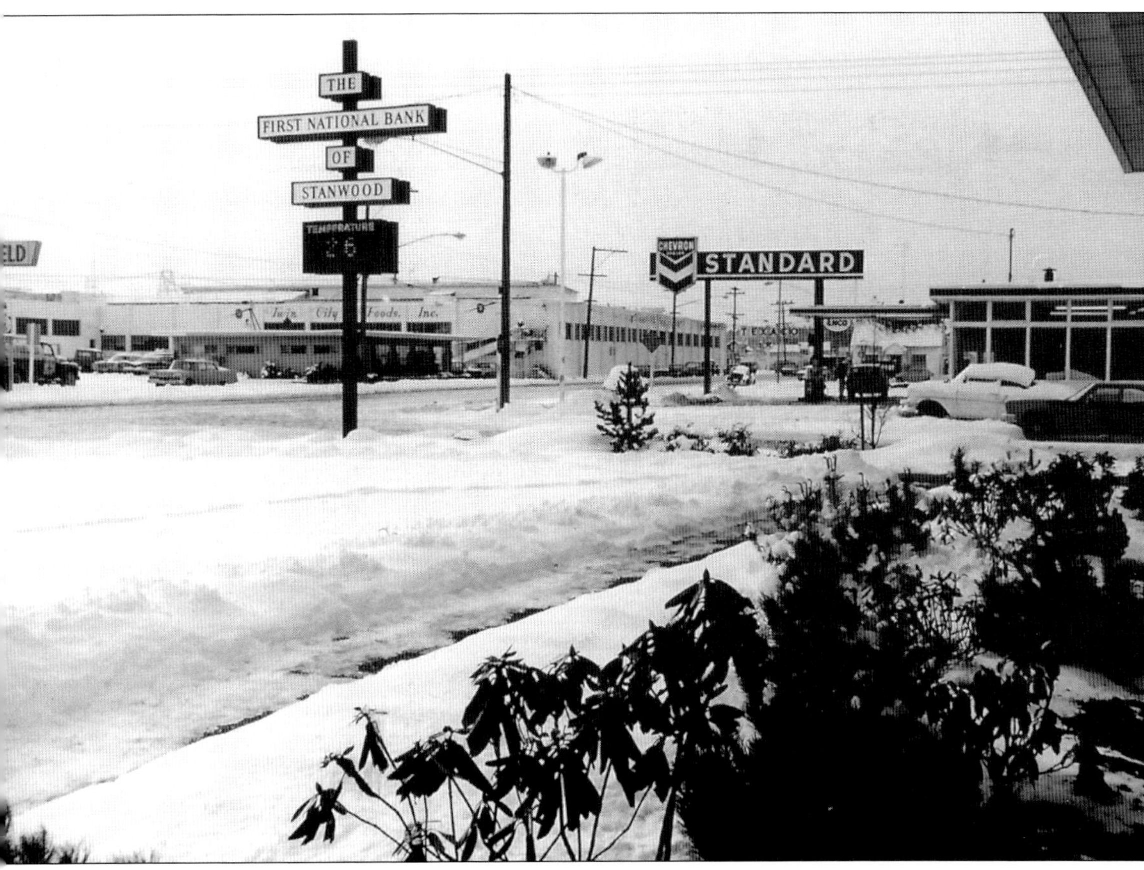

Main and Market Streets, Looking West. This photograph shows the Twin City Foods building after a 1969 snowstorm from the front of the First National Bank of Stanwood. At this location in 1918, the Lien family had a small canning operation that became the Lien Bros. Packing Co., which ran until 1941. Twin City Foods was established in 1945 by the Lervick family when they purchased the Lien Processing Company. A year after Twin City Foods was established, it shipped its first carload of quick-frozen peas to the Chicago market. The first peas were from the Franklin Hanson Farm on the Stillaguamish River. The family soon expanded to frozen potatoes, corn, beans, and carrots. In 1961, the company rebuilt its cold and dry storage buildings. By then, it was the main employer in the area. The company grew through mergers and purchases of other companies as a private label processor for retail in-house brands. In 1996, a significant fire destroyed the property, which was quickly rebuilt. It discontinued fresh packing in 2009 and became a repacking facility until it moved these operations out of Stanwood in 2018. Operations continued in Ellensburg and Pasco. Across the street in this photograph on the right is a Chevron station on the site of the old livery stables. The gas station was rebuilt as Bob's Market & Deli convenience store in the 1970s.

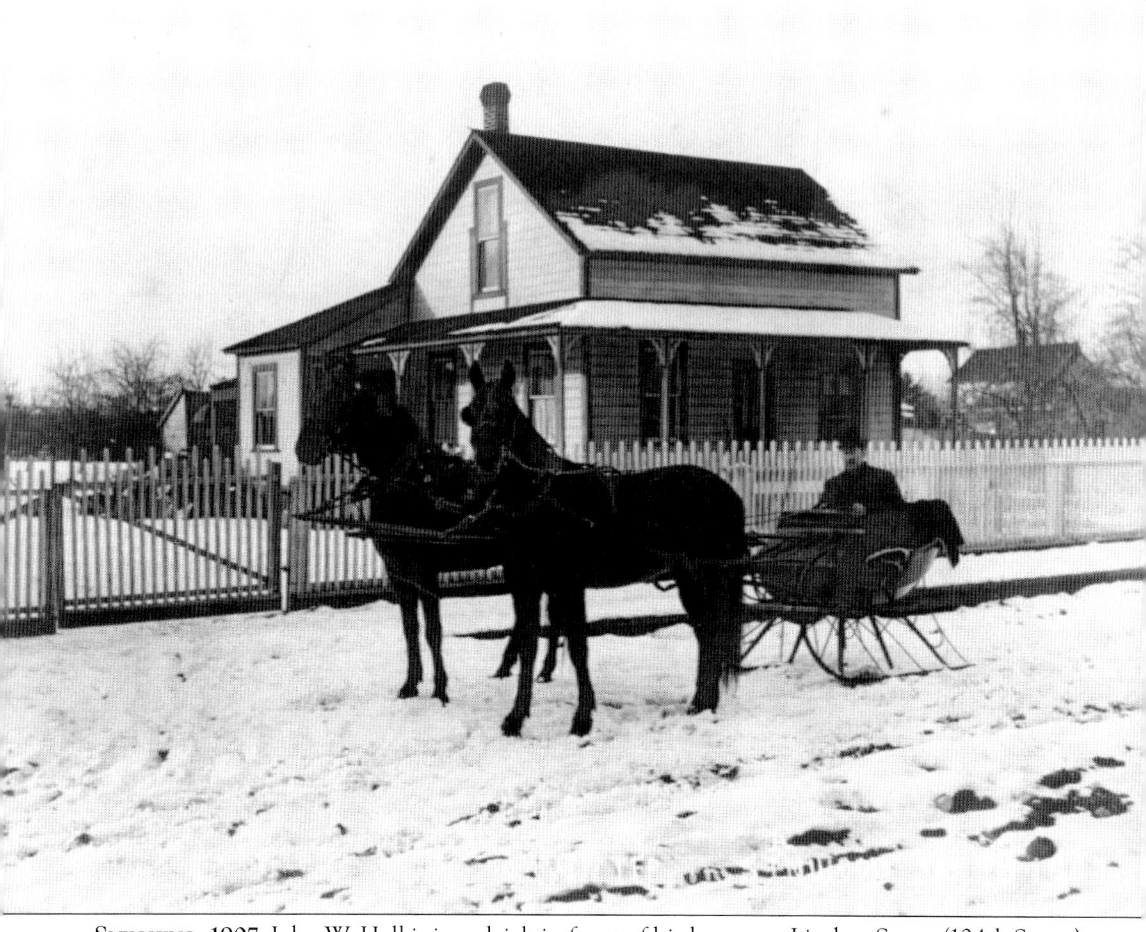

Sleighing, 1907. John W. Hall is in a sleigh in front of his house on Lindsey Street (104th Street). Hall was from Kansas. He and his wife, Alice, came to Stanwood soon after their marriage in 1890. He started out as a teamster for Robert Bates and later established the Stanwood Livery, carrying mail and passengers on a stagecoach drawn by four mules at first. He turned his attention to the establishment of the H&H Railroad between the two towns. (Photograph by John T. Wagness.)

Eight

Songs, Sports, Schools, and Churches

Gatherings of people for music, learning, sports, and general fellowship were strong in the community. Special celebrated events included a 1908 visit from Roald Amundsen, a Norwegian polar explorer who had visited Stanwood to give a lecture at the Oddfellows Hall to raise funds for his next expedition.

Stanwood's Fritjov Lodge of the Sons of Norway was organized in 1910 to promote and preserve the heritage and culture of Norway. Its members were vital to the local culture as singers and musicians as well as business and religious leaders in the Stillaguamish Valley. In 1927, women's first names began to appear in the register; the first five listed were Caroline Ostraat, Jennie Moe, Magda Kjelstad, Ingeborg Stene, and Emma Gunderson. The Sons of Norway building was dedicated in 1914 and had been moved from across the street; the second story was removed.

In 1939, Crown Prince Olaf and Princess Martha of Norway attended a special ceremony dedicating the Toftezen Memorial at the Lutheran Cemetery. Zakarias Martin Toftezen was the first Norwegian in Washington State; he arrived first on Whidbey Island, and his family settled in Stanwood.

The Stanwood School District, like many of the schools, began humbly, sometimes in a home. There were schools surrounding Stanwood in Florence (1872), Norman (1882), Victoria (1906), Silvana (1892), Freeborn (1894), Village (1907), Woodland (1904), Warm Beach (Birmingham, 1905), Bluff (or Prestlien School, 1890s), and Cedarhome (1870s). Stanwood's school district number changed to 99 in 1908. In 1929, a vote to unite Stanwood and East Stanwood lost by six votes. In 1937, District 333 consolidated the island district with the newly formed 315. In 1944, it was established as Twin City Joint Consolidated School District 401.

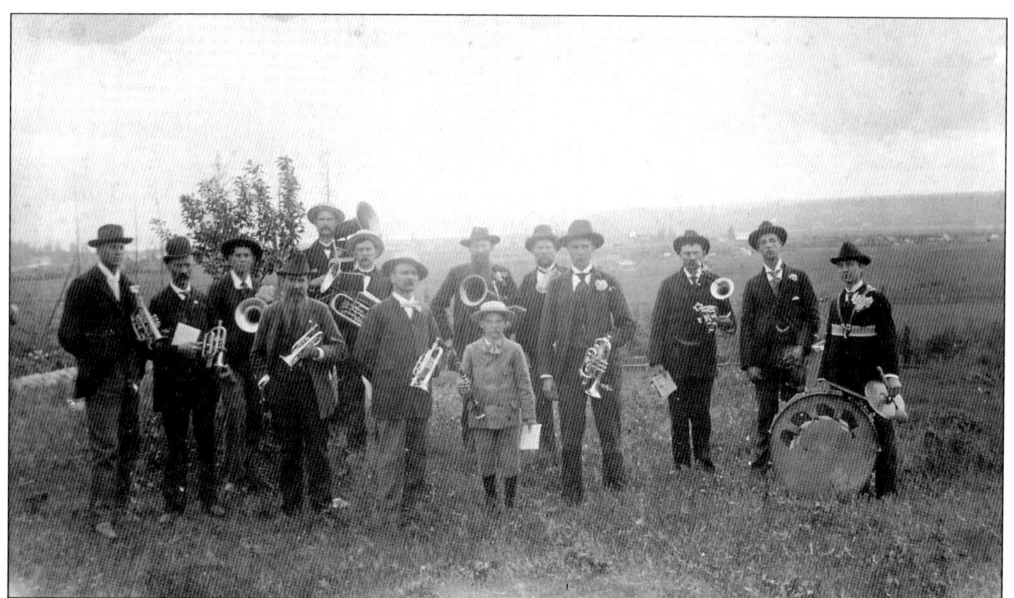

Ancient Order of United Workmen Musicians. This fraternal lodge was organized about 1895, and its first officer was D.O. Pearson, one of the musicians seen in the center back. The group was directed by J.T. (or T.K.) Logen and was popular in the 1896 elections. Others in the group include N.R. Olson, John Logen, John W. Hall, and Otto Rabel. (Photograph by O.S. Van Olinda.)

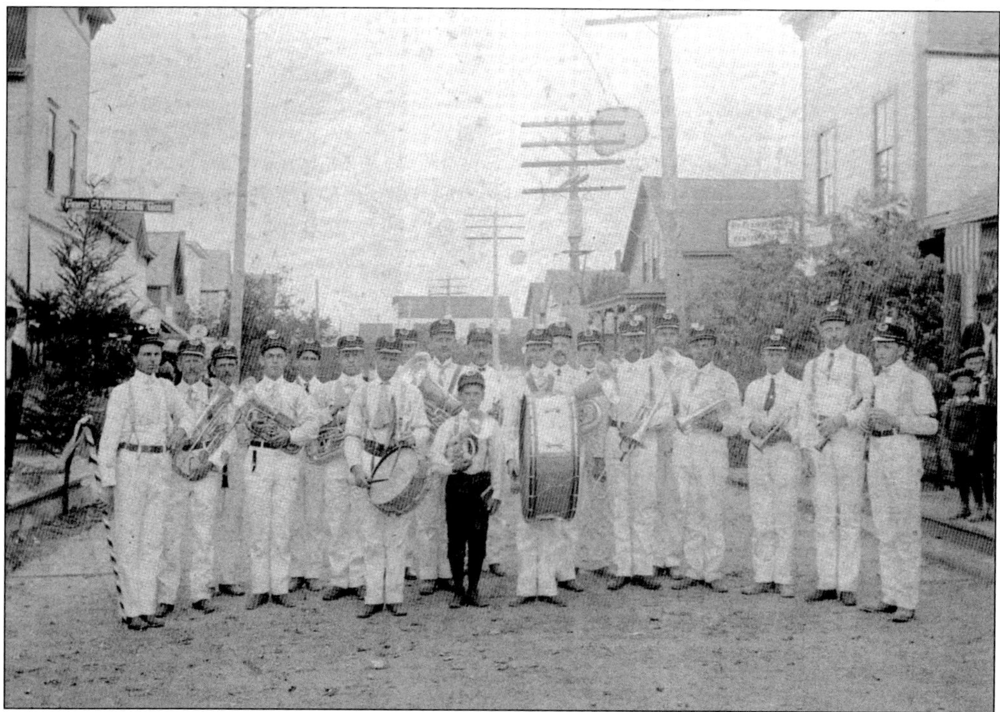

Stillaguamish Band. The Stillaguamish Band poses for a portrait on the unpaved Market Street. This view looks north, with the dentist's office on the right, the furnishings store on the left, and the Masonic Hall in the distance. Recognized individuals include Dan Lien, Andrew Lekness, and Otto Lien.

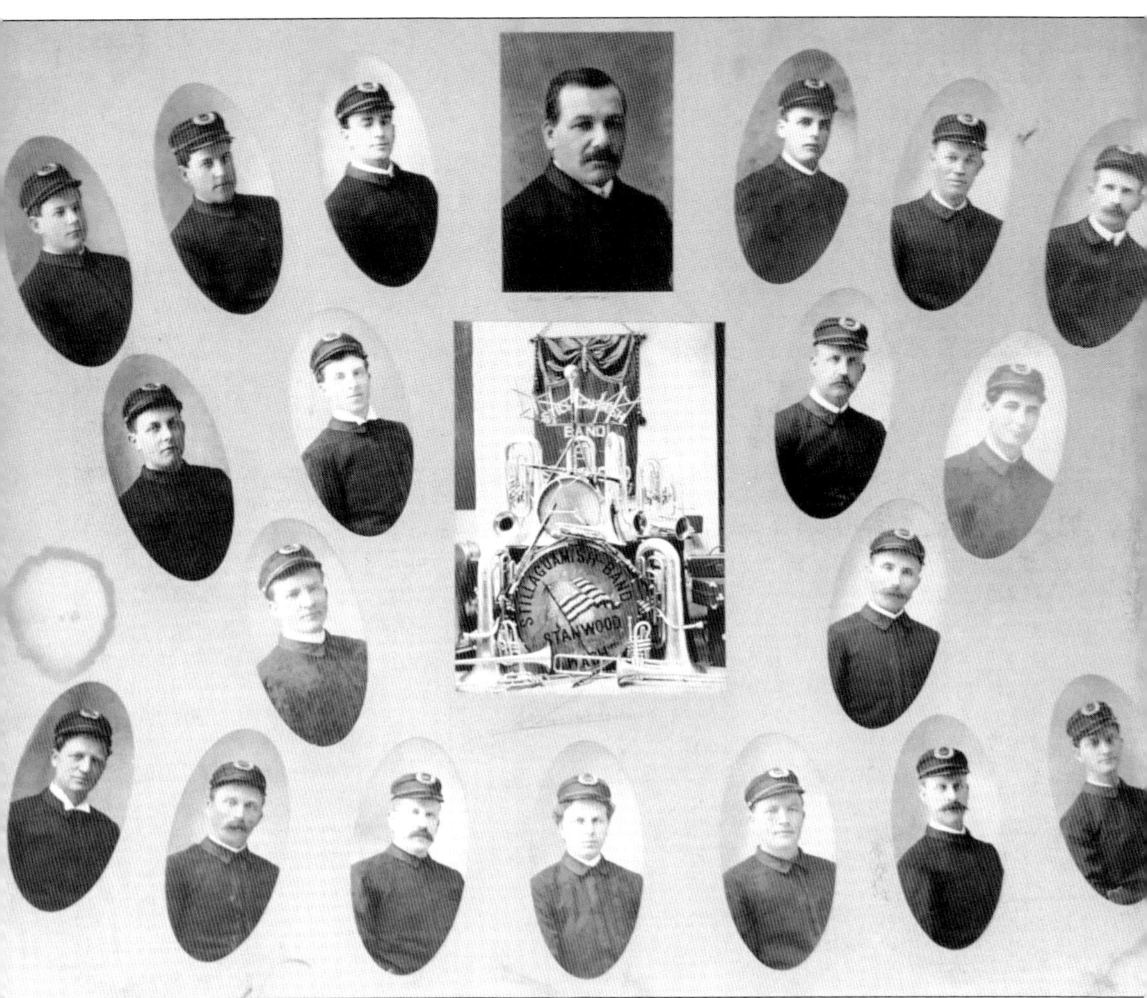

MEMBERS OF THE STILLAGUAMISH BAND. The band had 24 pieces in its repertoire and was composed of talented musicians mostly of Norwegian heritage. The band instruments pictured include a drum, a bass drum, horns, a tuba, a clarinet, and a trombone, along with a baton and a banner in the background. The Reverend Helge M. Tjernagel is pictured in the middle of the top row. Other band members include Trygve Lien, Dan Lien, Torger Logen, Gunder Naas, Elias Brue, Peter Logen, Bernard Gedstad, Otto Lien, Edwin Egge, Martin Leque, Magnus Thomle, Jens Gulstad, Lyder Brue, Martin Hackenstad, Bernard Lien, Andrew Lekness, Iver Thomle, Conrad Lien, and Ed Johnson; others are unidentified.

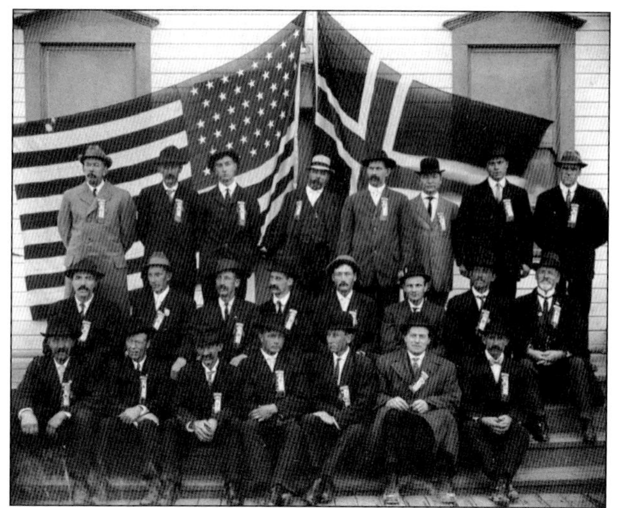

LOGE FRITJOV NO. 17 SONNER AF NORGE. The Sons of Norway No. 17 Fritjov Lodge was founded on April 24, 1910. Names listed include Knut Husby, Ole Kristofferson, Ole Dahl, Knut Dalsbo, Lars Langland, Ole Birkestol, Lars Husby, Ole Kaldseth, John Waldseth, Sigurd Hall, Pete Arnesen, John Haagensen, Peter Wold, Erik Oien, Carl Ryan, John Erstad, Halvard Rodseth, A.E. Klaeboe, Sivert Rinseth, Mr. Halvorson (the tailor), and Casper Harvold. (Photograph by John T. Wagness.)

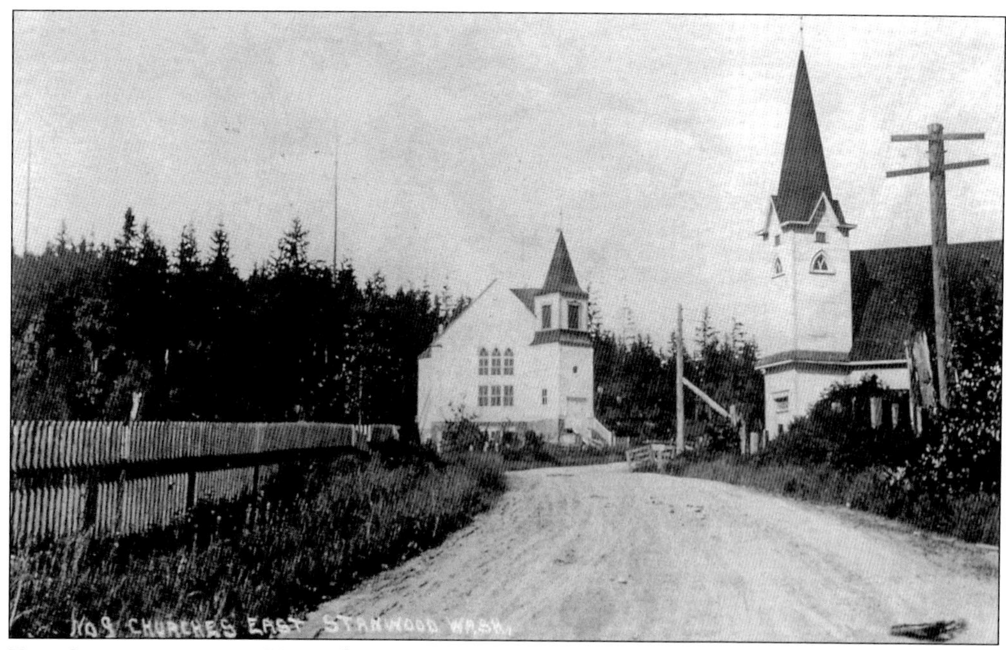

TWO CHURCHES ON THE HILL. The Zion Lutheran Church is on the left in the photograph. It was built in 1910 and burned in April 2003. The United Lutheran Church, on the right, was established about the same time. Members of the congregations eventually left the buildings and went to services in the Little White Church on the Hill, which became part of the Zion Lutheran Church and Salem Lutheran Congregation. Eventually, its members joined the current Peace Lutheran Church in Silvana, up the river.

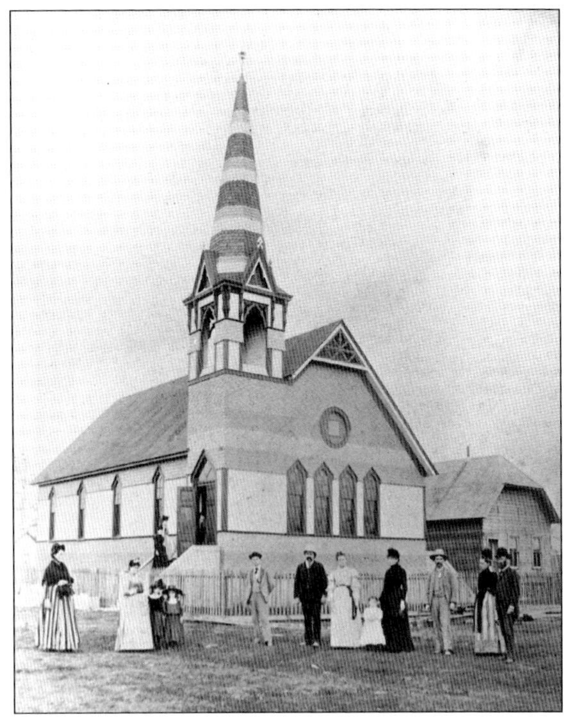

Methodist Church. The Methodist church was built in 1890; however, Methodist circuit riders were already in the area. In 1877, when Pearson arrived, a Reverend Derrick held a preaching service at the home of the Hancock family. The first regular preaching service was held in 1881, and in 1889, a down payment was made. The actual date of the "founding of the charge" was in 1884. The building was 30 by 60 feet with a tall spire.

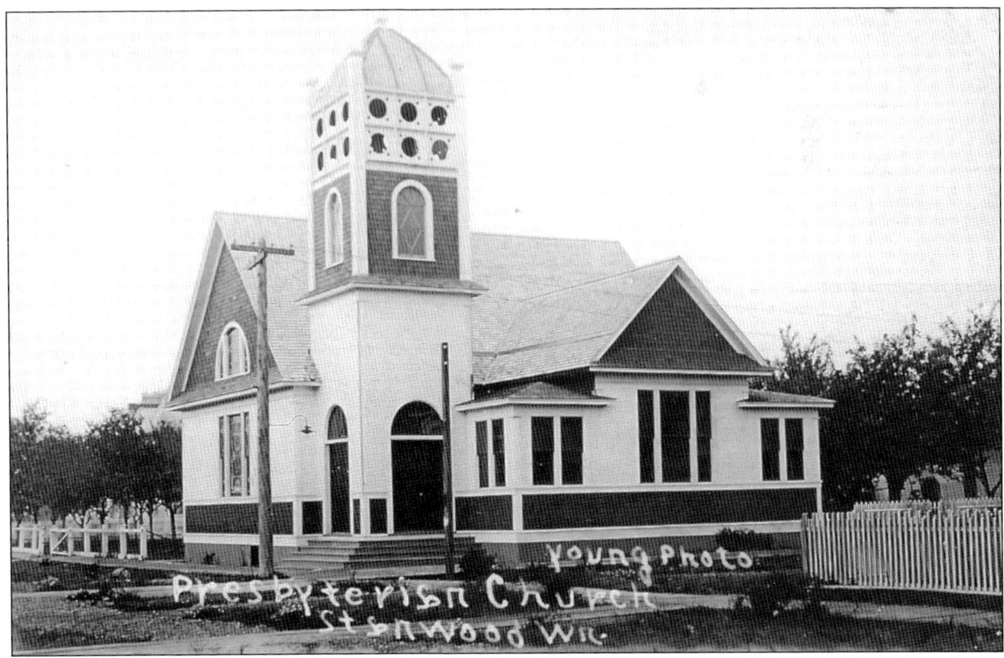

The Presbyterian Church. The Presbyterian church was organized in 1906, and its building was dedicated in July 1909 at the intersection of Pearson and Union Streets. In 1915, there was a popular new pastor, H.T. Murray, who also provided services to a Camano Island congregation at the Camano Schoolhouse. It had several owners and renters. The stained-glass window was removed in the 1970s. The Northwest Coast Presbytery (Presbyterian Church USA) purchased the building in 2015. (Photograph by Robert A. Young.)

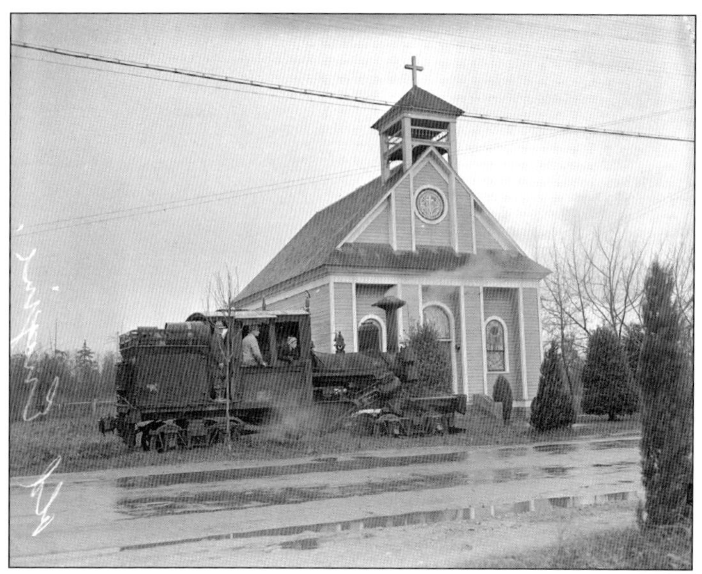

The First Catholic Church. This photograph captures the last run of the H&H Railroad and its old Climax engine through town. It is passing in front of the first Catholic church in Stanwood. The church was located on a small plot of land that had been purchased out of Francis Giard's large farm. The congregation completed this church in 1908. It was used until 1964, when the new church was completed up on the hill. The original church was torn down in 1965.

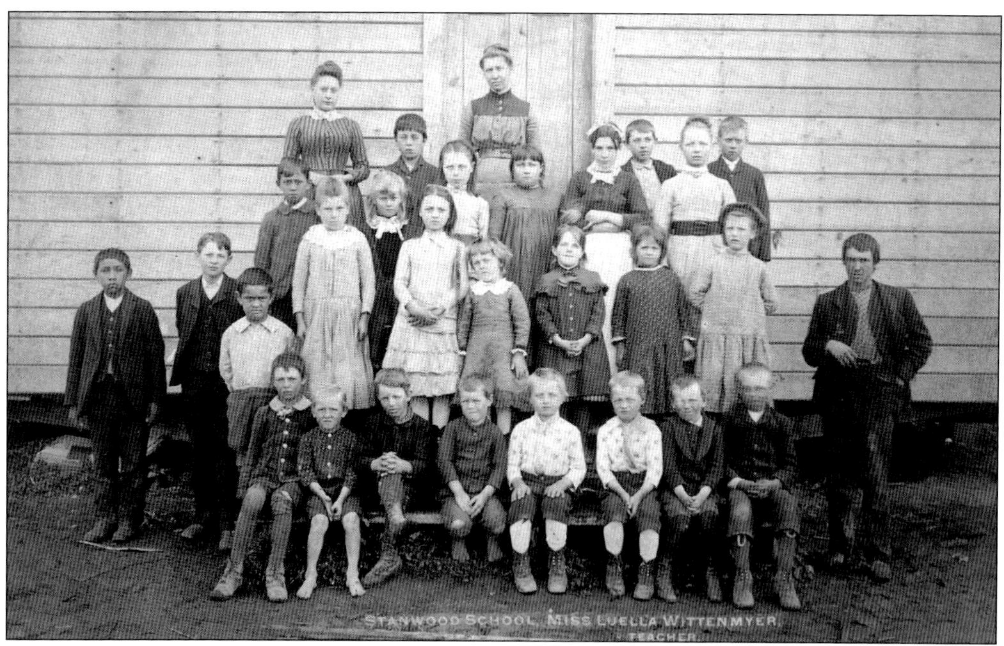

Stanwood School Students, 1880s. There was a little old schoolhouse on the "old river road" in a lot just south of the J.E. Hamilton Lumber Company on Ninety-Eighth Avenue. It is also known as the Floe Road or Leque Road, which connects across State Route 532. The building was moved to the Hamilton Lumberyard and is still there. The children in this photograph grew up in Stanwood's earliest days before many houses were built and before the 1892 fire. They were the Pearson children, the McLaughlan mill owners' children, the Caldon children, Matterands, Leque, Brownell, Harvey, Irvine, and Ulvestad. Pictured on the far left is Sep Irvine, the son of Jack Irvine with his first wife, Emma, who identified as Indian in the 1883 census. Dawn Brownell was his stepsister, the daughter of Lizzie Post Brownell, Jack Irvine's second wife.

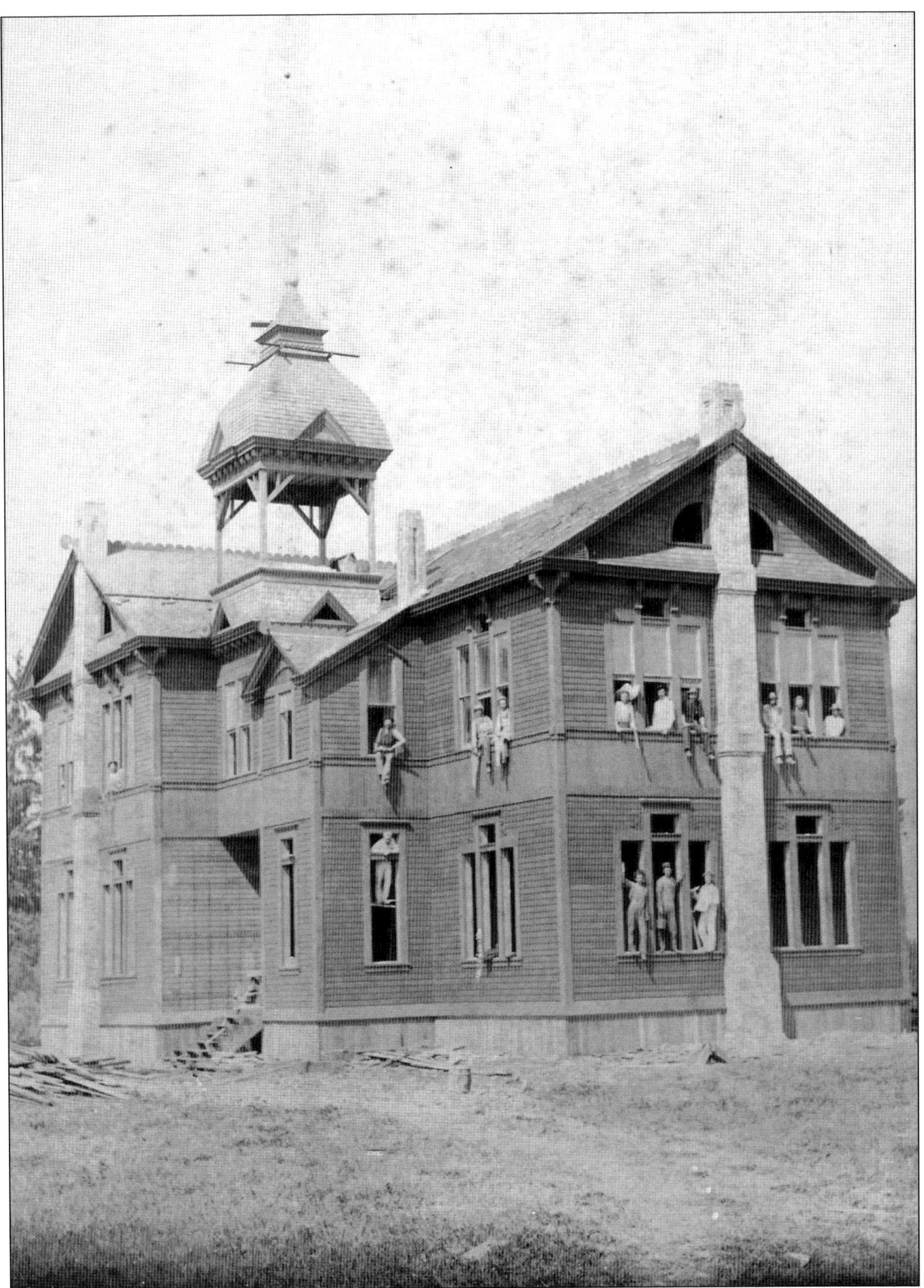

Stanwood School, North Street. The first Stanwood School was established through the efforts of Clara Stanwood Pearson. This view shows the children in the open unfinished windows before the school construction was completed, perhaps much to the dismay of parents. The school began as Snohomish County School District No. 4, established before it was built in 1872. (The Florence School was School District No. 3, also established in 1872.)

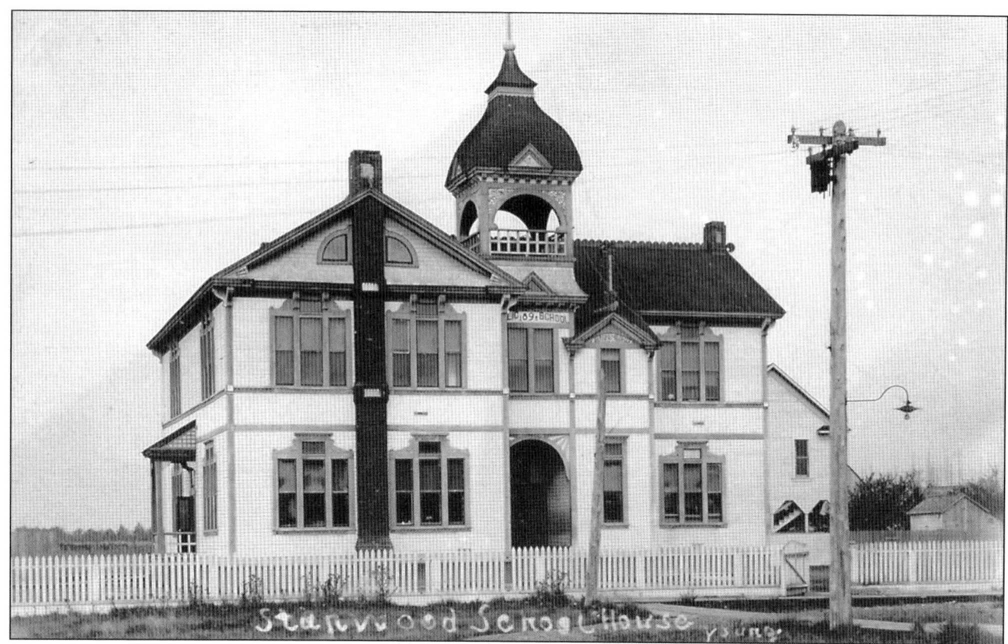

The North Street School. This beautiful school was completed in 1892 and included an elaborate tower for the school bell. This grand two-story school was a combined grade school and high school until the new high school next door was built in 1914. In 1938, it was sold to wreckers, and the materials were offered as used lumber and fixtures.

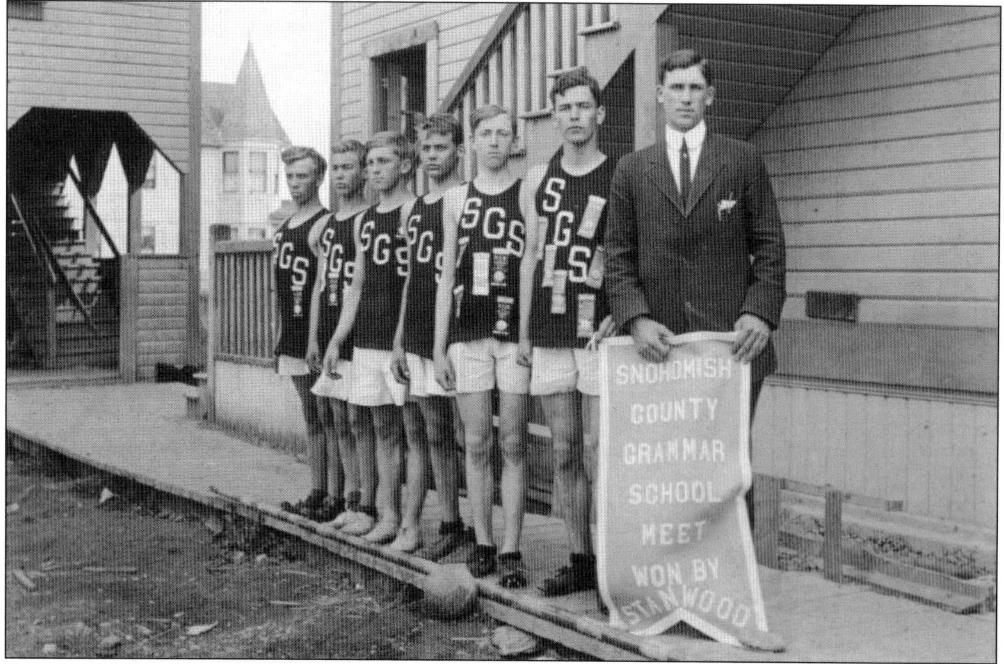

Snohomish County Grammar School Winners. In the early part of the 20th century and before, sometimes grade school or eighth grade was all the children could afford or were suited to. Grade school sports accomplishments were just as important as in later grades. The location is in the school building on North Street.

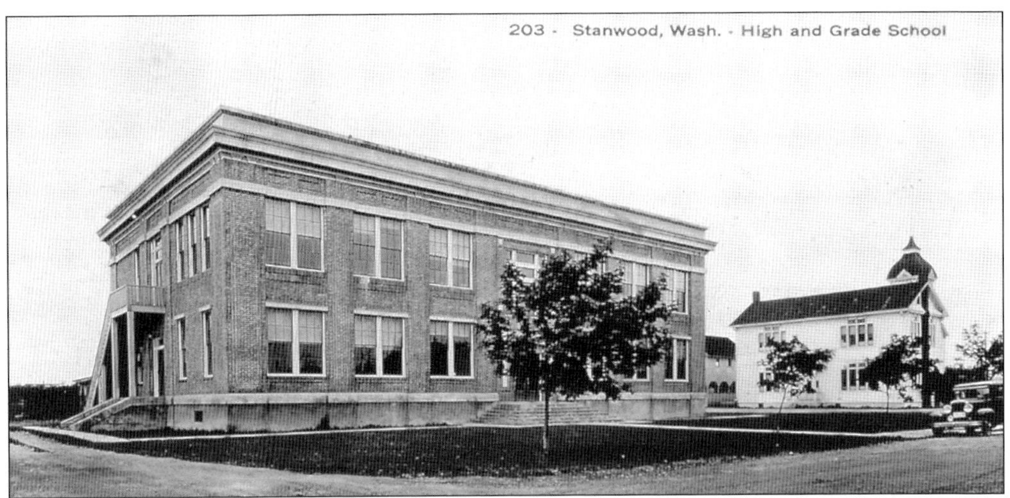

Stanwood High School and Grade School (Right). The brick high school building was dedicated in January 1914 on North Street just west of the 1892 grade school. The brick high school became a grade school after the grade school was demolished in 1938. High school students went to the new Stanwood Union High School between the two towns in 1939. The current Stanwood Elementary School on this property was dedicated in September 1956 with Pearl Wanamaker, Washington State school superintendent, who had been a teacher at the Mabana School on Camano Island in 1918.

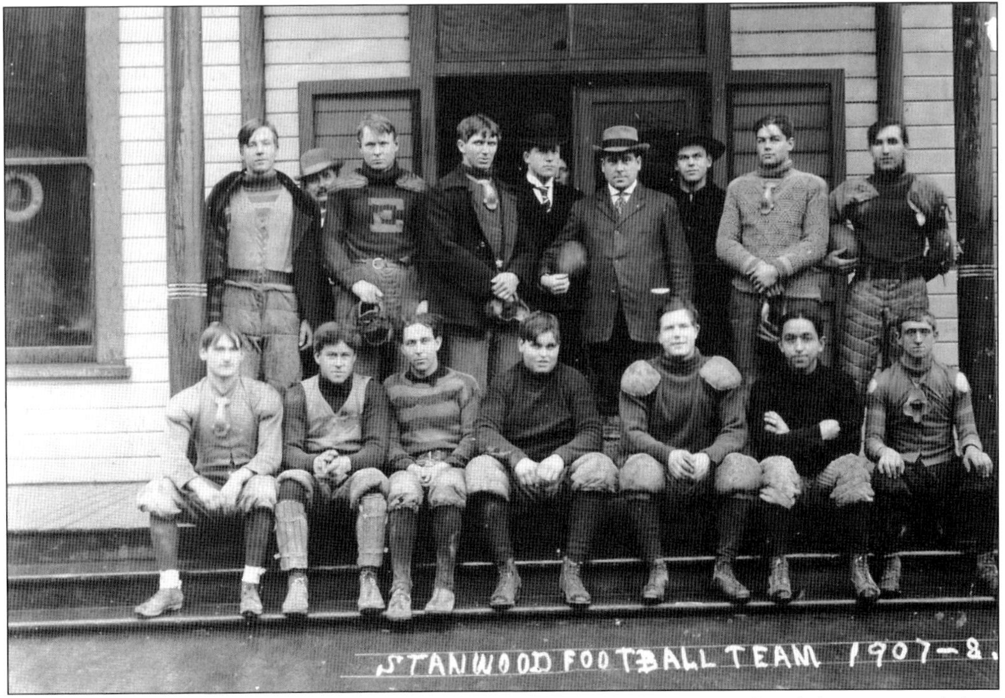

Stanwood Football Team, 1907–1908. Coach Jack O'Connor is pictured with his team and their uniforms/protective gear of the day. They are in the doorway of the grade school because there was no high school yet. Dr. Jack J. O'Connor was a dentist who attended Portland Dental College, where he was on the college team. In about 1909, he voluntarily coached the track and football teams to be prizewinners while working for Dr. Edward L. Hogan. (Photograph by John T. Wagness.)

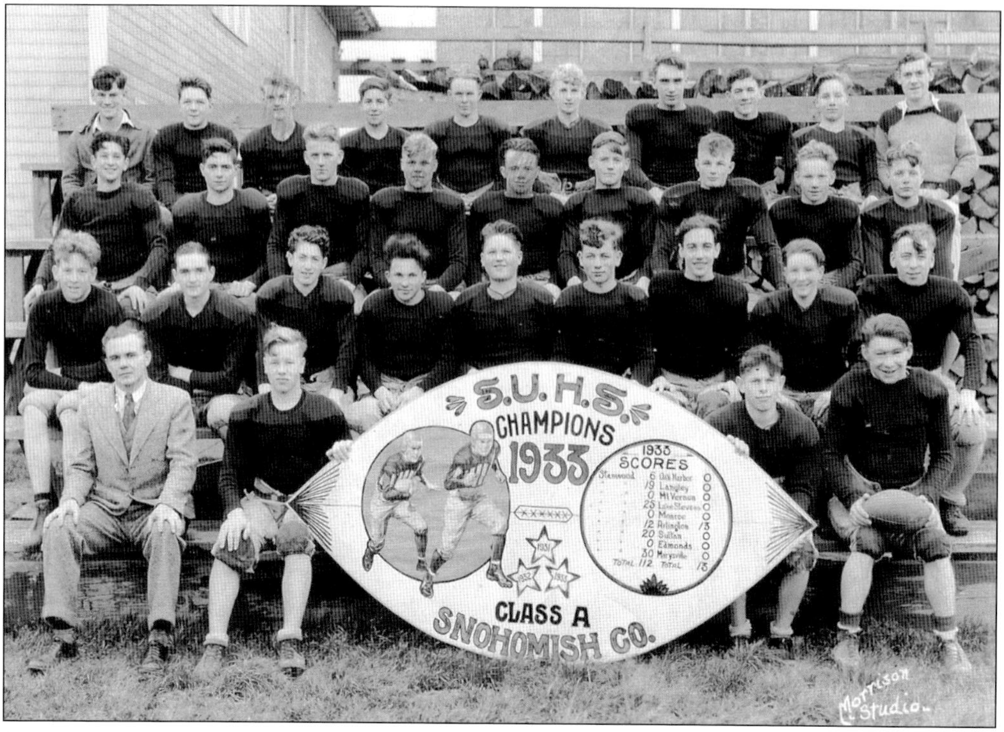

STANWOOD UNION HIGH SCHOOL CHAMPIONS, 1933 AND 1934. Stanwood High School's football team were also champions in 1931, 1937, 1940, and 1941. In 1933, Stanwood High School became Stanwood Union High School. Their yearbook was titled *ESACHES* (pronounced as it is spelled: "s-h-s") from 1913 until 1943. Over the years, the yearbook had several interesting names. In 1914, the title was *Klosh Illihe*, meaning "good land" or "garden." Later, it was called *Cardinal Memories* and the *Spartan Epic*.

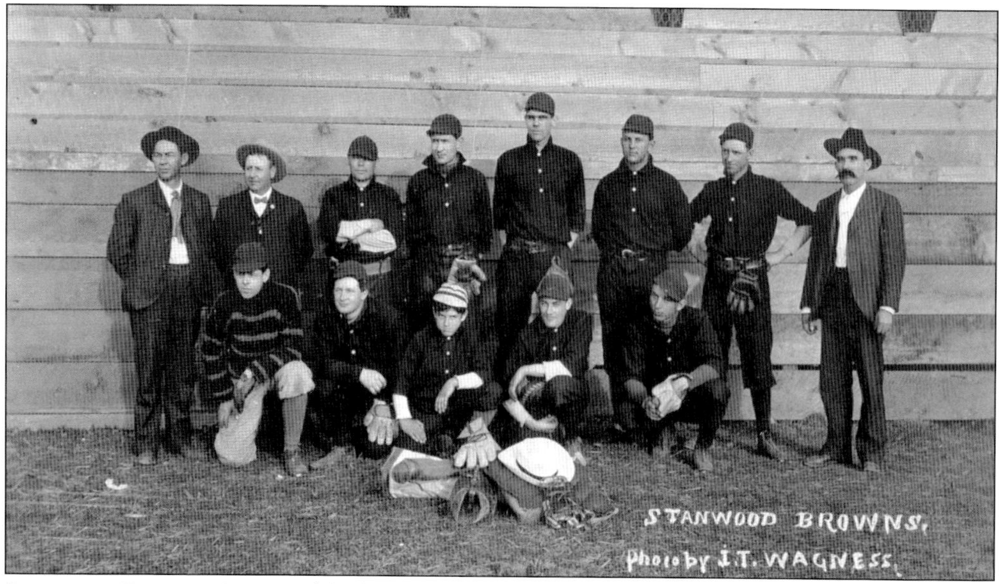

STANWOOD BROWNS. Stanwood had a baseball team in 1891 named the Stanwood Browns. They played teams from Fir, Florence, and Milltown, among others. (Photograph by John T. Wagness.)

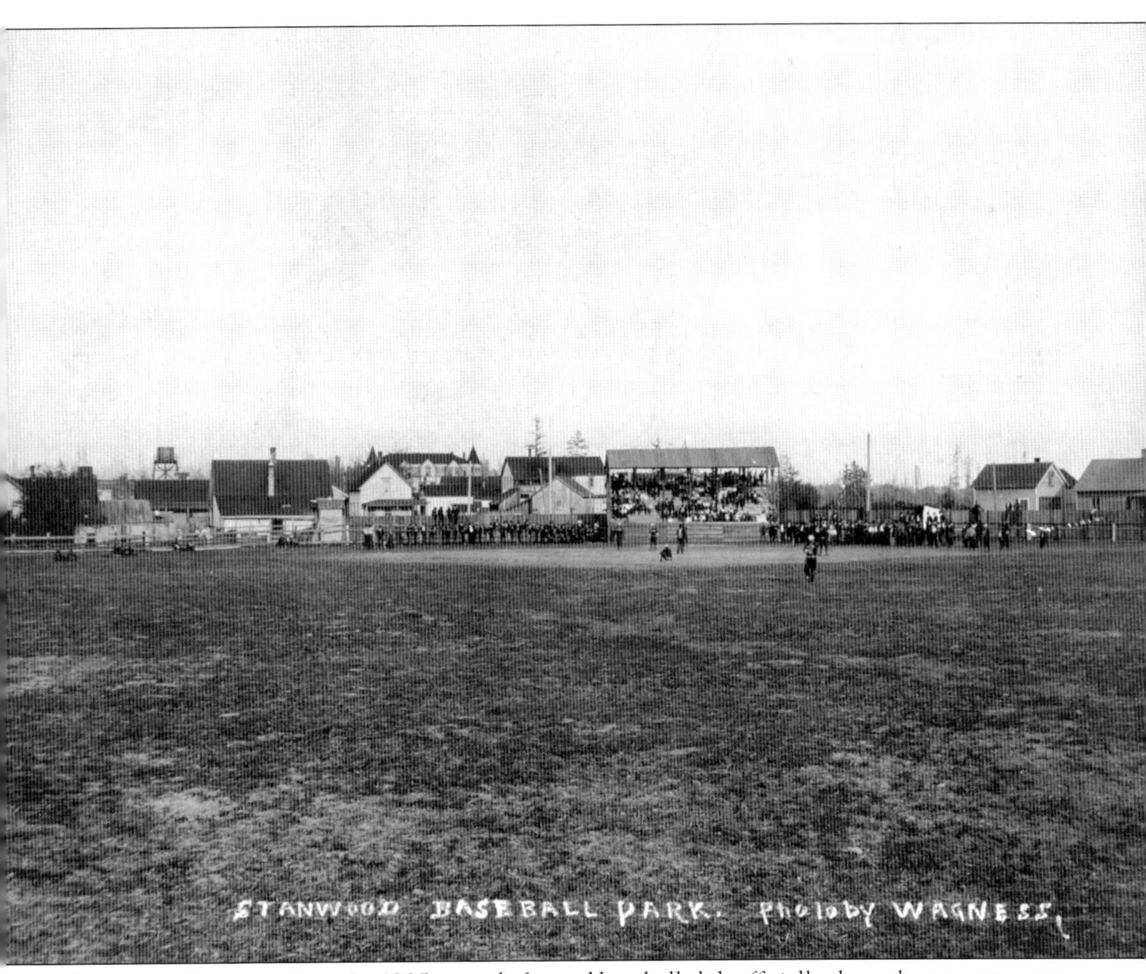

Stanwood Baseball Park. In 1905, a newly formed baseball club officially chose the property west of town and east of the Ovenell Farm for its baseball park. J.W. Hall leased the land, but when he extended the H&H Railroad toward the Stanwood Lumber Company mill, the park was moved to the area near the Stanwood Elementary School. In 1928, to raise funds to purchase equipment, there was a special baseball game featuring the nine children of the John T. Wagness and John Sande families in a friendly rivalry. The Sande family prevailed 18 runs to 6. (Photograph by John T. Wagness.)

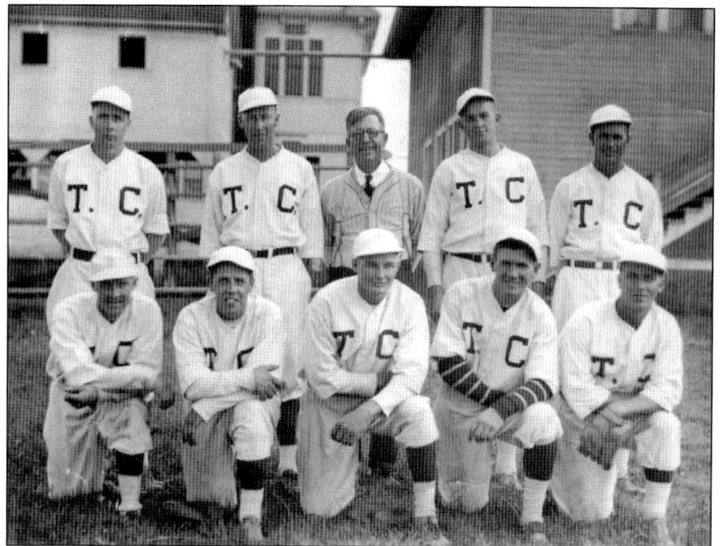

Twin City Baseball Players. The Twin City baseball team is pictured here around 1940. The players include (first row) George Perry, Ray Sande, Orville Fure, and two unidentified; (second row) Elmore Sigerstad, manager Gus Helland, Magnar Lervick, and two unidentified.

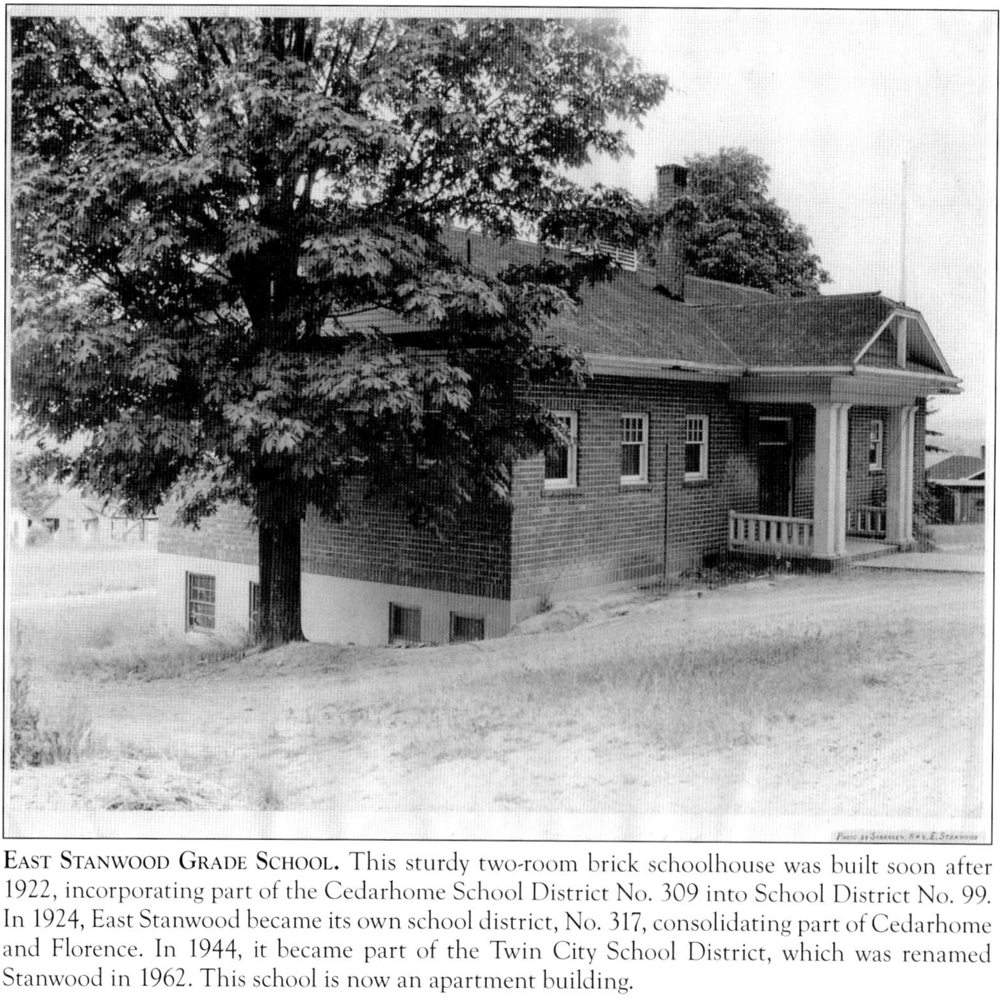

East Stanwood Grade School. This sturdy two-room brick schoolhouse was built soon after 1922, incorporating part of the Cedarhome School District No. 309 into School District No. 99. In 1924, East Stanwood became its own school district, No. 317, consolidating part of Cedarhome and Florence. In 1944, it became part of the Twin City School District, which was renamed Stanwood in 1962. This school is now an apartment building.

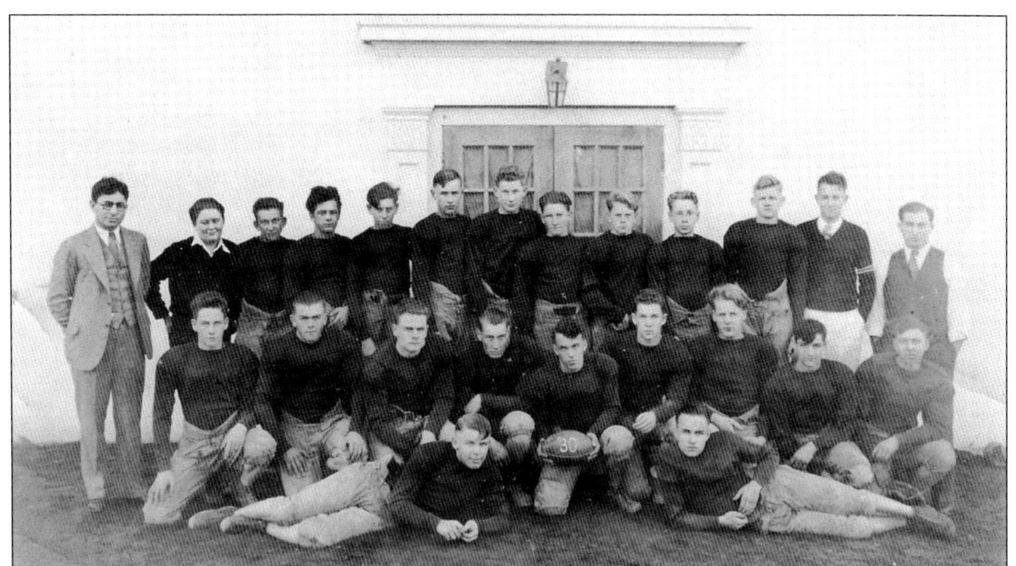

Lincoln High School Football Team, 1930 Champions. On the left is principal Alfred Tunem, whose excessive disciplinary actions toward students inspired students to walk out in protest. In January 1944, eighty-six students protested what they termed "Low grades and too much discipline." It was only a one-day strike, but Principal Tunem left that year after 15 years as superintendent.

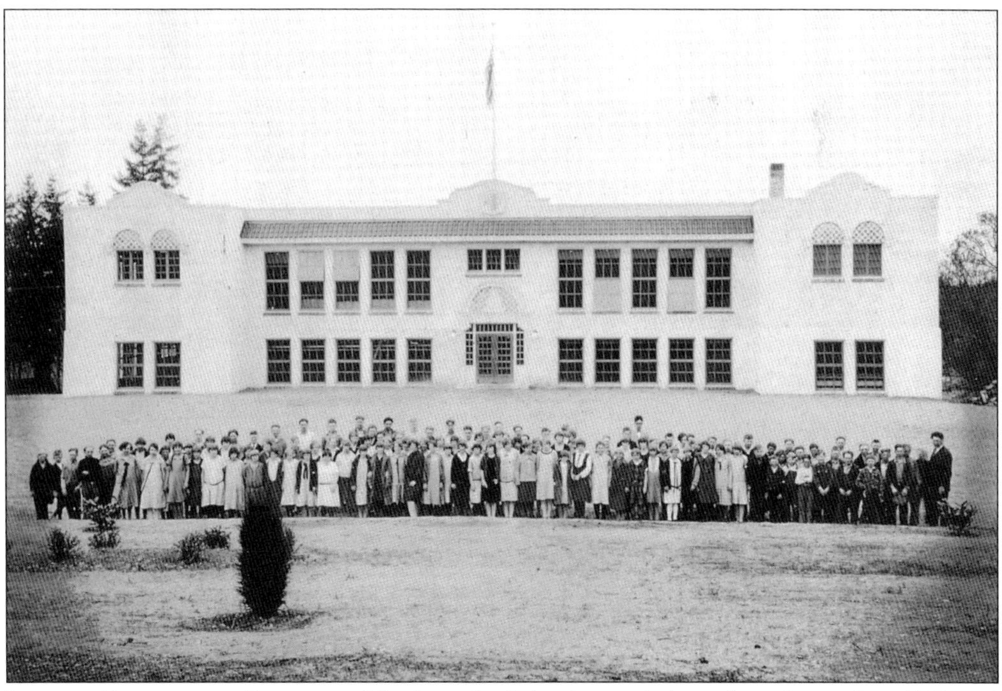

Lincoln School and Students. The Lincoln School was dedicated in September 1929 and became Lincoln High School in 1932, with a new addition in 1939. In 1962, Lincoln High School opened as a junior high school for students in the seventh, eighth, and ninth grades. Sophomores would attend Stanwood High School. The building is now the Stanwood Senior Center. In 1972, the center began using part of the building, and the building was remodeled in 1989.

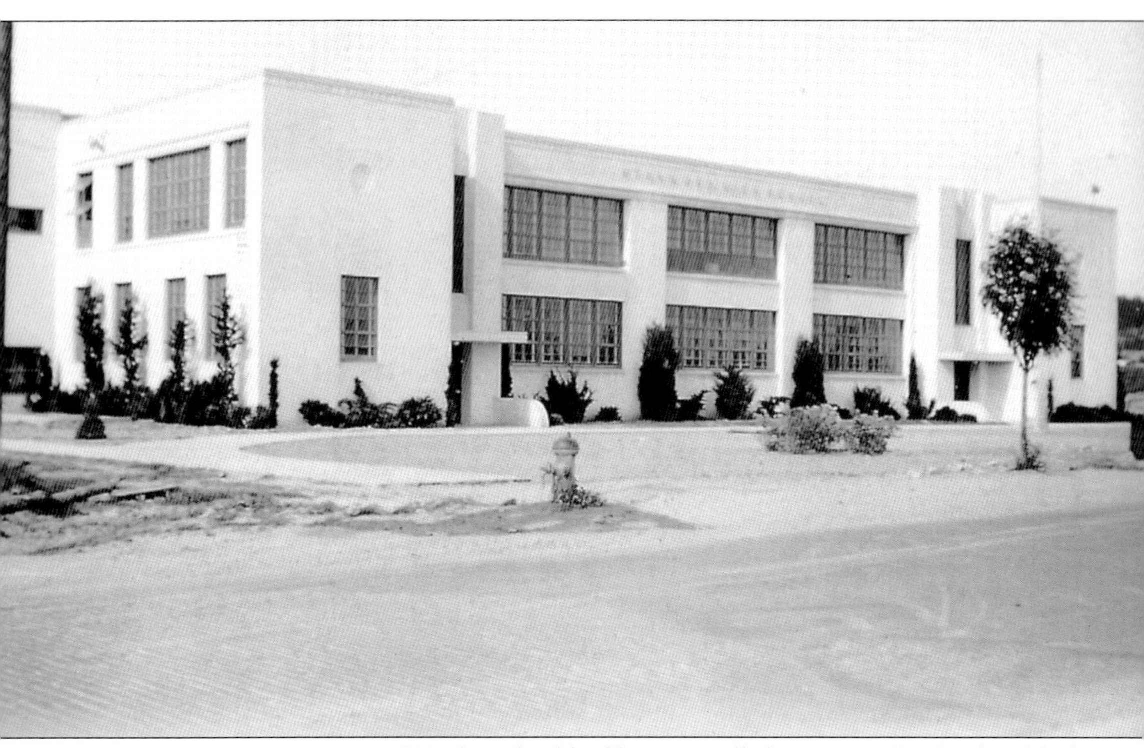

STANWOOD HIGH SCHOOL. In 1929, this school building was called Union High School and had 195 students. It was built deliberately between the two towns at a time when there was significant resistance to consolidation. After consolidations in 1937 and again in 1944, it became Twin City High School and the district was officially named the Twin City Joint Consolidated School District 401. In 1962, it became Stanwood School District again. The name changed again in 1999 to the Stanwood Camano School District. In 1972, this building became Stanwood Middle School when the new high school on the highlands was dedicated.

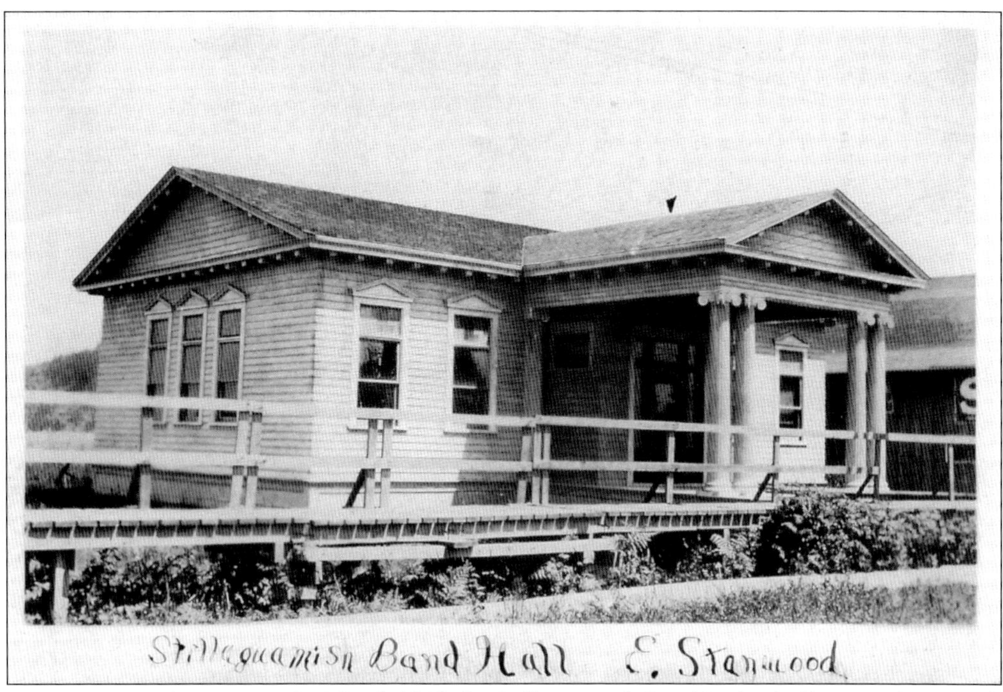

STILLAGUAMISH BAND HALL. In March 1915, the Stillaguamish Band built a hall in East Stanwood, though the location is not known. In June, the band made it known that it did not like its original East Stanwood location because it could not offer open-air concerts. In the meantime, Stanwood wanted a library somewhere on the Pacific Highway between the two towns. In 1914, Jack and Lizzie Irvine had both left bequests to support the building of a library in Stanwood. They stipulated that it had to be under the jurisdiction of Stanwood. The town called for an election to extend the boundaries to a point halfway to East Stanwood.

IRVINE PUBLIC LIBRARY. Fundraising followed, and in 1919, the band offered its building to the library if the Four Leaf Clover Club, the friends of the library group of the day, would pay to move it. Ultimately, the city purchased a library site on the Lien property beyond the curve leading to East Stanwood. In January 1922, the library officially opened. The library used the band hall for almost 50 years. In 1970, when a new library was built, the hall was purchased for $25 by the Twin Cities Gun Club and was moved east of East Stanwood on Sixty-Fourth Avenue NW.

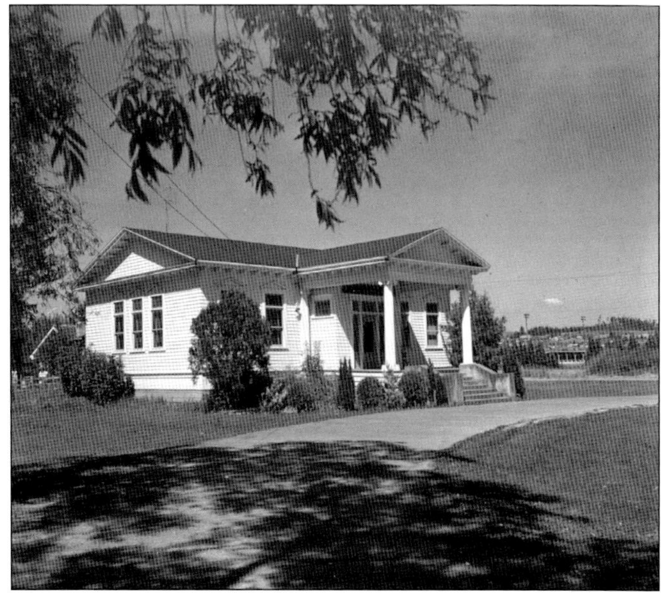

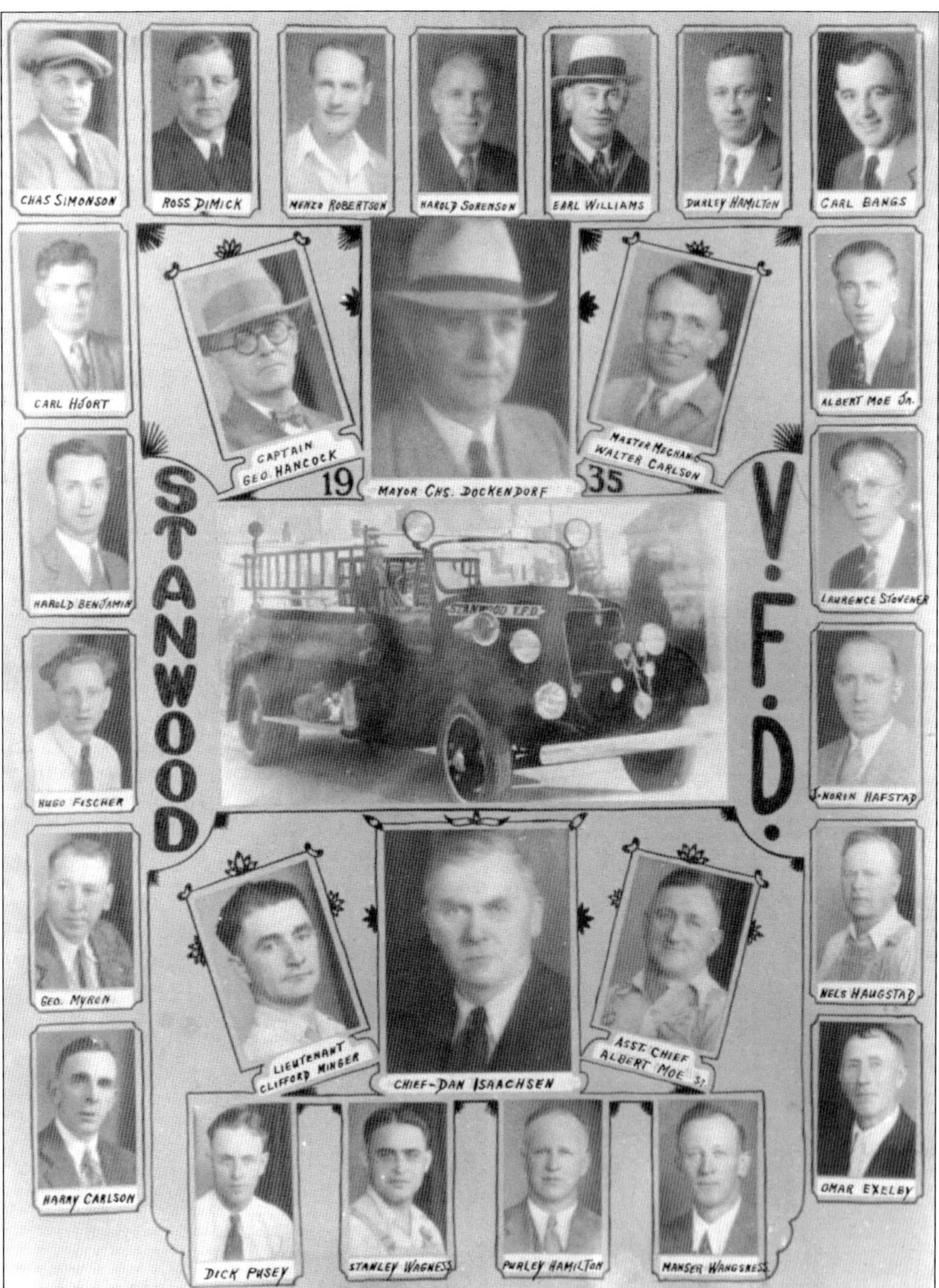

Stanwood Volunteer Fire Department (SVFD), 1935. Members of this 1935 Stanwood Fire Department were Carl Bangs, Harold Benjamin, Harry Carlson, R.S. Dimick, Mayor Charles Dockendorf, Omar Exelby, Hugo Fischer, Norin Hafstad, Durley Hamilton, George Hancock, Nels Haugstad, Carl Hjort, Clifford Minger, Albert Moe, Albert Moe Jr., George Myron, S.R. Pusey, Menzo Robertson, Charles Simonson, Harold Sorenson, Lawrence Stovner, Earl Williams, and Stanley Wagness. The photograph also includes other local officials.

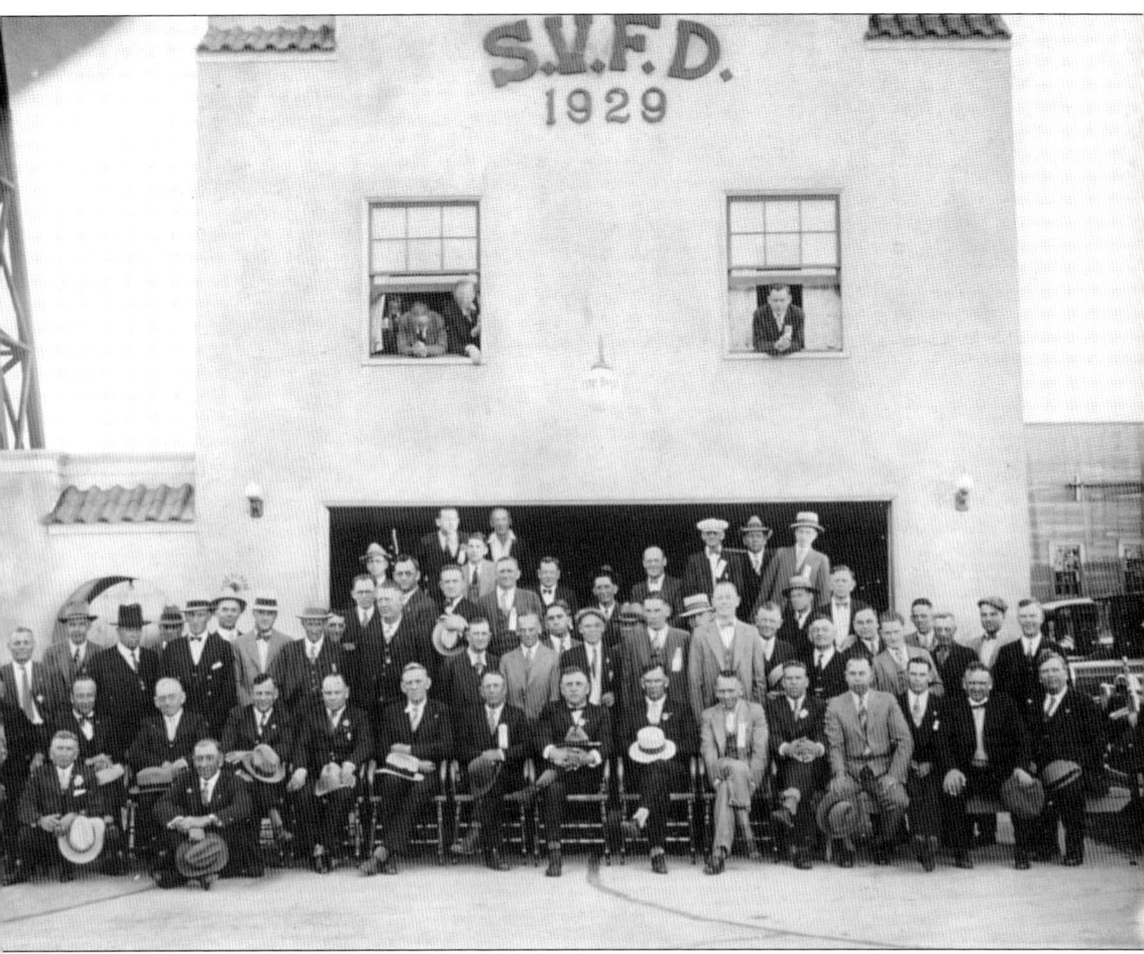

SVFD, 1929. The occasion for this photograph is the new fire station. This Spanish Revival–style building is on the west end of Stanwood on the opposite corner from the city hall. This photograph was taken at its original location on the property where the Twin City Food buildings were in 1929. The building was moved in 1954. It was sold by the City of Stanwood as surplus property in 2006. It is now a popular pub and restaurant. (Photograph by John T. Wagness.)

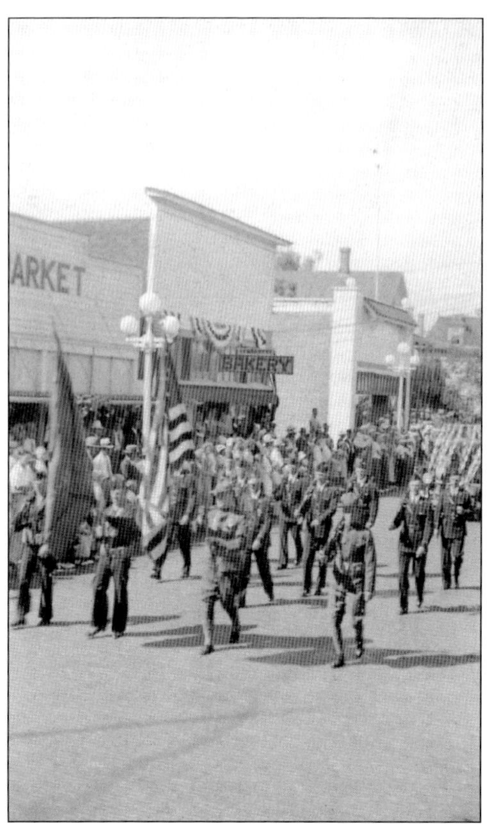

HARVEST JUBILEE PARADE, ABOUT 1934. This photograph shows another parade thought to be a Harvest Jubilee parade in which local servicemen are marching. The jubilee was an annual festival from 1939 until the early 1940s. They are passing the Palace Market at Broadway. The market was owned by Carl Bangs from the 1920s until 1962.

HARVEST JUBILEE CHILDREN'S PARADE, AUGUST, 1939. The jubilee included a full schedule of events including a band concert, races, boxing, wrestling, dancing, log bucking, log chopping, and baseball pitching contests. The parade passes the Palace Market on the corner of Market Street and Broadway. The Palace Market has since been a gas station and is now Bob's Market.

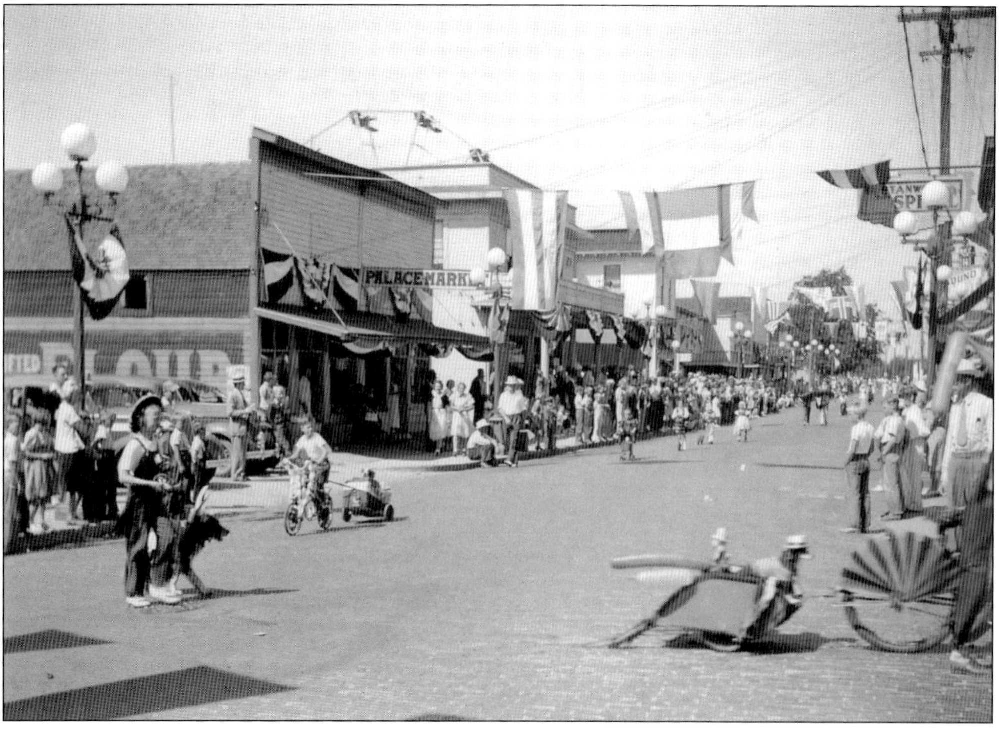

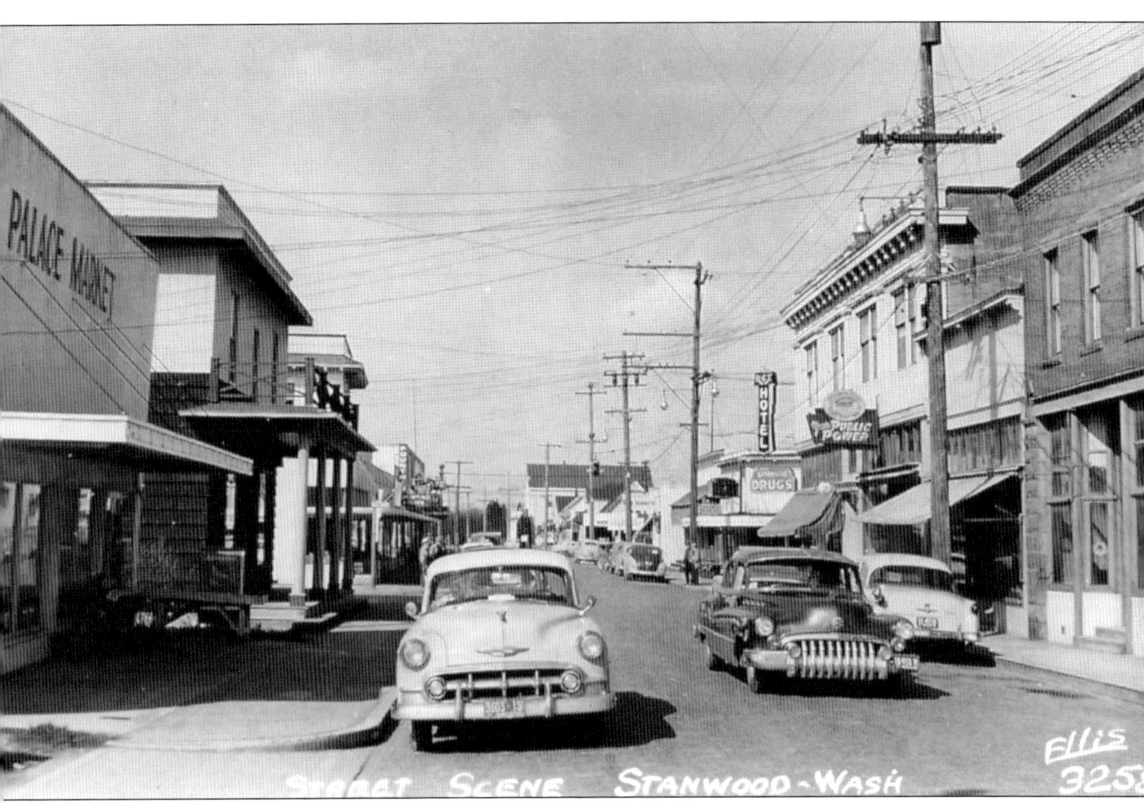

Street Scene. The Palace Market is shown here again on the left with a different, modernized facade, 1950s automobiles, and a remodeled Stanwood Hotel. On the right, the second story of the Knudson Building contained the modern 15-room Rex Hotel, established in November 1914 by Charles and Amelie "Millie" Dockendorf to compete with the Hotel Stanwood directly across the street. Charles Dockendorf served as mayor from 1922 to 1925 and again from 1930 to 1947. (Photograph by J. Boyd Ellis.)

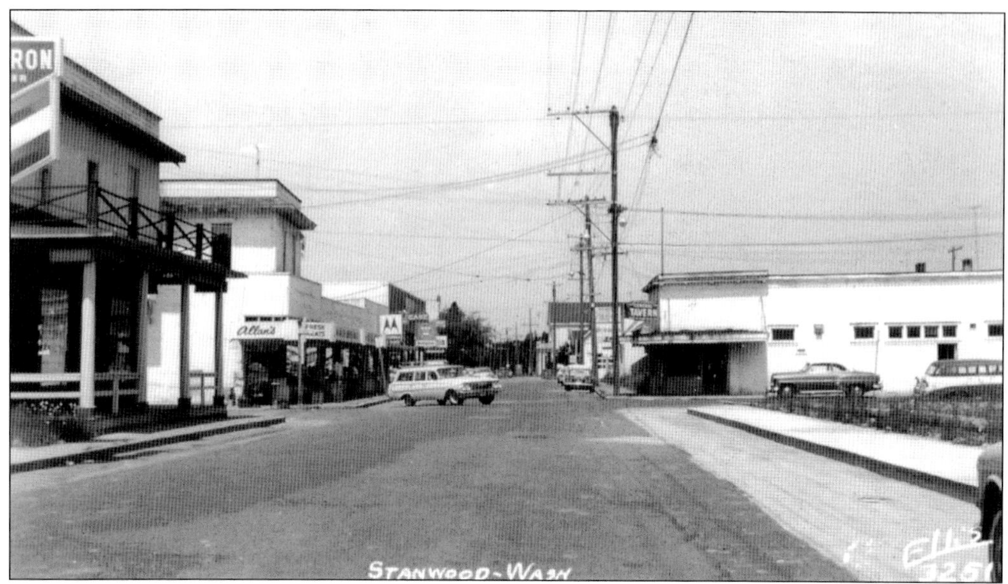

STANWOOD, WASHINGTON. Seen here is Market Street with the Ketchum Store, now Allan's Cash Grocery, which closed in 1968 after 29 years in business. The lot of the Palace Market is a Chevron station, according to the sign. The Central Tavern has replaced the Folly Theater. In 1942, the Central Tavern opened with a joint Central Café, operated by Mel Burrill. (Photograph by J. Boyd Ellis.)

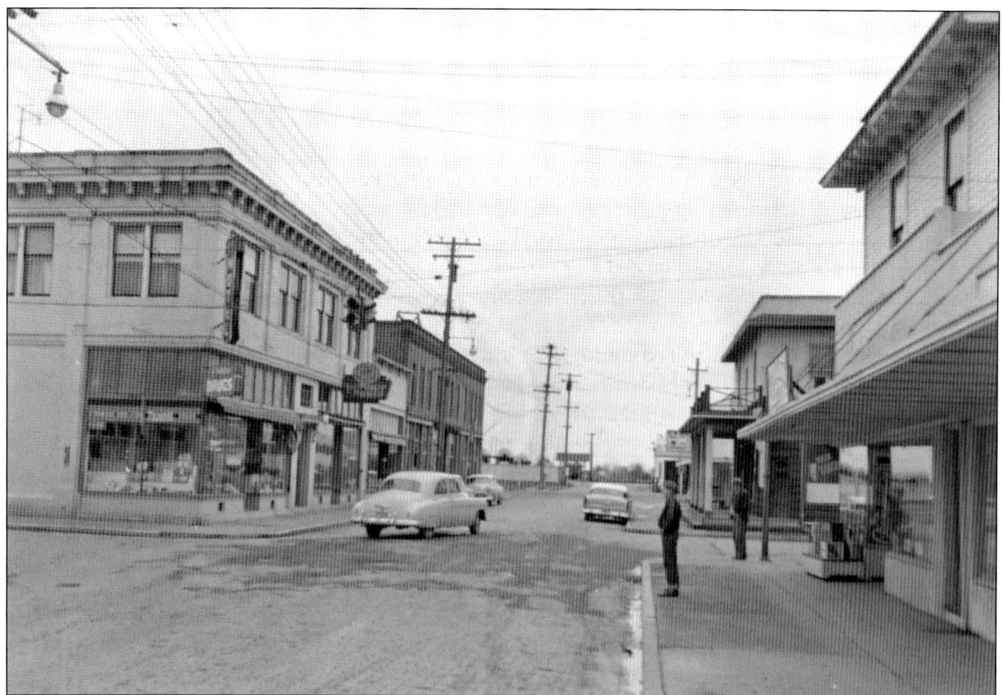

STREET VIEW, MARKET STREET. This view looks west toward the parking lot of Twin City Foods and the river beyond. The two classic brick buildings of Stanwood's Times Square appear here shortly before they were demolished. The Knudson Building and the original bank building were soon replaced by the new Seattle First National Bank in 1966.

Nine

Two Towns Become One Again

There had long been controversy over the possible merger of the two towns. Until 1960, both towns were small and had been struggling with duplication of services and buildings, not to mention wastewater treatment. The fire department had two buildings, and there were, of course, two city administrations. School district consolidation had finally been worked out in 1944, but the impending need for coordinated water and sewage management was critical. At least two votes were held previously, and East Stanwood voted against it.

Studies had been in process with consulting engineers in the late 1950s to help develop better wastewater treatment. Though the council of each city backed an improved and unified sewer processing system, the consulting firm reported that the treatment system could not be funded without the consolidation of the two towns. The Washington State Health Department ruled there could be no more building or expansion without a sewage treatment plant. Since neither town could afford a plant on its own, they were forced to consider merging. Acquiring the privately run water system was also considered. The *Twin City News* strongly backed the project. The vote in East Stanwood was 147 to 51 in favor and, in Stanwood, 218 in favor compared to only 26 against.

In 1957, money was allocated for the highway bridge to go over the railroad tracks. This changed the nature of Stanwood dramatically. State Route 532 (formerly Highway I-Y) bypassed most of the business district on the highway west to Camano Island. In 1969, State Route 532 was completed Its west end approached the 1949 Mark Clark bridge directly and connected without curving along Saratoga Street. It also changed the main intersections into town, providing two more. After the merger, Francis Giard's farm was sold in 1964 to a partnership. The 18-acre tract became the Viking Village Shopping Center, which was accessible from the new Highway I-Y/ State Route 532.

The two outgoing councils met in their respective town halls to conduct their last business. Their final order of business was approval of an ordinance terminating the activities of the Town of East Stanwood. The new council met at the Stanwood Town Hall with Idan Gilbertson to authorize the application for a federal grant to take care of the cost of the $520,000 sewer system and disposal facility that had been proposed. Costs of roads and streets are a constant for any city, but for Stanwood, flooding is an added burden requiring special attention and a heavy weight for those tasked to minimize bad outcomes and perhaps find innovative solutions.

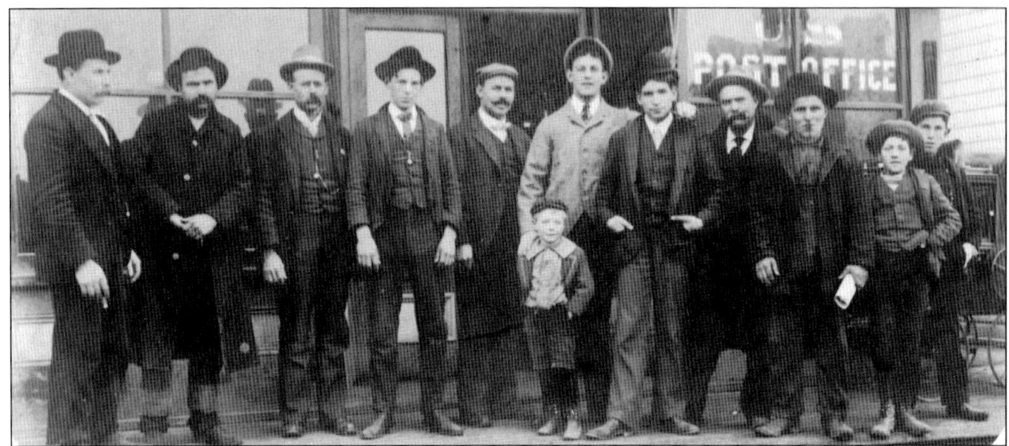

US Post Office. The post office was the beginning of Stanwood and, as written earlier, usually in an early mercantile or hotel. It has had five official buildings since its establishment at Centerville. Many of the town's founding businessmen are in this photograph. Postmasters included George Kyle, Robert Freeman, Henry Oliver, Michael McNamara, D.O. Pearson, John T. Logan, Andrew Tackstrom, Arthur E. Hall, Daniel C. Pearson, William Rouse, Trygve Lien, Alf Willard, and Laurence C. Johnson. Postmasters of East Stanwood included Carl J. Gunderson from 1913 until 1935, Marie Wenberg from 1935 until 1945, and Lars Sagen from 1945 until 1961, when it merged with the Stanwood Post Office.

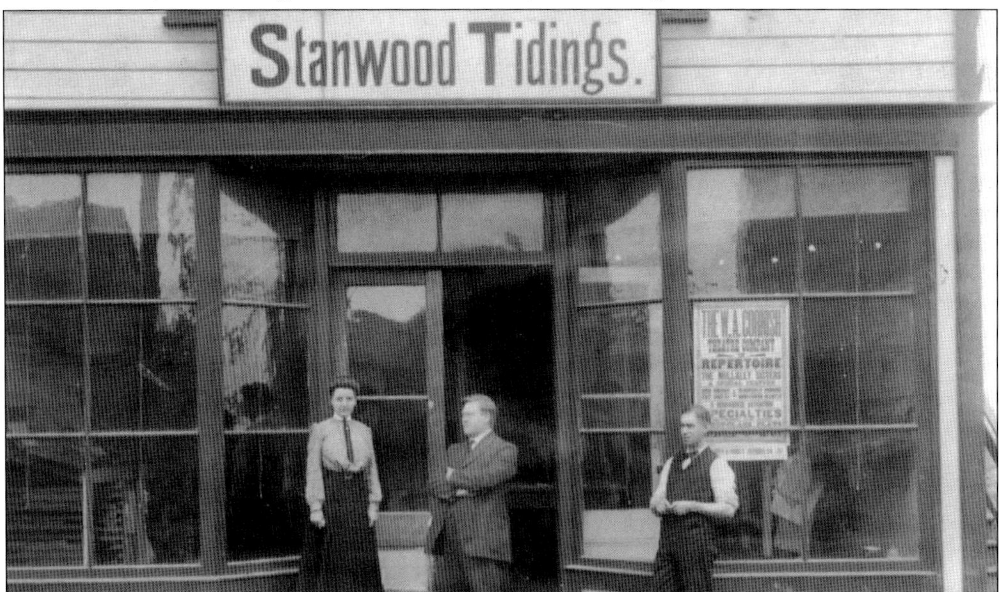

Stanwood Tidings. A newspaper for the Stanwood area began with the *Stanwood Post* from 1890 to 1895, though there are no existing issues. The *Stanwood (Weekly) Press* began in 1897 and ended in 1900. There is one known existing issue of the *Stillaguamish Valley News*, published in 1902. The *Stanwood Tidings* was published from 1903 to 1917; *Stanwood News*, 1920–1930; *Twin City News*, about 1930–1959; *Stanwood News*, 1960–1980; and *Stanwood Camano News*, 1981–present. Cliff Danielson became the publisher in 1958 and renamed the paper the *Stanwood News*. In 1981, he changed it again to the *Stanwood Camano News*. David Pinkham became owner-editor in 1985 and sold it in 2015 to Pioneer News Group. Since then, it has had a succession of corporate owners. It is hoped that the community can keep a news office in Stanwood, though economic forces continue to threaten the existence of small presses.

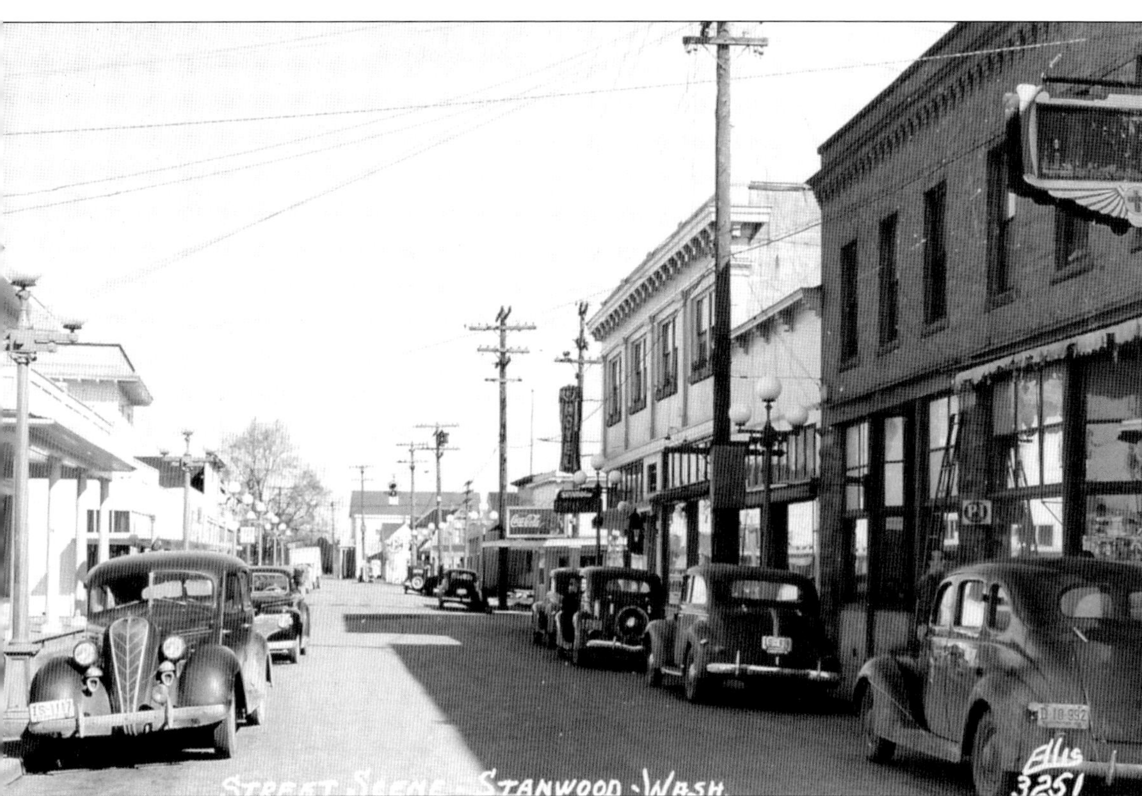

STREET SCENE, STANWOOD. This 1940s view shows the brick streets still in good condition. The Masonic Hall still towers down the street. The Central Café advertises Coca-Cola in the distance. It is difficult to tell, but the sign on the top right of the photograph says "Stanwood Hospital," which was on the second floor of the brick building after the bank moved to Main Street. The Signal gas station is in the distance, and its building is still standing as an auto glass company. (Photograph by J. Boyd Ellis.)

Mayors of Stanwood, Washington

1903 - 1905	Pearson, D. O.
1907 - 1909	A. B. Klaeboe
1910 - 1911	George J. Ketchum
1912 - 1915	D. O. Pearson
1916 - 1917	L. H. Jacobsen, M. D.
1918 - 1920	George J. Ketchum
1920 - 1922	Conrad Lien (resigned) succeeded by Nels Olsen
1922 - 1925	Charles Dockendorf
1926 - 1929	Ole. E. Thompson
1930 - 1947	Charles Dockendorf
1948 - 1951	Ed Bryant
1952 - 1959	Albert C. Moe

Consolidation June 1960

1960 - 1968	Idan Gilbertson
1969 - 1975	Donald Moa
1976 - 1985	Kenneth E. Day
1986 - 1993	Robert N. Larson
1994 - 1995	Donald K. Moa
1995 - 2003	Matthew J. McCune
2004 - 2005	H. W. Kuhnly
2006 - 2013	Dianne White
2014 - 2020	Leonard Kelley (resigned)
2020 - 2021	Elizabeth Callaghan
2021 -	Sid Roberts

East Stanwood Mayors

1922 - 1931	Francis Giard
1932 - 1935	Charles E. Yngve
1936 - 1938	Harold Greer
1939 - 1943	Charles. R. Amundson
1944 - 1951	James J. Hansen
1952 - 1958	Ira Armintrout
1958 - 1960	John G. Hanson

STANWOOD MAYORS, 1903–2021. This list of Stanwood mayors is as up-to-date as possible. Many of the mayors were popular and served several terms. Though the city built the city auditorium, later city hall, from 1934, Lawrence Stovner used his building, known as the Twin City Dairy (next to D.O. Pearson's store) as his office as city clerk and his side business as real estate agent, accountant, and tax preparer. The Twin City Foods used the auditorium building during this time. Stovner sat on the town council since 1934 with the exception of four years and was with the fire department for 35 years.

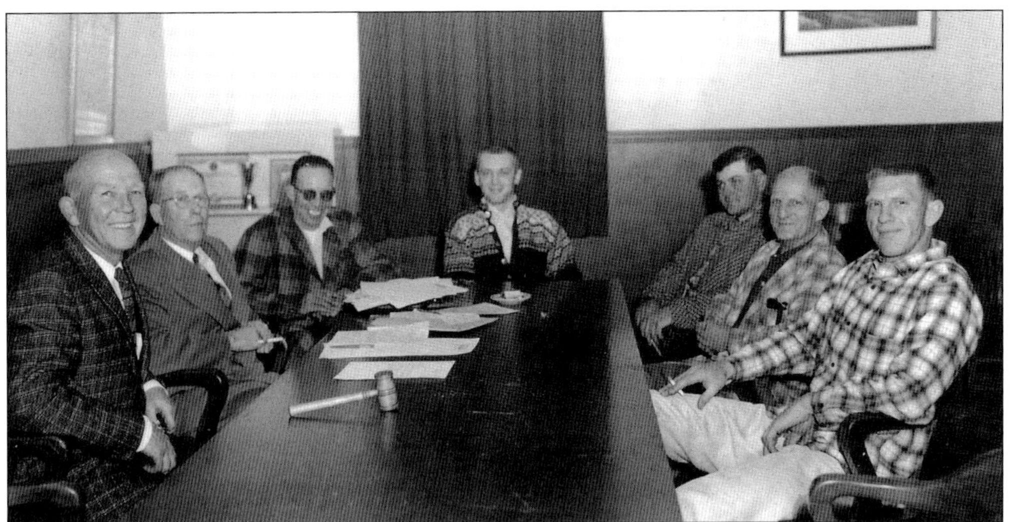

THE NEW CITY COUNCIL. In 1960, Stanwood merged to be able to resolve problems of pollution in the Stillaguamish River and improve efficiencies in civic management. City officials and business groups came together to propose a merger on the ballot in March 1960. The vote in East Stanwood was 147 to 51 in favor of consolidation, and in Stanwood it was 218 to 26 in favor. Idan Gilbertson was elected mayor, and Lawrence Stovner was clerk and treasurer. The council members were Cliff Fosse, Glenn Larson, Jim Hendershot, Don Moa, and Francis Giard Jr. Because of the vote, they were finally able to apply to the federal government to help cover the $520,000 sewage treatment system and lagoon installation.

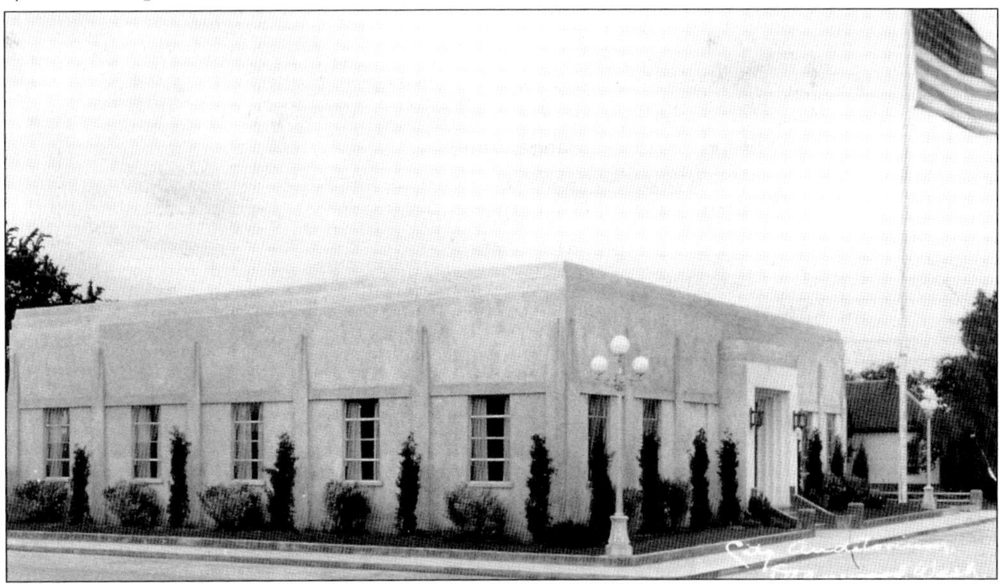

CITY AUDITORIUM. The Stanwood City Auditorium was built in 1932 and eventually became the current city hall. It was dedicated in 1936 as the city hall and was a special project of five-term mayor Charles Dockendorf. It was designed by Alf Christian Willard, who was also a contractor and later postmaster of Stanwood. Partially funded by the Works Progress Administration in 1944, it was paid for "with virtually no extra cost to the taxpayers, representing an investment of about $20,000,"according to the January 6, 1944, *Twin City News*. The first city hall was built in 1904 and had its own jail and courtrooms.

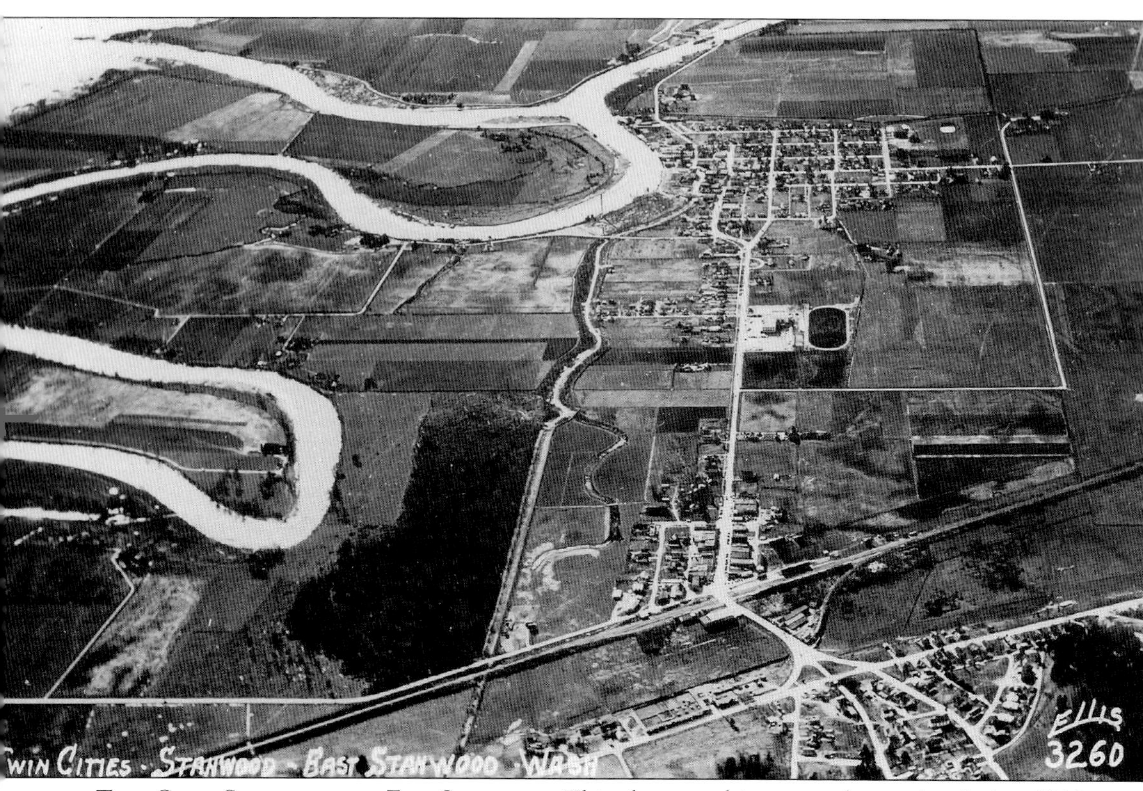

Twin Cities Stanwood and East Stanwood. This photographic postcard was taken before 1960, when State Route 532 (Highway I-Y) was constructed and the railroad crossing bridged. It shows the winding of Irvine Slough before its course was changed to build 532. This aerial photograph was taken by either J. Boyd Ellis (1894–1983) or his son Clifford, who took over the Arlington business in the later years. They produced some of the region's most important views of the growth and economic development of towns and cities. J. Boyd opened his Photo Arts Studio in Arlington in 1921. He managed to make a living in the business and must have been traveling all the time. His photographic postcards are probably held in all of the regional museums, but the primary collection is held by the Stillaguamish Valley Museum in Arlington.

Bibliography

"Achievement Number." *Stanwood Tidings*, June 14, 1916.

An Illustrated History of Skagit and Snohomish Counties, Their People, Their Commerce and Their Resources with an Outline of the Early History of the State of Washington. Chicago: Interstate Publishing Co., 1906.

Conant, Roger, and Susan H. Armitage. *Mercer's Belles: The Journal of a Reporter*. Pullman: Washington State University Press, 1992.

Conroy, Dennis, and Carol Husby Ronken. *Pioneers of the Stillaguamish*. Camano Island, WA: Cascade Writing, 2005.

Essex, Alice. *The Stanwood Story*. 3 vols. Stanwood, WA: *Stanwood Camano News*, 1971–1998.

Hanks, Richard A. *To Seek the Smiles of Dame Fortune: Stanwood Tales of the Last Great Gold Rush*. Camano Island, WA: Coyote Hill Press, 2022.

Iverson, O.B. "Experiences and Observations on Two Continents." *Stanwood News*, November 12, 1920, and December 10, 1920.

Joergenson, Gustaf B. *History of the Twin Cities Country*. Stanwood, WA: *Twin City News*, 1948–1949.

Klaeboe, A.B. "Stanwood, Washington." *The Coast: Alaska and the Greater Northwest* 16, no. 5 (November 1908): pp. 326–328.

Stanwood, Washington–Metropolis of the Stillaguamish Valley. Everett, WA: Commercial Clubs of Stanwood and East Stanwood, c. 1913.

"Stillaguamish River." *Northern Star* (Snohomish), April 8, 1976.

Suttles, Wayne, and Barbara Lane. "Southern Coast Salish." *Handbook of North American Indians*, vol 7. Washington, DC: Smithsonian Institution, 1990.

Whitfield, William. *History of Snohomish County, Washington*. Chicago: Pioneer Historical Pub. Co., 1926.

Discover Thousands of Local History Books Featuring Millions of Vintage Images

Arcadia Publishing, the leading local history publisher in the United States, is committed to making history accessible and meaningful through publishing books that celebrate and preserve the heritage of America's people and places.

Find more books like this at
www.arcadiapublishing.com

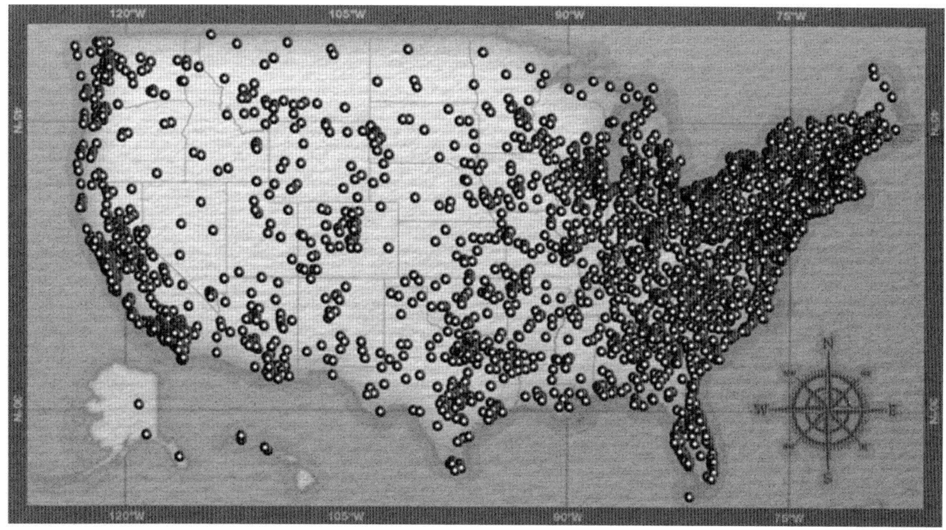

Search for your hometown history, your old stomping grounds, and even your favorite sports team.

Consistent with our mission to preserve history on a local level, this book was printed in South Carolina on American-made paper and manufactured entirely in the United States. Products carrying the accredited Forest Stewardship Council (FSC) label are printed on 100 percent FSC-certified paper.

MADE IN THE

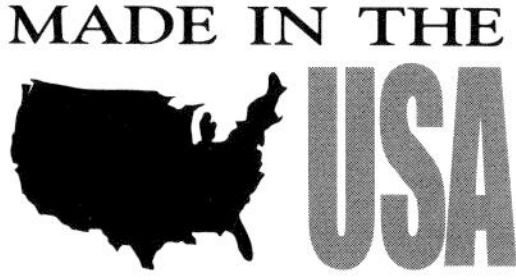